AF897080

Palgrave Studies in Governance, Leadership and Responsibility

Series Editors
Simon Robinson, Leeds Beckett University, Leeds, UK
Georgiana Grigore, School of Business, University of Leicester, Leicester, UK
Alin Stancu, Bucharest University of Economic Studies, Bucharest, Romania
Anna Sörensson, Mid Sweden University, Östersund, Sweden

The fall-out from many high profile crises in governance and leadership in recent decades, from banking to healthcare, continues to be felt around the world. Major reports have questioned the values and behaviour, not just of individual organizations but of professionals, industries and political leadership. These reports raise questions about business corporations and also public service institutions. In response this new series aims to explore the broad principles of governance and leadership and how these are embodied in different contexts, opening up the possibility of developing new theories and approaches that are fuelled by interdisciplinary approaches. The purpose of the series is to highlight critical reflection and empirical research which can enable dialogue across sectors, focusing on theory, value and the practice of governance, leadership and responsibility.

Written from a global context, the series is unique in bringing leadership and governance together. The King III report connects these two fields by identifying leadership as one of the three principles of effective governance however most courses in business schools have traditionally treated these as separate subjects. Increasingly, and in particular with the case of executive education, business schools are recognizing the need to develop and produce responsible leaders. The series will therefore encourage critical exploration between these two areas and as such explore sociological and philosophical perspectives.

Anna Sörensson · Maria Bogren ·
Georgiana Grigore · Alin Stancu ·
Anders Lundström
Editors

Creating New Roles for a Sustainable Economy

Digitalization, Green Enterprises and Organizational Challenges

palgrave
macmillan

Editors
Anna Sörensson
Mid Sweden University
Östersund, Sweden

Inland Norway University of Applied Science
Rena, Norway

Maria Bogren
Mid Sweden University
Östersund, Sweden

Nord University
Steinkjer, Norway

Georgiana Grigore
School of Business
University of Leicester
Leicester, UK

Alin Stancu
Bucharest University of Economic Studies
Bucharest, Romania

Anders Lundström
Mid Sweden University
Östersund, Sweden

ISSN 2662-1304 ISSN 2662-1312 (electronic)
Palgrave Studies in Governance, Leadership and Responsibility
ISBN 978-3-031-61550-4 ISBN 978-3-031-61551-1 (eBook)
https://doi.org/10.1007/978-3-031-61551-1

© The Editor(s) (if applicable) and The Author(s), under exclusive license to Springer Nature Switzerland AG 2024

This work is subject to copyright. All rights are solely and exclusively licensed by the Publisher, whether the whole or part of the material is concerned, specifically the rights of translation, reprinting, reuse of illustrations, recitation, broadcasting, reproduction on microfilms or in any other physical way, and transmission or information storage and retrieval, electronic adaptation, computer software, or by similar or dissimilar methodology now known or hereafter developed.
The use of general descriptive names, registered names, trademarks, service marks, etc. in this publication does not imply, even in the absence of a specific statement, that such names are exempt from the relevant protective laws and regulations and therefore free for general use.
The publisher, the authors and the editors are safe to assume that the advice and information in this book are believed to be true and accurate at the date of publication. Neither the publisher nor the authors or the editors give a warranty, expressed or implied, with respect to the material contained herein or for any errors or omissions that may have been made. The publisher remains neutral with regard to jurisdictional claims in published maps and institutional affiliations.

This Palgrave Macmillan imprint is published by the registered company Springer Nature Switzerland AG
The registered company address is: Gewerbestrasse 11, 6330 Cham, Switzerland

If disposing of this product, please recycle the paper.

Contents

1 **New Roles for a Sustainable Economy** 1
Anna Sörensson, Maria Bogren, Georgiana Grigore, Alin Stancu, and Anders Lundström

Part I Digitalization, Green Businesses and Sustainability

2 **Green Business Model: The Digitization of Sustainability** 11
Maria Rosaria Marcone

3 **Bibliometric Analysis of Research on the Concept of CSR and Sustainable Development in E-commerce** 35
Anna Napiórkowska

Part II New Roles for Sustainability, SMEs and Social Entrepreneurship

4 **Takeaway Coffee: The Interplay Between Convenience and Sustainability** 71
Maria Sherrington

5 **Unleashing the Power of Social Entrepreneurs for Regional Development: Insights from Jämtland Härjedalen** 101
Konstantin Golpayegani and Ulrich Schmudde

6 **Corporate Social Responsibility Approach by SMEs' Managing Directors in the Hungarian City of Győr—Empirical Evidence** 121
Adrienn Reisinger

Part III Key Organizational Challenges for Sustainable Development

7 **The Systematic Sustainable Business Model (SBM) Approach—A Flexible Organizational Tool** 143
Åsa Devine and Michaela Sandell

8 **Citizens' Engagement in the Co-Creation of Smart City—An Empirical Study** 177
Małgorzata Wiścicka-Fernando

9 **Communicated Sustainability Values from Nature-Based Businesses—Different Industries Give Different Perspectives** 203
Anna Sörensson and Maria Bogren

10 **Sustainability Developments in Municipalities—What, Why, and How** 219
Anna Sörensson, Anders Lundström, Ida Hallqvist, and Jesper Vestlund

Index 249

Notes on Contributors

Maria Bogren is Associate Professor of Organization and Leadership at Nord University, Norway. Bogren's research interests are broad, mainly in areas such as Working Life Research, Entrepreneurship, Sustainability and Marketing. She led the research project 'Cross-border career choices in the Nordic region's green belt' (2022) and is currently involved in the research project 'Limitless Competence' (2024–2026). She is a member of the following research networks: The Network for Working Life Research (NAFS), Mid Sweden University, Sweden and The Institute for Sustainable Social Development (INDESS), University of Cadiz, Spain.

Åsa Devine Ph.D., is a senior lecturer in Marketing at the AACSB-accredited School of Business and Economics at Linnaeus University, Sweden. Devine has a background in Industrial Engineering and Ergonomics and presented her Ph.D. in International Strategy with a focus on SMEs. Her current research interest lies within the domain of sustainability encompassing both organizational sustainable conduct and sustainable consumer behavior and intent.

Konstantin Golpayegani is Ph.D. Candidate in Business Administration at Mid Sweden University, Östersund. He is originally from Denmark but with international roots. Having such an idiosyncratic root, he is able to speak 7 languages more or less fluently. His research at Mid Sweden University is on '*The Mediating role of co-opetition between start-ups in developing Business Model Innovation*'. He holds an M.Sc. degree in Business Development and Internationalization from Umeå University, Sweden, and a B.A. in International Sales and Marketing Management from IBA Kolding, Denmark. Honorably mentioning the M.Sc. thesis which was about '*Authentic Leadership with a role to play in emotional commitment and organizational culture*'.

Georgiana Grigore is Associate Professor in Marketing at the University of Leicester, School of Business. She is also chair of an annual international conference in 'Social Responsibility, Ethics and Sustainable Business', which she co-founded in 2012. Her major area of research is in marketing and corporate responsibility concepts and practices, including changes that result from digital media. In the last years, she has published several books, including 'Corporate Responsibility and Digital Communities' and 'Corporate Social Responsibility in the Digital Age' that explore a contemporary intersection of two fields: corporate responsibility and digital technology. Her publications also include applications of post-psychoanalytic theories to consumer-brand relationships and shopping in Marketing Theory. Her research received external funding, including from Arthur W. Page Center (2014/2015 and 2015/2016) and British Academy/Leverhulme (2017/2019). She completed an EU-funded doctorate in Marketing at the Bucharest University of Economic Studies using relationship-marketing theory to examine the impact of corporate responsibility on stakeholders. Prior to her doctorate, she received a master's degree in Strategic Marketing and a bachelor's degree in Marketing from the same university. Before her Ph.D., Georgiana was a marketing specialist and consultant in the retail industry and a trainer for a series of practitioner workshops and marketing and corporate responsibility courses.

Ida Hallqvist is a student at Mid Sweden University in Östersund, Sweden.

Anders Lundström, Professor Emeritus at Mid Sweden University in Sweden, was one of the creators and managing director of the Swedish Foundation for Small Business Research (FSF) and invented the Global Award for Entrepreneurship Research in 1996. Anders Lundström has been chairing three world conferences in the areas of entrepreneurship, small business and innovations. He has created the IPREG (Innovative Policy Research in Entrepreneurship and Small Business), an international network consisting of research organizations in 14 European countries. He has been president of ICSB (International Council of Small Business) a worldwide network organization. He has been working as a full professor and project manager at Mid Sweden University for a multidisciplinary EU-funded project, SESPA, of social/societal entrepreneurship with 25 researchers from six different disciplines. He has also been Visiting Professor in China.

Maria Rosaria Marcone is Full Professor on Business Economics, 'Marche Polytechnic University'—Italy, where she teaches 'Business Strategies' and 'Operations and Logistics' at the master's degree Economics and Management. Publications in 'International Journal of Production Research', 'Journal of Knowledge Economy', 'International Journal of Information Technology and Management'.

Anna Napiórkowska is Assistant Professor at the Department of International Business in the Collegium of World Economy at the SGH Warsaw School of Economics. Author or co-author of publications in the field of corporate social responsibility, ethical leadership, CSR legalization, retail chains' CSR strategies in peer-reviewed journals and scientific books.

Adrienn Reisinger (Dr. habil) got the Ph.D. degree in 2010 at the Széchenyi István University, Győr, Hungary and the habilitation degree in 2017. Now she is working at the University at the Kautz Gyula Faculty of Business and Economics as a university associate professor and she is the vice-dean of scientific cases.

Michaela Sandell M.Sc. and M.Phil., is a lecturer in Marketing at the AACSB-accredited School of Business and Economics at Linnaeus University, Sweden. Sandell has a broad academic background in Business Administration and East Asian Studies, subsequently with a focus on Relationship Marketing and Strategy. Currently, her main research interests include sustainability, business ethics and culture.

Ulrich Schmudde who is originally from the famous Black Forest region in south-western Germany, is Ph.D. Candidate in Business Administration at Mid Sweden University, Östersund. He possesses both an M.Sc. and B.Sc. degree from Mid Sweden University, and prior to that studied at Worms University of Applied Sciences in Germany. Among other responsible positions, he worked as Head of Marketing and Tourism Development at a German municipality before pursuing a Ph.D. He even possesses an associate degree as an industrial management assistant which was issued by the German Chamber of Commerce (DIHK). His research field is on value proposition, value capture and sustainable development of destinations that stand in the shadow of high-profile destinations.

Maria Sherrington is Senior Lecturer in Marketing at the University of Central Lancashire in the UK where she specializes in sustainable and social marketing. Her research mission is to understand how marketing can be harnessed to affect consumer behavior change to address the current climate emergency.

Anna Sörensson is Associate Professor in Marketing at Mid Sweden University, Sweden and Inland Norway University of Applied Science, Norway. She has a Ph.D. in Business Administration within international marketing from Åbo Akademi (Finland). Her research focuses on sustainable businesses, the tourism industry and entrepreneurship. She is co-editor of the book series: Palgrave Studies in Governance, Leadership and Responsibility.

Alin Stancu is Professor of Corporate Social Responsibility and Public Relations in the Department of Marketing at The Bucharest University of Economic Studies, Romania. His main areas of research include customer care, consumer experience, corporate responsibility and public relations. He is the co-founder of The International Conference on Social Responsibility, Ethics and Sustainable Business (https://www.csrconferences.org) and co-editor of the book series: Palgrave Studies in Governance, Leadership and Responsibility.

Jesper Vestlund is a student at Mid Sweden University in Östersund, Sweden.

Małgorzata Wiścicka-Fernando works as an assistant professor at the University of Szczecin in the Department of Marketing. Her main research areas are Relationship Marketing, Sustainable Marketing, Consumer Behavior, and Communication. She is the author of (more than thirty) many scientific publications written in Polish, English, and German. She participated in scholarships in Germany, China, Sri Lanka, Turkey, and Georgia. She is a consultant for advertising agencies.

List of Figures

Fig. 2.1 Evolutionary phenomena in the way of doing business in sustainable era (*Source* Our elaboration) 12
Fig. 2.2 A conceptual model (*Source* Our elaboration) 18
Fig. 2.3 A new construct model (*Source* Our elaboration based on empirical investigation. *Legend* DI: digital innovation; GBMI: green business model innovation) 25
Fig. 3.1 Flow chart indicating research steps (*Source* Own elaboration) 39
Fig. 3.2 Published works in the years 2001–2021 (*Source* Own study based on Scopus database) 40
Fig. 3.3 Number of authors of publications from individual countries (*Source* Own study based on Scopus database. The data shows the countries of origin of at least three authors) 41
Fig. 3.4 Discipline of published works (*Source* Own study based on Scopus database. A publication may be assigned to more than one discipline) 45

Fig. 3.5	Keywords in the analyzed publications ($N = 127$) (*Source* Own elaboration based on Scopus database using VOSviewer software. The colors indicate the years of publication [according to the legend])	48
Fig. 3.6	Diversification of research in CSR, sustainable development and e-commerce (*Source* Own elaboration)	61
Fig. 6.1	Carroll's pyramid model for CSR (*Source* Compiled by the author based on Carroll, Archie B. "The Pyramid of Corporate Social Responsibility: Toward the Moral Management of Organizational Stakeholders." *Business Horizons* 34, no. 4 [1991]: 39–48)	124
Fig. 8.1	The conceptual framework of the study	185
Fig. 10.1	Agenda 2030 and its 17 SDGs	225

List of Tables

Table 2.1	Exemplary field investigation protocol	20
Table 2.2	Multiple examples of analysed supply chains	22
Table 3.1	Number of publications in 2001–2021	41
Table 3.2	Publication authors by country	42
Table 3.3	Publications in individual journals	43
Table 3.4	Number of citations for publications by country	45
Table 3.5	Publications with the highest number of citations	46
Table 3.6	Clusters of articles published in 2021 ($N = 38$)	50
Table 4.1	Holbrook's (1999) typology of consumer value	76
Table 4.2	Interviewee details	78
Table 4.3	Holbrook's (1999) typology of consumer value applied to takeaway coffee	90
Table 5.1	Thematic analysis	110
Table 6.1	Comparison of large and small business CSR based on Jenkins	126
Table 6.2	Characteristics of the sample, $n = 50$	128
Table 6.3	CSR in SMEs based on firm size and age	129
Table 7.1	A literature review resulted in 14 scientific articles focused on developing SBM tools	149
Table 7.2	Maximize material and energy efficiency—Archetype 1	158

Table 7.3	Closing resource loops—Archetype 2	160
Table 7.4	Substitute with renewables and natural processes—Archetype 3	161
Table 7.5	Deliver functionality rather than ownership—Archetype 4	161
Table 7.6	Adopt a stewardship role—Archetype 5	162
Table 7.7	Encourage sufficiency—Archetype 6	164
Table 7.8	Giving—Archetype 7	164
Table 7.9	Repurpose for society/environment—Archetype 8	165
Table 7.10	Inclusive value creation—Archetype 9	166
Table 7.11	Develop sustainable scale-up solutions—Archetype 10	167
Table 7.12	The systematic sustainable business model (SBM) approach integrating the core characteristics of SBM	172
Table 8.1	Selected definitions of a smart city	180
Table 8.2	Examples of two smart city rankings	181
Table 8.3	Demographic characteristics	188
Table 8.4	Summary of Chi-square test	189
Table 8.5	The willingness to co-create the smart city	189
Table 8.6	The willingness to co-create the smart city based on the gender group	190
Table 8.7	The activities in which respondents would like to be involved	192
Table 8.8	Other activities that citizens would like to be involved to co-create a smart city	192
Table 8.9	Experience in the co-creation of a smart city	192
Table 8.10	Citizens' experience in the co-creation of the smart city	193
Table 8.11	Activities that citizens already engaged in to co-create smart city	194
Table 9.1	Selected nature-based companies for the study	209
Table 9.2	Summary for the two groups	214
Table 10.1	SDGs—values for some regions and local communities	234
Table 10.2	Different rankings for different SDGs in the regions of Västernorrland and Jämtland/Härjedalen	234

1

New Roles for a Sustainable Economy

Anna Sörensson, Maria Bogren, Georgiana Grigore, Alin Stancu, and Anders Lundström

This book comes at a time where we ask how the academic community might work toward ethical, responsible, and sustainable business alternatives, and so where it fits within current global developments. We are experiencing an energy crisis that may be turning policy away from an

A. Sörensson (✉) · M. Bogren · A. Lundström
Mid Sweden University, Östersund, Sweden
e-mail: anna.sorensson@miun.se

G. Grigore
School of Business, University of Leicester, Leicester, UK

A. Stancu
Bucharest University of Economic Studies, Bucharest, Romania

A. Sörensson
Inland Norway University of Applied Science, Rena, Norway

M. Bogren
Nord University, Steinkjer, Norway

© The Author(s), under exclusive license to Springer Nature Switzerland AG 2024

A. Sörensson et al. (eds.), *Creating New Roles for a Sustainable Economy*, Palgrave Studies in Governance, Leadership and Responsibility,
https://doi.org/10.1007/978-3-031-61551-1_1

emphasis on sustainability and toward security. There is also a cost-of-living crisis that similarly detracts from efforts toward responsible and ethical business practice. Both are connected to a war in Europe resulting in wider global political unease with new risks to human welfare. Wars and energy crises invite comparisons with similar past events. At the same time, we are also experiencing something of a new industrial revolution in the form of digital technologies and especially artificial intelligence.

These challenges invite a consideration of new roles for a sustainable economy, as well as new possible routes to sustainability. And then there is the culture wars. Ken Peattie introduced us to these ideas in the last two years. Whether or not we accept the metaphor of culture wars, organizations are increasingly drawn into debates around representation, diversity, inclusion, and identity with little clarity over how they might be ethically navigated.

We therefore take stock and reflect on what roles might be created to enable a sustainable economy. Sensitivity to corporate social responsibility, and ideas, agendas, principles, practices, and arrangements of sustainability are areas that require creating new roles and entrepreneurial approaches. In this book, we want to address the emerging roles of existing businesses, markets, approaches, and practices for a sustainable economy.

The book brings together best papers presented at the 9th International Conference on Social Responsibility Ethics and Sustainable Business, held at Mid Sweden University in September 2022. This conference invited submissions that explore the new roles in a sustainable economy. Previously, we have published best papers from the ICSR conference on topics such as: 'Corporate Responsibilities, Sustainability and Markets' (Simões et al. 2022) that brought together CSR, sustainability and ways in which these principles and practices lead to the development of new markets, which might then affect organizations and their ecosystems; 'Corporate Responsibility and Sustainability during Coronavirus Crisis' (Sörensson et al. 2021) which provides an international examination of corporate responses to the pandemic in a variety of industries; 'Values and Sustainable Development' (Farache et al. 2020) which connects the concepts of financial value and/or moral values with

CSR activity; 'Responsible People' (Farache et al. 2019) which put a spotlight on the role of individuals in promoting social change, including studies from developing and developed countries; or 'Corporate Responsibility and Digital Community' (Grigore et al. 2018) which reflected on the evolving nature of CSR and its relationships with digital economy. In this year's book, we present chapters that include current thinking and developments by both academics and practitioners, combining theoretical foundations with practical insight on the roles that might contribute to sustainable sectors and economies. As such, this book is different in that it invites readers to imagine new roles that can shape businesses and societies, moving them closer to achieving sustainability goals.

Specifically, we ask: What new roles are existing businesses adopting in their practices in social responsibility and sustainability? How does the integration of sustainability and corporate social responsibility strategies and practices change the ways in which organizations operate? What types of markets are emerging for sustainable businesses? What is the role of social enterprises and non-profit organizations in shaping new roles and markets for a sustainable economy? These questions are answered in the three parts of the book.

There is an obvious link with the sustainability goals as the book invites readers to consider what are the new roles that best contribute to sustainable sectors and economies. The UN Sustainable Development Goals for 2030 reflect a worldwide common agenda for sustainable development. These 17 goals all include potential corporate engagement and specify the framework for corporate actions. Therefore, unpacking new roles for sustainability, including what these may mean for digitalization, green businesses, SMEs or social entrepreneurship, offers resources to help organizations in their attempts to reach sustainability goals.

1.1 Digitalization, Green Businesses, and Sustainability

In the first part, we explore digitalization, green businesses, and sustainability. In Chapter 2, Marcone looks at green business models and the digitalization of sustainability. Results are presented from an ongoing case study on green management with particular reference to the most relevant strategic decisions by manufacturing companies and the concomitant design by management of new governance systems and new structures or dashboards to evaluate the competitive performance of the company. The focus of the chapter is to highlight how new digital technologies, especially those implemented in operations, represent the ideal prerequisite for allowing manufacturing companies to formulate the most appropriate strategies to successfully attack current competitive contexts. Disruptive technological innovations generate new business models within companies, in the technological-production chains, and favor the re-design of business performance evaluation models and buyer–supplier relationships. In Chapter 3, Napiórkowska performs a bibliometric analysis of research on the concept of CSR and sustainable development in e-commerce. An analysis of articles published since 2000 was carried out using the Scopus database and the VOSviewer software. Content analysis of the latest research was performed using MAXQDA, a text analysis software. The content analysis shows clusters with current research topics in the field of CSR, sustainable development, and e-commerce.

1.2 New Roles for Sustainability, SMEs, and Social Entrepreneurship

In the second part, we consider the new roles for sustainability and their importance for SMEs and social entrepreneurship. In Chapter 4, Sherrington sets the spotlight on takeaway coffee and the interplay between convenience and sustainability. The purpose was to investigate how consumer sustainability attitudes and practices transfer to takeaway coffee consumption. Takeaway coffee was found to be dominated by self-oriented values, with taste and convenience as supreme elements that drive consumption. Other-oriented value elements such as sustainability received low priority in purchase decisions. In the interplay between convenience and sustainability, convenience was found to have the upper hand. In Chapter 5, Golpayegani and Schmudde focus on the contributions of social entrepreneurs to the regional development in a case study from Sweden. The results from the conducted 20 semi-structured interviews showed that social entrepreneurship alone is not sufficient to generate regional development but with the support of a Quadruple Helix collaboration the social entrepreneurs can play an important role. In Chapter 6, Reisinger studies corporate social responsibility approach by SMEs' managing directors in a Hungarian city. Results from interviews with 50 SMEs in Győr show that in medium-sized companies managing directors know more likely the term CSR but it does not relate to their CSR knowledge or use of CSR term.

1.3 Key Organizational Challenges for Sustainable Development

In the third and final part, we end with a reflection on the key organizational challenges for sustainable development, including how these might be addressed by academics and practitioners. In Chapter 7, Devine and Sandell present the systematic sustainable business model (SBM) approach as a flexible organizational tool. This approach allows for depicting to what extent an organization is involved in a variety of environmental, social, and economic sustainability-related activities. Each sustainability activity is scrutinized against the value being created, delivered, and captured. This flexible organizational tool allows for mapping of an organization's sustainability conduct, following progress over time, and comparisons between different organizations. In Chapter 8, Seid Hassen, Alemu Kesto, and Nigussie study the impact of working and living condition sustainability pillar on certificate achievement with the case of coffee exporting sector in Ethiopia. The result shows that the internal management system, government authority, and certification schemes monitoring system negatively affect working and living condition criteria compliances which in turn lead to certification delay and extra cost for closing the non-conformities in general which affects the certificate achievement of the coffee exporters. In Chapter 8 Wiścicka-Fernando conduct an empirical study in Poland of Citizens' engagement to co-create a smart city. Citizens' engagement in the development of the smart city is significant. The results of this study can be used to inform sustainable development-oriented decisions and can become key for the regional policy-making process and other researchers interested in smart city development. In Chapter 9 Sörensson and Bogren focus on how entrepreneurs in nature-based businesses communicate sustainability values with their stakeholders. Data were collected from 100 nature-based businesses in Sweden, which were selected from various categories. The results show that there are differences between the different categories of companies, and the companies are grouped into two types. In Chapter 10 Sörensson, Lundström, Hallqvist, and Vestlund address municipalities' challenges when implementing Agenda 2030 in their operations. The results show that the municipalities invest to varying degrees in the 17 SDGs and that the focus is on issues that the municipalities see as central to developing and achieving growth in their municipality. The focus is mainly on the own operations more than how Agenda 2030 is to be implemented in relation to the surrounding society.

References

Devine, A., & Sandell, M. (2023). The Systematic Sustainable Business Model (SBM) Approach—A Flexible Organizational Tool. In Sorensson et al. (eds) *New Roles for a Sustainable Economy.* Cham: Palgrave Macmillan.

Farache, F., Grigore, G., Stancu, A., & McQueen, D. (Eds.). (2019). *Responsible People: The Role of the Individual in CSR, Entrepreneurship and Management Education.* Springer.

Farache, F., Grigore, G., Stancu, A., & McQueen, D. (Eds.). (2020). *Values and Corporate Responsibility: CSR and Sustainable Development.* Springer Nature.

Golpayegani, K., & Schmudde, U. (2023). The Contributions of Social Entrepreneurs to the Regional Development: A Case Study in Jämtland

Härjedalen. In Sorensson et al. (eds) *New Roles for a Sustainable Economy.* Cham: Palgrave Macmillan.

Grigore, G., Stancu, A., & McQueen, D. (2018). *Corporate Responsibility and Digital Communities*. Cham: Palgrave Macmillan.

Hassen, F.S., Kesto, D.A., & Nigussie, Y. (2023). Impact of Working and Living Condition Sustainability Pillar on Certificate Achievement: The Case of Coffee Exporting Sector in Ethiopia. In Sorensson et al. (eds) *New Roles for a Sustainable Economy.* Cham: Palgrave Macmillan.

Marcone, M. (2023). Green Business Models: The Digitization of Sustainability. In Sorensson et al. (eds) *New Roles for a Sustainable Economy*. Cham: Palgrave Macmillan.

Napiórkowska, A. (2023). Bibliometric Analysis of Research on the Concept of CSR and Sustainable Development in E-commerce. In Sorensson et al. (eds) *New Roles for a Sustainable Economy*. Cham: Palgrave Macmillan.

Reisinger, A. (2023). Corporate Social Responsibility Approach by SMEs' Managing Directors in a Hungarian City of Győr—Evidence from Interview Research. In Sorensson et al. (eds) *New Roles for a Sustainable Economy.* Cham: Palgrave Macmillan.

Sherrington, M. (2023). Takeaway Coffee: The Interplay Between Convenience and Sustainability. In Sorensson et al. (eds) *New Roles for a Sustainable Economy*. Springer Nature.

Simões, C., Stancu, A., & Grigore, G. (Eds.). (2021). *Corporate Responsibility, Sustainability and Markets: How Ethical Organisations and Consumers Shape Markets*. Springer Nature.

Sörensson, A., Tesfaye, B., Lundström, A., Grigore, G., & Stancu, A. (Eds.). (2021). *Corporate Responsibility and Sustainability During the Coronavirus Crisis: International Case Studies*. Springer Nature.

Wiścicka-Fernando, M. (2023). Citizens' Engagement to Co-Create a Smart City—An Empirical Study. In Sorensson et al. (eds) *New Roles for a Sustainable Economy.* Cham: Palgrave Macmillan.

Part I

Digitalization, Green Businesses and Sustainability

2

Green Business Model: The Digitization of Sustainability

Maria Rosaria Marcone

2.1 Introduction

Since sustainability is a new economic model the attention of scholars and economic operators must necessarily pay particular attention to business production systems and to new ways of managing these business systems and new relationships within supply chains.

The research work presents the first results of an ongoing study on green management with particular reference to the most relevant strategic decisions on a wide range of evolutionary phenomena in the way of doing a new way of doing business that induces management at the concomitant design of (1) new green business model (see point 1 in Fig. 2.1), of (2) new digital technological implementation (see point 2 in Fig. 2.1) and of (3) the reconfiguration of sustainable supply chains (SC). These supply chains appear as new governance systems and, in

M. R. Marcone (✉)
Business Economics, Marche Polytechnic University, Ancona, Italy
e-mail: m.r.marcone@staff.univpm.it

© The Author(s), under exclusive license to Springer Nature Switzerland AG 2024

A. Sörensson et al. (eds.), *Creating New Roles for a Sustainable Economy*, Palgrave Studies in Governance, Leadership and Responsibility,
https://doi.org/10.1007/978-3-031-61551-1_2

the concrete, they become new managerial structures that demand the design and the application of more adequate dashboards to evaluate the competitive performance of the company.

The focus of the paper is mainly to highlight how new digital technologies, especially those implemented in operations, in new material design and in new digital governance platforms at the supply chain level, represent the ideal prerequisite for allowing manufacturing companies to formulate the most appropriate sustainable strategies to successfully attack current competitive contexts.

In strategic management studies, traditionally focused on the decisions' formulation, increasing importance is recognized in the analysis of how changes are generated and the evaluation of the effects they generate (Hock et al. 2015). The widest vision of business strategy studies increasingly incorporates the innovative processes that sustain the sustainability aspects into their productive processes, products and services. While extant research on the linkage between sustainability has gained attention, should be noted that in the past years, prior research has predominantly focused on firm's sustainable phenomena, analysing their impact on firm's sustainable performances (e.g. financially

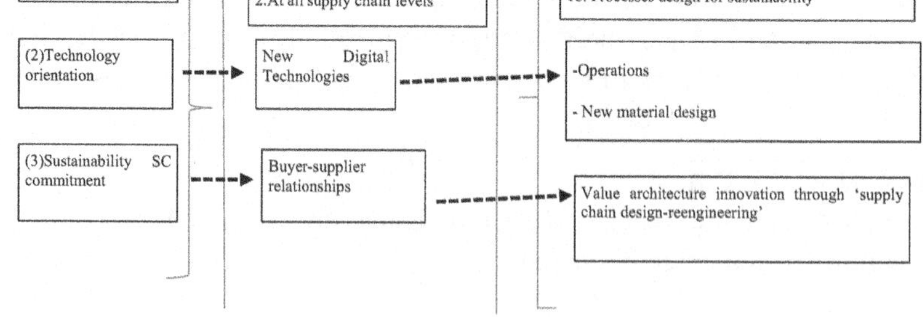

Fig. 2.1 Evolutionary phenomena in the way of doing business in sustainable era (*Source* Our elaboration)

and environmentally) and on sustainable innovative products (considered as final output), neglecting the supply chain innovative mechanisms that leverage sustainability. While findings from previous studies suggest that sustainability may drive business model innovation, it still lacks empirical evidence on whether and how innovative processes for the sustainability may influence the evolvement of business model (BM) in firms belonging to the given supply chain and also may improve buyer–supplier relationships in a new sense (Fig. 2.1).

The contribution examines the critical yet underexplored role of innovative processes diffusion in sustaining digital innovation in business model strategies of the firms belonging to the supply chain systems more and more deveining evolutive in a sustainable sense. The study of the evolutionary view of disruptive innovation diffusion in the supply chain is empirically assisted by the investigation of the roles played by case studies—distinct yet interconnected parties (agri-suppliers, food manufacturing systems, manufacturing firms, platforms or hub academies)—within innovation supply chain systems as well as the research opportunities it brings. Height are those studied (see text Table 2.2).

We want to contribute to the improvement of the innovative sustainability research by analysing supply chain strategic orientation and its direct influence on competitive outcomes of the innovative processes of the supply chain actors. Moreover, we extend our previous research on the linkage between innovation and sustainability, which mainly relied on qualitative case studies.

Numerous managerial studies have made use of the theoretical framework focused on resources—resource-based view (RBT) approach—to analyse how various forms of integration between actors-firms in the supply chain impact on their performance (Flynn et al. 2010; Cao and Zhang 2011; Schoenherr and Swink 2012; Felsberger et al. 2022). The resource-based approach also makes it possible to estimate the value of the 'relational resources' that are developed in the 'buyer–supplier' relationships.

2.2 Company Innovative Strategies for Sustainable Competition

Digital Technologies

Disruptive[1] technological innovations generate the adaptation of del dashboard to evaluate new business model redesign activities within companies, regarding in particular their technological-production activities, and require the redesign of business performance evaluation models. In addition, digital technologies permeate the supply chain relationships, since they are used for designing multi-sided platforms within a given supply chain, within which they represent new governance model.

Studies focused on R&D that impact on the improvement of business competitive performance (including business productivity) must necessarily be based on theoretical study frameworks that consider complementary intangible investments such as business process redesign, the co-invention of new products and business models, and investments in human capital. Although the effects of complementary investments and their spillovers are often mentioned in the literature, there is a lack of in-depth research (Nonnis et al. 2023).

It is something further than the classic absorptive capacities (AC) (Cohen and Levinthal 1990; Riikkinen et al. 2017) that has the potential to explain performance and competitive advantage. Research on AC is cross-disciplinary and involves theories on dynamic capability, network structures and knowledge management (Apriliyanti and Alon 2017). Seminal scientific research converges in defining AC as a multidimensional theoretical construct, based on ability developed in learning processes or in knowledge processes. The analysis of the relationships

---

[1] The 5 faces of 'disruption' have been presented by Clayton Magleby Christensen. In fact, development of an overwhelming wave that is at the same time efficient, proactive, inclusive, constructive and in favor of society.

Disruptive innovations are not breakthrough innovations or 'ambitious start-ups' that drastically change the way business is done, but rather consist of simple, accessible and affordable products and services. These products and services appear modest at first, but over time have the potential to transform an industry.

between AC and its knowledge dimensions is important (Knoppen et al. 2022).

Some scientific studies suggest that a firm's commitment to sustainability drives innovations and thus may give firms an opportunity to gain a competitive advantage by changing the current business model innovation and furthermore that sustainability seems to be directly linked to such type of innovation (Spieth and Schneider 2016; Foss and Saebi 2018; Sovacool et al. 2020).

Some authors studied the effect of emerging digital technologies on the operations management through co-creation and found a positive impact on efficiency, safety and ecological sustainability. These technologies will create new potential for firms changing strategic management, which may lead to improved sustainable competitiveness.

Technology orientation refers to a constant monitoring of technological developments and a constant search for new technologies beyond current products. Kennedy et al. (2017) found that the choice to increase sustainability intensifies technological knowledge in order to develop solutions to sustainability issues and gain possible competitive advantages. Likewise, new technologies could create opportunities to conform with governmental regulations regarding material usage, energy usage and production emissions, which might be required to avoid fines. New technologies can also change the production processes and the procurement practices. Digital technologies might enable new disruption channels and may develop the potential to design new supply chain structure (value creation architecture) (Teece 2010).

Sustainability

While it is commonly believed that sustainability and sustainable development are interchangeable terms, they are in themselves different. Their natural difference lies in the fact that sustainable development is the journey, the path and the process to achieve sustainability. More recently, economic operators and business managers have become aware that environmental sustainability is an indispensable value, not only to be safeguarded, but even to be increased. Sustainability is the company's capital, that is a potential competitive advantage (King et al. 2006; Krause et al. 2009). Sustainability is made up of a plurality of elements unthinkable until a few years ago: in addition to the patrimonial and financial capital, partly tangible (machinery, land, buildings) and intangible (know-how, reputation, value of the brand, etc.), is made up of natural capital (raw material extraction methods, water purification, renewable energies, ecosystem services, etc.), human capital (resources, motivation, training) and the value of capital of a given society (education system, culture, infrastructure, etc.). Furthermore, there is awareness that sustainable companies can evaluate and monitor their environmental performance targets, thus expanding the more usual company performance evaluation metrics. Sustainable development is currently a key element in the processes of formulation of the competitive strategies of many companies we will take care of the manufacturing, energy and agrifood sectors (Dyllick and Muff 2016). The sustainable development of the company's business presupposes that additional objectives with respect to the traditional ones (economic-financial objectives) are considered both in the formulation of growth strategies and in the planning of modern internal and inter-firm governance procedures. The study of corporate business sustainability reveals the importance of the parameters aimed at assessing the eco-efficiency of corporate activities (from the business case to the natural case) (Dyllick and Muff 2016).

Business Model

The business model is the operational aspect of the company strategy. More analytically, it is the company's way of working which, having to be redefined in dynamic competitive situations, is the result of continuous reconfigurations of the operating processes and parts of the company's production structure referable to them (re-engineering).

The business model must necessarily be restructured by companies that intend to anticipate the signs of change coming from outside (sector's structure, market needs, development of technologies, etc.) or that even want to act proactively in the external context. The business model modification is concretely and profitably possible in the production structures which adapt with agility (operational agility) to the new competitive ways.

The business model modification and the resulting creation of value are sources of a competitive advantage which is also modified, since it is different, sometimes significantly, from the past.

A conceptual model is developed to examine whether the goals of firms implementing new business models (BM), which are essentially the marginal edge and the growth-oriented strategy (Latifi et al. 2021), affect a firm's overall performance. In fact, earning edge and growth strategy (in Fig. 2.2 they appear as 'first level performance') are two essential performances, which however generate significant effects on company under-performance or second-level performances (such as revenue growth, efficiency growth, operational capabilities). According to some scholars, a plausible approach may be to analyse mediating and moderating factors that allow firms to translate BM into higher performance (Guo et al. 2017). According to these scholars, the mediating factors are precisely the three elements, revenue growth, efficiency growth, operational capabilities, which in this work are the detailed or second-level performances, in practice those which more analytically allow us to interpret the quality of the impact of the new digital business models on the green sustainability and on the competitiveness of the company (Fig. 2.2).

The business model is defined as new when it is the result of the planning, by managers, entrepreneurs and investors, of a system of activities that is radically new in terms of strategic objectives, operational structure and forms of governance (architectural novelty of the business) or of a supply chain system, in which activities with elements of novelty (goals, structure, governance) integrate with unmodified activities (complementary novelty of the business) (Teece 2010; Zott and Amit 2010; Spieth et al. 2016).

The production of scientific contributions on the subject of the business model is extremely active and lively. For further insights, please refer to the reflections that some authors have launched on the topics listed below: Brucherer et al. (2012) recognizes two important 'macro-dimensions' among the causes of modification of business models, the

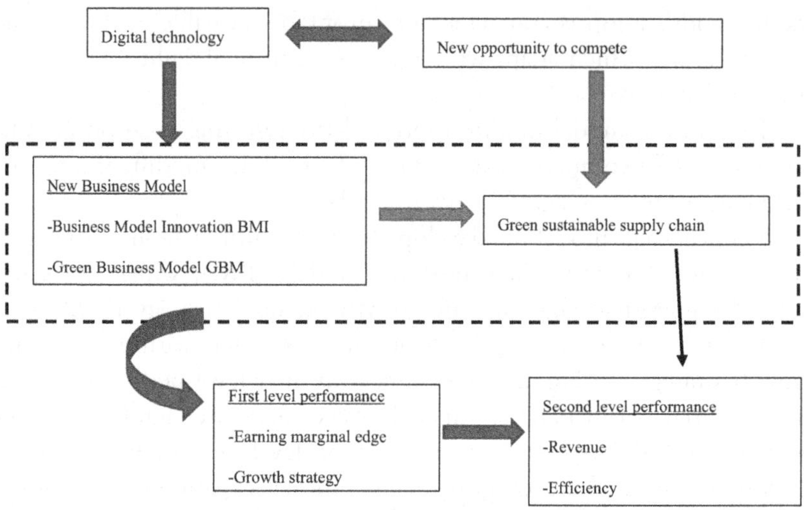

Fig. 2.2 A conceptual model (*Source* Our elaboration)

market and the industry; Teece (2010) argues that the criticality of the operational meaning of the business model lies in the connection that it makes possible between the 'micro-foundations' or 'micro-elements' constituting the business strategy and the competitive performance it actually achieves; Schneider and Spieth (2013) are among the most convinced supporters of the business model as an operational process in continuous evolution.

Digital Innovation in Green Sustainable Supply Chains

The companies that attribute strategic importance to environmental issues are those that recognize a new opportunity to compete. They are inclined to make huge investments aimed at the adoption of non-polluting technological solutions in production systems, as well as to start internal training activities to increase the skills of human resources in environmental matters and also to design specific and well-detailed internal organizational procedures. See the impact of the green sustainable SC in more detailed performance (or 'second-level performance') in Fig. 2.2. This is the case of companies that use production technologies fuelled by renewable energy sources and reduce CO_2 emissions, or that use materials for whose production the production contexts of the countries of origin are not compromised. Among the companies that adopt this strategy, we can mention those that use the residues or scraps of the manufacturing cycles in further industrial transformation processes. The development of digital technologies creates competitive opportunities for firms in repositioning in international supply chains. While research on the linkage between sustainability and innovation mainly focused on how firms develop sustainable innovations, a deeper understanding of sustainability's effects on supply chain strategies and inter-firm planning processes requires more insights (Adams et al. 2016; Klein et al. 2021).

2.3 Methodology

This is qualitative research. First, we continuously visited and revisited the international managerial literature and systematized and re-systematized the conceptual categories which are the focus of this study, and which could contribute to increasing the knowledge base of management scholars. The analysis of the international managerial literature has favoured the inclusion of articles and research contributions based on the following criteria: articles should include hypotheses concerning the relation between digital BMI by introducing a new system of creating, delivering and capturing value; references are made to new supply chain relationships. We continuously collected and re-analysed information (quantitative data, such as revenue, investment efforts in innovative procedures and processes), internal and external resources involved (organizational, managerial and above all research skills applied to production departments) and analysis of the procedures put in place to innovate, such as evolved internal and external relationships to the company; those external to the company, but within the supply chain to which it belongs; those external to the company and the supply chain.

The survey was administered after in SMEs' sample after forward and back translation procedures. Before administering the survey, we subjected the design of the questionnaire to two rounds of pre-testing with (a) first level area managers and representatives of trade associations and (b) technicians from various managerial areas and actors in the field of start-ups. So even if the number of companies is limited, the questionnaire was administered in two different steps to many people (see text Table 2.1).

The value of qualitative research is also that of proceeding in a positive-interpretative way: in fact, the presentation of the case study allows us to interpret its relation to theoretical. Since our purpose has been to systematize and conceptualize an empirical phenomenon and thereby contribute to the enrichment of the managerial theory (Eisenhardt 2021), rather than verifying or falsifying already established constructs, we are not claiming that our findings are universal nor that they reveal statistically significant relationships.

An interpretative, qualitative approach, utilizing selected multi-case study interviews, is chosen because it helps to navigate and understand the complex issues that are associated with the data quality concept, and its relation to the factors involving managerial practices to implement a

Table 2.1 Exemplary field investigation protocol

More precisely, the elements of the digital supply chain projects that have been investigated have been those deemed capable of influencing the relational structure established between the partners. In this study the following are considered:
• procurement policies (single, dual and multi-sourcing), • attitude and commitment to collaborative improvement projects with supply chain partners (especially at the 'supplier-side' level), • the position of the company within the SC, • the extension of the interdependencies between the companies within the SC (relative importance of a customer for the supplier's business and criticality of the supplies), • the duration of the relationship and the types of past experiences, • technological or procedural links between companies, • the existence of legal constraints, such as patents, contracts, etc., • the bargaining power and influence of the parties, • the length and complexity of the supply chain.

new business model and to build facilities in modern relationships within supply chain.

The constructs were developed after a comprehensive review of previous literature. Industry 4.0 leads to the age of digitization. Everything is digital and intelligent: business models, environments, production systems, machines, operators, products and services. New disruptive technologies provide supply chains with broad prospects for gaining competitive advantage and a good foundation for future sustainable supply chain practices, paving the way for adopting new business models and improving the manufacturing process. We approach this task through a literature review and multiple examples of supply chains (see text Table 2.2). These are supply chains located in Italy and sectoral interdependencies in technology value chains are analysed.

2.4 Digital Business Model in Digital Supply Chain Reconfiguration

A new conceptual model is shown in Fig. 2.3. Although some previous steps of the research still in progress have been analysed, in the present work we want to show some preliminary systematizations even if scientific reflection activities are still ongoing and discussions with national and international scientific representatives are scheduled in the next international conferences.

Transitions towards sustainability are highly dependent on the development and diffusion of emerging technologies causing changes both in the demand for materials such as minerals and metals and in the firm's productive processes (productive processes redesign, production servitization, etc.). Industry 4.0 leads to the age of digitization. Everything is digital and intelligent: business models, environmental relationships, production systems, industrial machinery, products and services and supply chain relationships. It has been stated that the change of the business model is concretely and profitably possible in the productive structures that with agility (operational agility) are adapted to the new modalities to compete. Among the most convinced supporters of the

Table 2.2 Multiple examples of analysed supply chains

Firms	Some business information	Sustainable strategies
1	• Born, 2015 • Localization, Tanzania • Supply chain platform that is internationalized, generating the technological leap	*Milk supply chain* Leading Italian company in the production of milk, promoter of the motto 'there is no quality without social responsibility', is engaged by many in the planning and support of social and cultural initiatives both in Italy and in poor countries. Among the most significant examples, we can mention the Africa Milk Project which allowed the construction of a dairy in Tanzania. The dairy, from a funded project, has become a company that allows small producers in rural communities to autonomously take charge of project activities. By replicating the cooperative model on which the Italian company is based, an economic project has been successfully launched, sustainable over time, in one of the poorest areas of Tanzania

Firms	Some business information	Sustainable strategies
2	• Born, 1978 • Location: Florence (Italy) • Supply chain re-engineering (in 'supplier-side' perspective)	*Organic food* Favouring the supply chain of Italian (or even regional) raw materials is the strategy pursued by the company that specialized in the production of organic food. Objectives: the choice makes it possible to reduce costs (almost in procurement and in production areas), to increase the resilience of the supply chain, to involve the players in the supply chain in innovative-digitalized processes Product strategy: sustainable and organic food (suppliers that do not use herbicides, pesticides, chemical fertilizers, GMOs) exclusively plant-based (i.e. vegetable). Organic, healthy products characterized by a high nutritional profile, but also by unique recipes in terms of flavour and formulation. Target products: (1) Rich in and (2) free from foods
3	• Born, 2022 • Location, Parma (Italy) • New supply chain design in a 'district area'	*Biotech Hub* Modification of the business model of the leading pharmaceutical company that designs the new Italian supply chain of biotechnological drugs Objectives: *progress in science, technology, innovative* drugs, technological hub in a 'district area'. Increase Italian biopharmaceutical exports

(continued)

Table 2.2 (continued)

Firms	Some business information	Sustainable strategies
4	• Location: Marghera and Gela (Italy) • Supply chain internationalization • Supply chain platform redesign	Green sustainability—Precision agriculture sector Production of eco fuels: no more palm oil, but (1) frying oils (used), animal fats discarded from slaughterhouses and other biomass; (2) from Kenya, non-edible cotton, castor and croton oils From Kenya arrives in Gela, in November 2022, the first load of vegetable oil produced in the Makueni experimental farm, where castor, croton and cotton seeds are pressed, vegetable raw materials that are not in competition with the food chain, grown in degraded areas, harvested from spontaneous trees or resulting from agricultural by-products The Marghera biorefinery is the first in the world where hydrogenated biofuels are produced to replace diesel, naphtha, LPG and kerosene for aircraft. Gela plant: production capacity—at full capacity, 20,000 tonnes/year; in 2023 it will reach 5000 tonnes
5 6 7 8	• Born, 2022 • Location: Parma, Perugia, Puglia • Supply chain collaboration among 200 Italian producers (suppliers-agronomists) and 7000 hectares of crops will be digitized • Digitized supply chain platform (technological leap)	4 companies in the agrifood chain (with well-known and established brands in the world) have joined an open platform project (i.e. accessible in 'as a service' mode via management software in the cloud) and capable of accompanying 'supplier-side' companies to gradually digitize, simplifying the collection and processing of data The platform project started in 2022, initially involving 103 operators in the supply chain and provides for the integration of data collected by IoT sensors, climate indicators and forecasting models to have full control of agronomic management and a more precise understanding of the environmental footprint of the supply chain itself

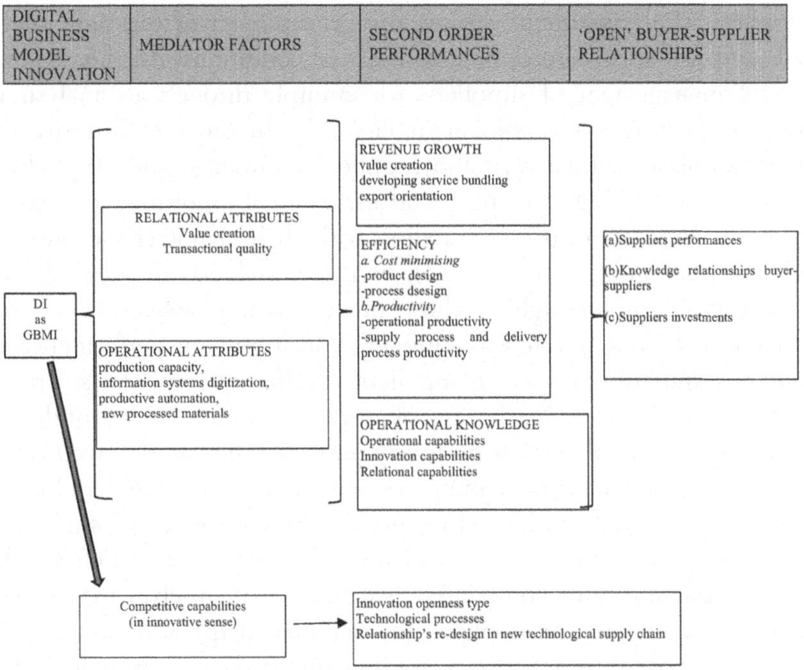

Fig. 2.3 A new construct model (*Source* Our elaboration based on empirical investigation. *Legend* DI: digital innovation; GBMI: green business model innovation)

business model as an operating process in continuous becoming, we remember Teece (2010) and Schneider and Spieth (2013).

New disruptive technologies provide supply chains with broad prospects for gaining competitive advantage and a good foundation for future sustainable supply chain practices, paving the way for adopting new business models and improving the manufacturing process. Another element enhancing the relations of new business models in the supply chain is the amplification of the added value generated.

Many studies have followed on the importance of relationships in SCs (Parmigiani and Rivera-Santos 2011; Cao and Lumineau 2015; Gölgeci et al. 2018). Having the availability of strategic resources is of fundamental importance because this allows for forging relationships with key suppliers who consequently allow the procurement of the right materials and will apply appropriate contractual conditions. All this requires careful management of suppliers, for example through an analysis of their performance (see point a in Fig. 2.3). In order to improve the synergies between their own and suppliers' knowledge, industrial client firms should be able to identify and use external innovative knowledge (radically innovative) in combination with their characteristic business activities (see point b in Fig. 2.3). Some research has focused, already in the past, on highlighting how procurement strategies have been transformed from rewards to supplier's contingent on performance to high-risk initiatives involving suppliers' specific investments (see point c in Fig. 2.3). Now, in the era of open innovation, one wonders if relations with suppliers that positively influence the competitive performance of manufacturing companies can be seen as closed industrial client–supplier relationships. In practice, the emergence of such relationships requires the formation of new relational assets which are the basis of the ability of companies to reposition themselves in the new structures of the offer or supply chain: they are perhaps even more important than those relational assets, traditionally dedicated to maintaining consolidated relationships, as well as identifying and planning new ones. Scholars are only now beginning to examine knowledge resources and the mechanisms underlying the competitive advantage driven by innovation that reconfigures the design processes of fashion collections. As knowledge resources are arguably of critical importance to innovation (Höber and Schaarschmidt, 2017), they are increasingly being made available by supply chain operators (manufacturers, suppliers, retailers, start-uppers, etc.) in the restructuring processes of innovative production chain phenomena (Salunke et al. 2019).

Although the RBV places emphasis almost exclusively on the benefits deriving from collaborations based on the development of resources that are specific (unique or dedicated) to each relationship, and therefore difficult to imitate, interactions between diversified supply chains emerge with ever greater force in global competition. Indeed, the analysis of the supply chain in the relational perspective considers the interdependence that is created between companies and the willingness that they have to initiate and control forms of interaction that increase the degree of integration of the supply chain. The concept of integration between different business units (companies), aimed at constituting a single 'business system', essentially refers to the quality of the collaboration between companies in the activation of innovative and complex technological processes, which, through the production and products and services at the 'downstream' stages, generate value. We found that innovative strategic orientation choices, such as digital technology orientation and green sustainability supply chain design, affect more important competitive supply chain outcomes and improve buyer–supplier relationships.

The relationships of the new business models within the supply chain are relatively stable, non-hierarchical in nature and based on interdependence, in the sense that what occurs in a relationship has an impact on the contents and processes of other companies belonging to the same supply chain. This relational dimension is based on a process of mutual convergence which, in order to be able to develop, requires the willingness of the parties to interact and establish mutual knowledge.

2.5 Some Final Reflections

The research work presents the first results of an ongoing study on green management with reference to the most relevant strategic decisions by companies, belonging in manufacturing, agrifood and energy sectors, and the concomitant design by management of new relational governance systems and new structures or dashboards to evaluate the competitive performance of the company.

The academic-scientific debate has been heavily focused in recent years on the issue of sustainability that has captured the attention of the financial and social disciplines. However, since this is a new economic model, the attention of scholars and economic operators (managers, institutions, etc.) must necessarily pay particular attention to business production systems and to new ways of managing these business systems within supply chains.

Following the research results obtained, it emerged that buyers and suppliers, developing relational skills, favour the profitable circulation of information, which is the basis of cooperation based on mutual trust. Such a strong degree of integration determines the reduction of conflicts and the formation of relational revenues. The integration of supply chain operators or supply chain integration (SCI) is made possible by the ability of companies to cooperate with 'critical suppliers and customers' and more and more cooperation involves business managers (intra-organizational collaboration), managers of different companies, but belonging to a group or to a multinational (cooperation between home-mother and subsidiary) and managers of completely autonomous companies (inter-organizational cooperation).

The paper presents modern and unusual innovative processes shedding new light on success factors in modern competitive contexts increasingly anchored to integrated and relational relationships (relationships) in sustainable supply chains.

At the conclusion of the study, the first cognitive results of which have been presented here, we would like to bring to the attention of the reader some observations. Firstly, the company's 'proactivity' towards environmental and social issues positively orients the opinion of the stakeholders. Secondly, the empirical findings make it possible to agree with those managerial studies which have highlighted how responsible management of the 'supply chain' increases the company's reputation, which is one of the critical success factors to be leveraged in international competitive processes and in international business markets (Tate et al. 2010). It is understandable how, even in business marketing, companies strive to demonstrate that the activities generate positive externalities both on the social and on the environmental context. Because transactions have evolved today: on the 'supply side' contractual relationships take place within a wide range of potential innovative relationships involving start-ups, innovation communities, young and competitive companies in new sectors, etc. It seems clear that transactional relationships are not to be considered as traditional ways of regulating supply chain relationships in supply chains characterized by consolidated or even mature technologies. Moreover, if a company competes mainly on product-service innovation, the type of relationship could depend on where the innovation is expected to emerge: many types of innovations (and therefore the technological assets) emerge outside the usual and close collaborations between suppliers and buyers.

The relationships between the operations in the supply chain are at the basis of the evolution of the value created by the supply chain. Upstream integration concerns partnerships or simply contractual relationships between purchasing companies and supplier companies. The need to involve suppliers in innovation processes, in the design processes of new business models, as well as to acquire relevant information on the evolution of technologies and on the behaviour of competitors, increases the need for coordination between companies in the supply chain, concretely achievable with the conclusion of long-term agreements, the establishment of more intense communication processes, the ability to manage joint decision-making processes and the development of relationships of trust.

References

Adams, Richard, Sally Jeanrenaud, John Bessant, David Denyer, and Patrick Overy. "Sustainability-Oriented Innovation. A Systematic Review." *International Journal of Management Reviews* 18, no. 2 (2016): 180–205. https://doi.org/10.1016/j.ibusrev.2017.02.007.

Apriliyanti, Indru Dwi, and Ilan Alon. "Bibliometric Analysis of Absorptive Capacity." *International Business Review* 26, no. 5 (2017): 896–907. https://doi.org/10.1016/j.ibusrev.2017.02.007.

Brucherer, Eva, Uli Eiser, Oliver Gassman. "Towards Systematic Business Model Innovation: Lessons from Product Innovation Management." *Creativity and Innovation Management* 21, no. 2 (2012): 183–198. https://doi.org/10.1111/j.1467-8691.2012.00637.x.

Cao, Zhi, and Fabrice Lumineau. 2015. "Revisiting the Interplay Between Contractual and Relational Governance: A Qualitative and Meta-Analytic Investigation." *Journal of Operations Management* 33–34, January (2015): 15–42. https://doi.org/10.1016/j.jom.2014.09.009.

Cao, Mei, and Qingyu Zhang. "Supply Chain Collaboration: Impact on Collaborative Advantage and Firm Performance." *Journal of Operations Management* 29, no. 3 (2011): 163–180. https://doi.org/10.1016/j.jom.2010.12.008.

Cohen, Wesley M., and Daniel A. Levinthal. "Absorptive Capacity: A New Perspective on Learning and Innovation." *Administrative Science Quarterly* 35, no. 1 (1990): 128–152. http://links.jstor.org/sici?sici=0001-8392%28199003%2935%3A1%3C128%3AACANPO%3E2.0.CO%3B2-5.

Dyllick, Thomas, and Katrin Muff. "Clarifying the Meaning of Sustainable Business: Introducing a Typology From Business-as-Usual to True Business Sustainability." *Organization & Environment* 29, no. 2 (2016): 156–174. https://doi.org/10.1177/1086026615575176.

Eisenhardt, Kattlehen. "What Is the Eisenhardt Method, Really?" *Strategic Organization* 19, no. 1 (2021): 147–160. https://doi.org/10.1177/1476127020982866.

Felsberger, Andreas, Fahham Hasan Qaiser, Alok Choudhary, and Gerald Reiner. "The Impact of Industry 4.0 on the Reconciliation of Dynamic Capabilities: Evidence from the European Manufacturing Industries." *Production Planning and Control* 33, nos. 2–3 (2022): 277–300. https://doi.org/10.1080/09537287.2020.1810765.

Flynn, Barbara, Huo Baofeng, and Xiande Zhao. "The Impact of supply Chain Integration on Performance: A Contingency and Configuration Approach." *Journal of Operations Management* 28, no. 1 (2010): 58–71. https://doi.org/10.1016/j.jom.2009.06.001.

Foss, Nicolai, and Tina Saebi. "Business Models and Business Model Innovation. Between Wicked and Paradigmatic Problems." *Long Range Planning* 51, no. 1 (2018): 9–21 https://doi.org/10.1016/j.lrp.2017.07.006.

Gölgeci, Ismail, William Murphy, and David Johnston. "Power-Based Behaviors in Supply Chains and Their Effects on Relational Satisfaction: A Fresh Perspective and Directions for Research." *European Management Journal* 36, no. 2 (2018): 278–287. https://doi.org/10.1016/j.emj.2017.03.011.

Höber, Björn, and Mario Schaarschmidt. "Transforming from Service Providers to Solution Providers: Implications for Provider-Customer Relationships and Customer-Induced Solution Innovation." *International Journal of Technology Management* 73, nos. 1–3 (2017): 1–15. https://doi.org/10.1504/IJTM.2017.082357.

Hock, Marianne, Thomas Clauss, and Esther Schulz. "The Impact of Organizational Culture on a Firm's Capability to Innovate the Business Model." *R&D Management* 46, no. 3 (2015): 433–450. https://doi.org/10.1111/radm.12153.

Guo, Hai, Jintang Tang, Zhongfeng Su, and Jerome Kats. "Opportunity Recognition and SME Performance: The Mediating Effect of Business Model Innovation." *R&D Management* 47, no. 3 (2017): 431–442. https://doi.org/10.1111/radm.12219.

Kennedy, Steve, Gail Whiteman, and Jan van den Ende. "Radical Innovation for Sustainability. The Power of Strategy and Open Innovation." *Long Range Planning* 50, no. 6 (2017): 712–725. https://doi.org/10.1016/j.lrp.2016.05.004.

King, Andrews, Stuart Burgess, Winnie Ijomah, and Chris McMahon. "Reducing Waste: Repair, Recondition, Remanufacture or Recycle?" *Journal of Sustainable Development* 14, no. 4 (2006): 257–267. https://doi.org/10.1002/sd.271.

Klein, Sascha, Patrick Spieth, and Sven Heidenreich. "Facilitating Business Model Innovation: The Influence of Sustainability and the Mediating Role of Strategic Orientations." *Journal of Product Innovation Management* 38, no. 2 (2021): 271–288. https://doi.org/10.1111/jpim.12563.

Knoppen, Desirée, Willem Saris, and Paolo Moncagatta. "Absorptive Capacity Dimensions and the Measurement of Cumulativeness." *Journal of Business Research* 139 (2022): 312–324. https://doi.org/10.1016/j.jbusres.2021.09.065.

Krause, Daniel, Stephan Vachon, and Robert Klassen. "Special Topic Forum on Sustainable Supply Chain Management: Introduction and Reflections on the Role of Purchasing Management." *Journal of Supply Chain Management: A Global Review of Purchasing and Supply* 45, no. 4 (2009): 18–25. https://doi.org/10.1111/j.1745-493X.2009.03173.x.

Latifi, Mohammad-Ali, Shahrokh Nikou, and Harry Bowman. "Business Model Innovation and Firm Performance; Exploring Causal Mechanisms in SMEs." *Technovation* 107 (2021): 102274. https://doi.org/10.1016/j.technovation.2021.102274.

Nonnis, Alberto, Ahmed Bonfour, and Keungoui Kim. "Knowledge Spillovers and Intangible Complementarities. Emprical Case of Eurepean Countries." *Research Policy* 52 (2023): 104611. https://doi.org/10.1016/j.respol.2022.104611.

Parmigiani, Anne, and Miguel Rivera-Santos. "Clearing a Path Through the Forest: A Meta-Review of Inter-Organizational Relationships." *Journal of Management* 37, no. 4 (2011): 1108–1136. https://doi.org/10.3846/tede.2018.5695.

Riikkinen, Rilana, Katri Kauppi, and Asta Salmi. "Learning Sustainability? Absorptive Capacities as Drivers of Sustainability in MNCs' Purchasing." *International Business Review* 26, no. 6 (2017): 1075–1087. https://doi.org/10.1016/j.ibusrev.2017.04.001.

Salunke, Sandeep, Jay Weerawardena, and Janet McColl-Kennedy. "The Central Role of Knowledge Integration Capability in Service Innovation-Based Competitive Strategy." *Industrial Marketing Management* 76, January (2019): 144–156. https://doi.org/10.1016/j.indmarman.2018.07.004.

Schneider, Sabrina, and Patrick Spieth. "Business Model Innovation: Towards an Integrated Future Research Agenda." *International Journal of Innovation Management* 17, no. 1 (2013). https://doi.org/10.1142/S136391961340001X.

Schoenherr, Tobias, and Morgan Swink. "Revisiting the Arcs of Integration: Cross-Validations and Extensions." *Journal of Operations Management* 34, nos. 1–2 (2012): 99–115. https://doi.org/10.1016/j.jom.2011.09.001.

Sovacool, Benjamin, Patrick Schmid, Andy Stirling, Walter Goetz, and Gordon MacKerron. "Differences in Carbon Emissions Reduction Between Countries Pursuing Renewable Electricity Versus Nuclear Power." *Nature Energy* 5, (2020): 928–935. https://doi.org/10.1038/s41560-020-00696-3.

Spieth, Patrick, and Sabrina Schneider. "Business Model Innovativeness. Designing a Formative Measure for Business Model Innovation." *Journal of Business Economics* 86, no. 6 (2016): 671–696. https://doi.org/10.1007/s11573-015-0794-0.

Spieth, Patrick, Dirk Schneckenberg, and Kurt Matzler. "Exploring the Linkage Between Business Model & Innovation and the Strategy on the Firm." *R&D Management* 46, no. 3 (2016): 403–413. https://doi.org/10.1111/radm.12218.

Tate, Wendy, Lisa Ellram, and John Kirchoff. "Corporate Social Responsability Reports: A Thematic Analysis Related to Supply Chain Management." *Journal of Supply Chain Management* 46, no. 1 (2010): 19–44. https://doi.org/10.1111/j.1745-493X.2009.03184.x.

Teece, Davide. "Business Models, Business Strategy and Innovation." *Long Range Planning* 43, nos. 2–3 (2010): 172–194. https://doi.org/10.1016/j.lrp.2009.07.003.

Zott, Cristhop, and Raphael Amit. "Buisness Model Design: An Activity System Perspective." *Long Range Planning*, 43 nos. 2–3 (2010): 216–226. https://doi.org/10.1016/j.lrp.2009.07.004.

3

Bibliometric Analysis of Research on the Concept of CSR and Sustainable Development in E-commerce

Anna Napiórkowska

3.1 Introduction

Since 2000, the sudden development of Internet technologies has revolutionized the way businesses sell their products and services. The crisis caused by the Covid-19 pandemic, affecting global economies, has forced organizations to redesign their operations to ensure the continuity of ongoing operations at a distance. Producers and retailers had to adapt their offers to the new demand requirements, especially through the use of digital technologies.[1] The internet, digitization and access

[1] Idiano D'adamo, Rocio González-Sánchez, Maria Sonia Medina-Salgado, Davide Settembre-Blundo, "E-commerce calls for cyber-security and sustainability: How European citizens look for a trusted online environment", *Sustainability (Switzerland)* 13/12 (2021), https://doi.org/10.3390/su13126752.

A. Napiórkowska (✉)
Collegium of World Economy, SGH Warsaw School of Economics, Warsaw, Poland
e-mail: atalip@sgh.waw.pl

© The Author(s), under exclusive license to Springer Nature Switzerland AG 2024

A. Sörensson et al. (eds.), *Creating New Roles for a Sustainable Economy*, Palgrave Studies in Governance, Leadership and Responsibility,
https://doi.org/10.1007/978-3-031-61551-1_3

to technology have changed modern consumption habits. Consumer purchasing preferences are changing from traditional sales channels to e-commerce. Whether these changes have beneficial or harmful effects on society is a subject of constant debate.[2] Today, businesses in almost every sector and location are considering e-commerce and its business and environmental implications. The negative effects are relatively easy to spot and often reported in the media, but the benefits of this change are often invisible.[3]

Changing the way consumers think and growing awareness of their impact on the natural environment has resulted in researchers being able to better understand ecological shopping behavior, especially in the context of online shopping.[4] Ethical consumption is one type of purchasing behavior through which consumers express their responsibility to society. By buying products for their positive qualities (e.g., organic products) or by boycotting products for their negative qualities (e.g., products made by child labor), consumers may translate their personal values and ethical concerns into purchasing decisions.[5]

Even before the COVID-19 pandemic, there was an increase in individual shipments, including in downtown areas. During the pandemic, through the implementation of restrictions (lock-down, home office, online education, etc.), the volume of transport and distribution of individual parcels (including groceries, deliveries of ready meals, etc.) increased in some cities by over 100 percent, causing major changes in

---

[2] Heleen Buldeo Rai, "The net environmental impact of online shopping, beyond the substitution bias", *Journal of Transport Geography* 93 (2021), https://doi.org/10.1016/j.jtrangeo.2021.103058.

[3] Travis Tokar, Robert Jensen, Brent D. Williams, "A guide to the seen costs and unseen benefits of e-commerce", Business Horizons 64/3 (2021), https://doi.org/10.1016/j.bushor.2021.01.002.

[4] Theresa Maria Rausch, Daniel Baier, Stefanie Wening, "Does sustainability really matter to consumers? Assessing the importance of online shop and apparel product attributes", *Journal of Retailing and Consumer Services* 63 (2021), https://doi.org/10.1016/j.jretconser.2021.102681.

[5] Chia-Nan Wang, Thanh-Tuan Dang, Ngoc-Ai-Thy Nguyen, "Outsourcing reverse logistics for e-commerce retailers: A two-stage fuzzy optimization approach", *Axioms* 10/1 (2021), https://doi.org/10.3390/axioms10010034.

their sustainability.[6] With regard to the environmental impact of online and multi-channel sales, on the one hand, the efficiency of home delivery compared to individual shopping trips was attributed and, on the other hand, attention was paid to complex consumer behavior. Despite intense efforts by researchers, the literature lacks a solid consensus, preventing policymakers and practitioners from implementing measures to improve sustainability and steer consumers toward sustainable practices.[7]

The aim of this study is to conduct a Systematic Literature Review (SLR) and a bibliometric analysis of publications in the field of Corporate Social Responsibility (CSR), sustainable development and e-commerce, as well as content analysis of the latest research in this area. The study was based on previous research with the use of SLR and bibliometric analysis, for example, Nagariya, Kumar and Kumar,[8] Khudzari et al.,[9] Leung, Sun and Bai.[10] Finally, SLR and bibliometric analysis of 127 scientific articles was carried out using the Scopus database and the VOSviewer software. Content analysis has been limited to the latest research, therefore, the content analysis of 38 articles published in 2021 was performed using MAXQDA, a text analysis software. As a result of the content analysis, five clusters with research topics in the field of CSR, sustainable development and e-commerce were created. To the author's knowledge, it is the first CSR, sustainable development and e-commerce study to combine SLR, bibliometric analysis and content analysis.

Based on the gaps identified in the literature, the aim of this study is to answer the question—what are the directions of research on the concept

[6] Tomas Settey, Jozef Gnap, Dominika Beňová, Michal Pavličko, Ol'ga Blažeková, "The growth of e-commerce due to COVID-19 and the need for urban logistics centers using electric vehicles: Bratislava case study", *Sustainability (Switzerland)* 13/10 (2021), https://doi.org/10.3390/su13105357.

[7] Buldeo Rai, "The net environmental impact of online shopping".

[8] Ramji Nagariya, Divesh Kumar, I. Kumar, "Service supply chain : From bibliometric analysis to content analysis , current research trends and future research directions", *Benchmarking: An International Journal* 28/1 (2021), https://doi.org/10.1108/BIJ-04-2020-0137.

[9] Jauharah Md Khudzari, Jiby Kurian, Boris Tartakovsky and G.S. Vijaya Raghavan, "Bibliometric analysis of global research trends on microbial fuel cells using Scopus database", *Biochemical Engineering Journal* 136 (2018), https://doi.org/10.1016/j.bej.2018.05.002.

[10] Xi Y. Leung, Jie Sun, Billy Bai, "Bibliometrics of social media research: A co-citation and co-word analysis", *International Journal of Hospitality Management* 66 (2017), https://doi.org/10.1016/j.ijhm.2017.06.012.

of CSR and sustainable development in e-commerce? In addition, the research aims to provide information on the publication trend—taking into account the publication year, country, author, discipline, and to identify the most influential publications in terms of citations.

3.2 Research Method

In this study, the SLR method was adopted for the identification, sorting and reporting of related articles.[11] In the first step of SLR, the articles were identified in the database through the keywords that make up the search string. The data was retrieved from Scopus, which allows to combine keywords with hyphens such as "AND", "NOT" and "OR" to generate relevant search results. When searching for relevant articles, three keywords and hyphens were combined: "CSR" OR "sustainability" AND "e-commerce". The Scopus database and the Web of Science database are indicated by researchers as the best tools for assessing the state of publication in a given area.[12] In addition, Scopus provides approximately 20 percent greater scope than WoS.[13,14] Scopus managed by Elsevier Publishing is the largest database of abstracts and citations of peer-reviewed literature in the fields of technology, medicine, social sciences, and arts and humanities.[15]

After entering the keywords "CSR" OR "sustainability" AND "e-commerce", the Scopus database indicated 391 publications. The list was filtered by selecting papers published in scientific journals (papers that were in the process of being published were rejected), in English

[11] E.g. Verónica Duque-Uribe, William Sarache, Elena Valentina Gutierrez, "Sustainable supply chain management practices and sustainable performance in hospitals: A systematic review and integrative framework", *Sustainability* 11/21 (2019), https://doi.org/10.3390/su11215949.

[12] Eric Archambault, David Campbell, Yves Gingras, Vincent Lariviere, "Comparing bibliometric statistics obtained from the web of science and Scopus", *Journal of the American Society for Information Science and Technology* 60/7 (2009), https://doi.org/10.1002/asi.21062.

[13] Matthew E. Falagas, Eleni I. Pitsouni, George A. Malietzis, Georgios Pappas, "Comparison of PubMed, Scopus, web of science, and Google Scholar: Strengths and weaknesses", *The FASEB Journal* 22 (2008), https://doi.org/10.1096/fj.07-9492LSF.

[14] Nagariya, Kumar and Kumar, "Service supply chain".

[15] Ibidem.

and which were scientific papers (conference materials, books, chapters in books, reviews were rejected). Finally, there were 209 articles left in the database.

In the next step, the articles were analyzed by reading the title, abstract and keywords. Articles not related to CSR, sustainable development and e-commerce were removed. Ultimately, 127 publications were selected for further SLR and bibliometric analysis. This study combines SLR with bibliometric analysis whose main goal is to find highly cited, reputable research papers. Citations can be obtained by citation analysis in VOSviewer software, where VOS stands for *visualization of similarities*. VOSviewer software provides information on the most cited articles, most engaged researchers, countries, and allows to generate keyword groups based on similar research topics.

The last step was to critically analyze the content of the newest articles and present the results. The content analysis of publications carried out with the use of MAXQDA allowed to identify clusters in order to obtain research topics and research direction. Figure 3.1 presents a chart indicating the progression of the study.

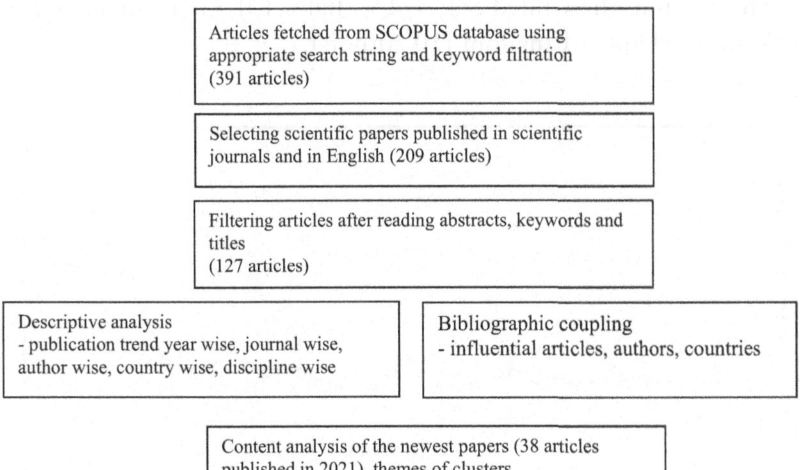

Fig. 3.1 Flow chart indicating research steps (*Source* Own elaboration)

3.3 Research Results

In the first phase, an analysis was carried out to identify the annual research progress and the most present journals, authors, countries and disciplines. Figure 3.2 shows the publication trend and covers the period from 2001 to 2021.

The first publication referring to the relationship between CSR and e-commerce was published in 2001. From this year to 2017, we observe a very weak upward trend, from one to a maximum of five articles. Not a single article was published in 2002, 2005, 2008, 2011 and 2012. Since 2018, we have noticed a rapid increase in publications (17 items in 2018 and 26 items in 2019). In the so-called pandemic year, that is, in 2020, only 16 papers have been published, which could be caused by the introduced restrictions, remote work and a situation of uncertainty. In turn, the year 2021 resulted in a record number of publications, a total of 38 articles were written. The exact number of publications in particular years is presented in Table 3.1.

Figure 3.3 presents data on the country of origin of the authors of the analyzed publications. Most authors (24) come from China, followed by researchers from the United States (15), Italy (13), Germany (11), India (11) and the United Kingdom (10 authors).

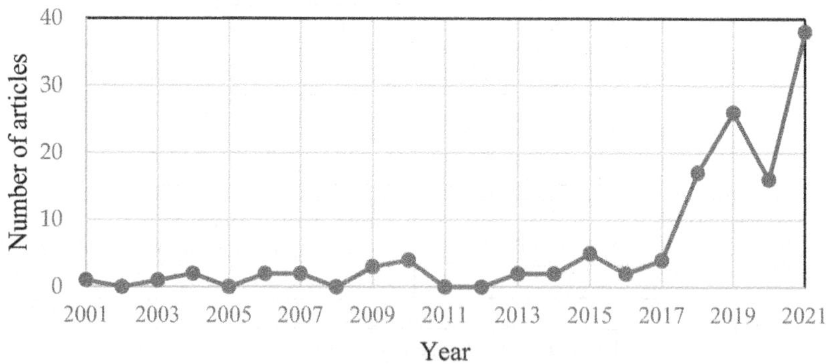

Fig. 3.2 Published works in the years 2001–2021 (*Source* Own study based on Scopus database)

Table 3.1 Number of publications in 2001–2021

Year of publication[a]	Number of publications
2021	38
2020	16
2019	26
2018	17
2017	4
2016	2
2015	5
2014	2
2013	2
2010	4
2009	3
2007	2
2006	2
2004	2
2003	1
2001	1

Source Own study based on Scopus database
[a]In 2002, 2005, 2008, 2011 and 2012, the number of published works is zero

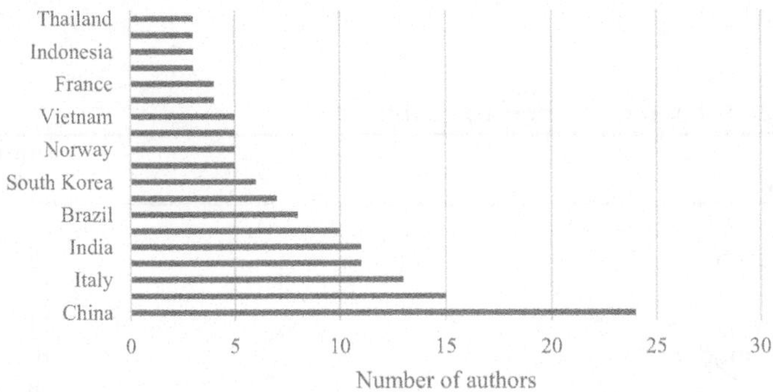

Fig. 3.3 Number of authors of publications from individual countries (*Source* Own study based on Scopus database. The data shows the countries of origin of at least three authors)

The exact number of authors of papers in individual countries is presented in Table 3.2.

Table 3.3 shows the number of analyzed articles in the journals in which they were published. The undisputed leader is the "Sustainability Switzerland" journal with the number of 36 publications. Then, with four articles each, are the journals "Journal of Cleaner Production" and "Transportation Research Part D Transport and Environment". Three papers were published in the "Sustainable Cities and Society" journal. The remaining 84 articles were published in as many as 68 different journals.

Figure 3.4 presents the disciplines in which the analyzed works were published. Most of the papers have been published in the field of Social Sciences (67 articles). The top five also includes Environmental Sciences—57 articles, Energy—51 articles, Business, Management and Accounting—45 articles and Engineering—24 articles).

In the second stage, bibliometric analysis was carried out to find the countries and authors with the highest publishing impact (in terms of citations).

Table 3.2 Publication authors by country

Country	Number of authors
China	24
United States	15
Italy	13
Germany	11
United Kingdom	10
Brazil	8
Spain	7
South Korea	6
Canada, Norway, Poland, Vietnam	5
Belgium, France	4
Greece, Indonesia, Malaysia, Thailand	3
Finland, the Netherlands, Slovakia, South Africa, Sweden, Taiwan, Turkey	2
Nepal, Nigeria, Peru, Romania, Russia, Serbia, Singapore, Ukraine, UAE	1

Source Own study based on Scopus database

Table 3.4 shows countries' contributions to the CSR, sustainable development and e-commerce literature based on the number of citations. The publications from the United States have the highest number of citations (331 citations). The top five also includes publications from China (230 citations), Italy (208 citations), Germany (145) and Brazil (91 citations).

Table 3.5 shows the 11 articles with the highest number of citations, together with the authors and the year of publication. The article with the highest number of citations (82) is entitled "A review of the environmental implications of B2C e-commerce: a logistics perspective", by Italian researchers (Riccardo Mangiaracina, Gino Marchet, Sara Perotti and Angela Tumino)[16] from the Polytechnic University of Milan and was published in 2015 in the "International Journal of Physical Distribution & Logistics Management".

The VOSviewer software also allows to analyze keywords in selected publications. On this basis, we can analyze the period of occurrence and relationships of individual keywords (Fig. 3.5).

Already on the basis of the analysis of the keywords themselves, it can be noticed that in 2021 (yellow) the researchers focused mainly on

Table 3.3 Publications in individual journals

Journal title	Number of publications
Sustainability Switzerland	36
Journal of Cleaner Production; Transportation Research Part D: Transport and Environment	4
Sustainable Cities and Society	3
Energies, Environmental Science and Technology; International Journal of Environmental Research and Public Health; International Journal of Logistics Systems and Management; International Review of Retail Distribution and Consumer Research; Journal of Industrial Ecology; Journal of Internet Banking and Commerce; Journal of Transport Geography; Sustainable Production and Consumption	2

(continued)

[16] Riccardo Mangiaracina, Gino Marchet, Sara Perotti, Angela Tumino, "A review of the environmental implications of B2C e-commerce: A logistics perspective", *International Journal of Physical Distribution & Logistics Management* 45/6 (2015), https://doi.org/10.1108/IJPDLM-06-2014-0133.

Table 3.3 (continued)

Journal title	Number of publications
Axioms, Boletin Tecnico Technical Bulletin, Business Horizons; Cogent Business and Management; Communications of the ACM; Computational Intelligence; Development Studies Research; Economies; Electronic Library; Emerald Emerging Markets Case Studies; Environmental Quality Management; Euro Journal on Decision Processes; Fme Transactions; Forests; Forum Scientiae Oeconomia; Future Generation Computer Systems; IPPTA Quarterly Journal of Indian Pulp and Paper Technical Association; Indian Journal of Marketing; Industrial Management and Data Systems; Information Communication and Society; Information Switzerland; Intellectual Economics; International Journal of Advanced Science and Technology; International Journal of Business And Society; International Journal of Business Performance Management; International Journal of Drug Policy; International Journal of Electronic Commerce; International Journal of Engineering Business Management; International Journal of Environment Workplace and Employment; International Journal of Fashion Design Technology and Education; International Journal of Grid and Utility Computing; International Journal of Information Science and Management; International Journal of Innovation Creativity and Change; International Journal of Internet Marketing and Advertising; International Journal of Logistics Management; International Journal of Logistics Research and Applications; International Journal of Operations and Production Management; International Journal of Physical Distribution and Logistics Management; International Journal of Production Economics; International Journal of Technology Marketing; International Journal of Transport Economics; Journal of Fashion Marketing and Management; Journal of Global Marketing; Journal of International Studies; Journal of Retailing and Consumer Services; Journal of Textile and Apparel Technology and Management; Logforum; Management Science Letters; Manufacturing and Service Operations Management; Plastics Engineering; Prabandhan Indian Journal of Management; Research in Transportation Economics; Rivista Di Studi Sulla Sostenibilita; Sadhana Academy Proceedings in Engineering Sciences; Scientific Papers of The University of Pardubice Series D Faculty Of Economics and Administration; Sustainability United States; System Dynamics Review; Technological Forecasting and Social Change; Territorio; Transport Reviews; Urbe; World Review of Entrepreneurship Management and Sustainable Development	1

Source Own study based on Scopus database

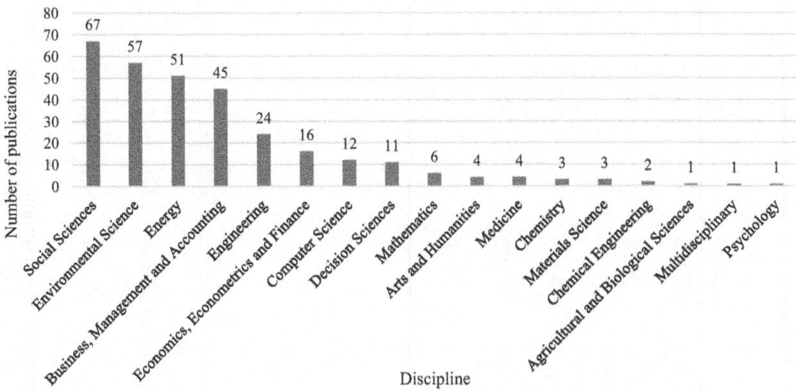

Fig. 3.4 Discipline of published works (*Source* Own study based on Scopus database. A publication may be assigned to more than one discipline)

Table 3.4 Number of citations for publications by country[a]

Country	Number of publications	Number of citations
United States	15	331
China	24	230
Italy	13	208
Germany	11	145
Brazil	8	91
Canada	5	68
India	11	60
South Korea	6	59
Nepal	1	58
Great Britain	10	56
Norway	5	56

Source Own elaboration based on Scopus database using VOS viewer software
[a]Countries with more than 50 citations are included

topics related to consumer behavior, last-mile logistics (last-mile delivery) or the Covid-19 pandemic. Attention is also drawn to the fact that in the center we observe keywords related to e-commerce and sustainable development, while the term corporate social responsibility is distant from the main keywords and their connections.

Table 3.5 Publications with the highest number of citations

Publication title	Author(s)	Publication year	Number of citations
A review of the environmental implications of B2C e-commerce: a logistics perspective	Mangiaracina et al.[17]	2015	82
Consumer motives for peer-to-peer sharing	Hawlitschek, Teubner and Gimpel[18]	2018	61
The effects of online service quality of e-commerce Websites on user satisfaction	Sharma and Lijuan[19]	2015	58
Limits to growth in the new economy: exploring the 'get big fast' strategy in e-commerce	Oliva, Sterman and Giese[20]	2003	53
Shared Mobility for Last-Mile Delivery: Design, Operational Prescriptions, and Environmental Impact	Qi et al.[21]	2018	47

[17] Ibidem.

[18] Florian Hawlitschek, Timm Teubner, Henner Gimpel, "Consumer motives for peer-to-peer sharing", *Journal of Cleaner Production* 204 (2018), https://doi.org/10.1016/j.jclepro.2018.08.326.

[19] Gajendra Sharma, Wang Lijuan, "The effects of online service quality of e-commerce websites on user satisfaction", *Electronic Library* 33/3 (2015), https://doi.org/10.1108/EL-10-2013-0193.

[20] Rogelio Oliva, John D. Sterman, Martin Giese, "Limits to growth in the new economy: Exploring the 'get big fast' strategy in e-commerce", *System Dynamics Review* 19/2 (2005), https://doi.org/10.1002/sdr.271.

[21] Wei Qi, Lefei Li, Sheng Liu, Zuo-Jun Max Shen, "Shared mobility for last-mile delivery: Design, operational prescriptions, and environmental impact", *Manufacturing and Service Operations Management* 20/4 (2018), https://doi.org/10.1287/msom.2017.0683.

Publication title	Author(s)	Publication year	Number of citations
Assessing the impact of ICT on UK general haulage companies	Davies, Mason and Lalwani[22]	2007	42
Comparative Energy, Environmental, and Economic Analysis of Traditional and E-commerce DVD Rental Networks	Sivaraman et al.[23]	2008	41
Renewable energy sources: Using PROMETHEE II for ranking websites to support market opportunities	Andreopoulou et al.[24]	2018	41
Public Transport-Based Crowdshipping for Sustainable City Logistics: Assessing Economic and Environmental Impacts	Gatta et al.[25]	2018	40
A multiobjective optimization model for sustainable reverse logistics in Indian E-commerce market	Dutta et al.[26]	2020	30
Business Network-Based Value Creation in Electronic Commerce	Kaufmann, Li and Heck[27]	2010	30

Source Own elaboration based on Scopus database using VOSviewer software

[22] Ian Davies, Robert Mason, Chandra Lalwani, "Assessing the impact of ICT on UK general haulage companies", *International Journal of Production Economics* 106/1 (2007), https://doi.org/10.1016/j.ijpe.2006.04.007.

[23] Deepak Sivaraman, Sergio Pacca, Kimberly Mueller, Jessica Lin, "Comparative energy, environmental, and economic analysis of traditional and E-commerce DVD rental networks", *Journal of Industrial Ecology* 11/3 (2008), https://doi.org/10.1162/jiec.2007.1240.

[24] Zacharoula Andreopoulou, Christiana Koliouska, Emilios Galariotis, Constantin Zopounidis, "Renewable energy sources: Using PROMETHEE II for ranking websites to support market opportunities", *Technological Forecasting and Social Change* 131 (2018), https://doi.org/10.1016/j.techfore.2017.06.007.

[25] Valerio Gatta, Edoardo Marcucci, Marialisa Nigro, Sergio Maria Patella, Simone Serafini, "Public transport-based crowdshipping for sustainable city logistics: Assessing economic and environmental impacts", *Sustainability (Switzerland)* 11/1 (2018), https://doi.org/10.3390/su11010145.

[26] Pankaj Dutta, Anurag Mishra, Sachin Khandelwal, Ibrahim Katthawala, "A multiobjective optimization model for sustainable reverse logistics in Indian e-commerce market", *Journal of Cleaner Production* 249 (2020), https://doi.org/10.1016/j.jclepro.2019.119348.

[27] Robert John Kauffman, Ting Li, Erick Van Heck, "Business network-based value creation in electronic commerce", *International Journal of Electronic Commerce* 15/1 (2010), https://doi.org/10.2753/JEC1086-4415150105.

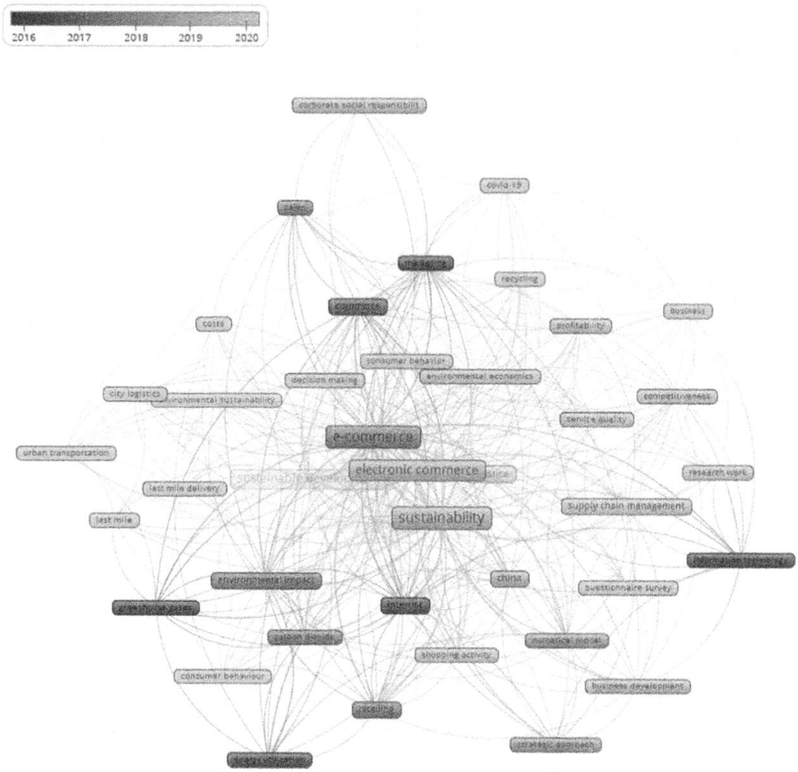

Fig. 3.5 Keywords in the analyzed publications ($N = 127$) (*Source* Own elaboration based on Scopus database using VOSviewer software. The colors indicate the years of publication [according to the legend])

In the next step of the study, the content of articles published in 2021 was analyzed. As a result of the analysis of 38 articles, using the MAXQDA software, five clusters were distinguished:

1. research related to consumer behavior,
2. research related to supply chain management,
3. research related to the influence of Covid-19,
4. research related to last-mile logistics,
5. research related to the impact of e-commerce on sustainability.

Table 3.6 presents the division of works into individual clusters with the authors and title of the publication.

The first cluster is characterized by research on consumer behavior. As noted by García-Jurado, Pérez-Barea and Fernández-Navarro,[28] social, ethical and environmental considerations arising from the purchase of products and services are increasingly taken into account in consumers' purchasing decisions. The authors refer to the profiles of socially responsible consumers and analyze the impact of product reviews on sales. Rausch et al.,[29] on the basis of the clothing industry, analyze the importance of sustainable development for consumers and the aspects that are important when making purchasing decisions by consumers. According to the survey results, clothing features such as fit, comfort and price-quality ratio are more important to consumers than CSR-related items. The most important attributes of sustainable clothing, however, are its durability, fair wages and working conditions, as well as an environmentally friendly production process. Interestingly, women more often indicated the importance of attributes related to sustainable development than men. Brand and Rausch[30] indicate significant differences in the willingness of consumers to pay a higher price for sustainable products depending on the environmental attitude of consumers. While very green consumers emphasize the importance of sustainability characteristics (e.g. materials, labels, country of origin), among less ecological consumers, price and then design are by far the most important determinants of their purchasing decisions. Rao et al.[31] indicate that the so-called green consumerism shapes positive and negative attitudes of consumers toward e-commerce. According to the researchers, consumers prefer ease of use and usability of e-commerce over positive environmental factors. The first cluster is dominated by quantitative research, with the use of questionnaires, conducted on consumers.

The second cluster consists of articles related to supply chain management. Izmirli et al.[32] analyze the policy of making inventories available

---

[28] García-Jurado, Pérez-Barea, Fernández-Navarro, "Towards digital sustainability".

[29] Rausch et al., "Does sustainability really matter to consumers?".

[30] Brand and Rausch, "Examining sustainability surcharges for outdoor apparel".

[31] Rao et al., "The e-commerce supply chain and environmental sustainability".

[32] İzmirli et al., "Omni-chanel network design towards circular economy".

Table 3.6 Clusters of articles published in 2021 ($N = 38$)

Authors	Publication title
Cluster 1—Consumer behavior	
García-Jurado, Pérez-Barea and Fernández-Navarro[33]	Towards Digital Sustainability: Profiles of Millennial Reviewers, Reputation Scores, and Intrinsic Motivation Matter
Dartnell and Kish[34]	Do responses to the COVID-19 pandemic anticipate a long-lasting shift towards peer-to-peer production or degrowth?
Rausch et al.[35]	Does sustainability really matter to consumers? Assessing the importance of online shop and apparel product attributes
Buldeo Rai[36]	Sharing is caring: How non-financial incentives drive sustainable e-commerce delivery

[33] Alejandro García-Jurado, Jose Javier Pérez-Barea, Francisco Fernández-Navarro, "Towards digital sustainability: Profiles of millennial reviewers, reputation scores and intrinsic motivation matter", *Sustainability (Switzerland)* 13/6 (2021), https://doi.org/10.3390/su13063297.

[34] Lewis R. Dartnell, Kaitlin Kish, "Do responses to the COVID-19 pandemic anticipate a long-lasting shift towards peer-to-peer production or degrowth?", *Sustainable Production and Consumption* 27 (2021), https://doi.org/10.1016/j.spc.2021.05.018.

[35] Rausch et al., "Does sustainability really matter to consumers?".

[36] Buldeo Rai, "The net environmental impact of online shopping".

Authors	Publication title
Brand and Rausch[37]	Examining sustainability surcharges for outdoor apparel using Adaptive Choice-Based Conjoint analysis
Rao et al.[38]	The e-commerce supply chain and environmental sustainability: An empirical investigation on the online retail sector
Caspersen and Navrud[39]	The sharing economy and consumer preferences for environmentally sustainable last mile deliveries
Xie et al.[40]	Assessing Consumer Preference for Overpackaging Solutions in E-Commerce
Li and Wu[41]	A Multi-Echelon Network Design in a Dual-Channel Reverse Supply Chain Considering Consumer Preference

(continued)

[37] Benedikt Brand, Theresa Maria Rausch, "Examining sustainability surcharges for outdoor apparel using adaptive choice-based conjoint analysis", *Journal of Cleaner Production* (2021), https://doi.org/10.1016/j.jclepro.2020.125654.

[38] Prakash Rao, Sreejith Balasubramanian, Nitin Vihari, Shazi Jabeen, Vinaya Shukla, Janya Chanchaichujit, "The e-commerce supply chain and environmental sustainability: An empirical investigation on the online retail sector", *Cogent Business and Management* 8/1 (2021), https://doi.org/10.1080/23311975.2021.1938377.

[39] Elise Caspersen, Stale Navrud, "The sharing economy and consumer preferences for environmentally sustainable last mile deliveries", *Transportation Research Part D: Transport and Environment* 95 (2021), https://doi.org/10.1016/j.trd.2021.102863.

[40] Guojie Xie, Lijuan Huang, Chrysostomos Apostolidis, Zuqing Huang, Weiwei Cai, Guokai Li, "Assessing consumer preference for overpackaging solutions in e-commerce", *International Journal of Environmental Research and Public Health* 18/15 (2021), https://doi.org/10.3390/ijerph18157951.

[41] Peng Li, Di Wu, "A multi-echelon network design in a dual-channel reverse supply chain considering consumer preference", *International Journal of Environmental Research and Public Health* 18/9 (2021), https://doi.org/10.3390/ijerph18094760.

Table 3.6 (continued)

Authors	Publication title
Cluster 2—Supply chain management	
Ma et al.[42]	Detecting the Crisis of Supply Chain Management on E-Commerce for Sustainability Using Q-Technique
Wang, Dang and Nguyen[43]	Outsourcing Reverse Logistics for E-Commerce Retailers: A Two-Stage Fuzzy Optimization Approach
İzmirli et al.[44]	Omni-Channel Network Design towards Circular Economy under Inventory Share Policies
de Sousa et al.[45]	Challenges, Opportunities, and Lessons Learned: Sustainability in Brazilian Omnichannel Retail
Zheng et al.[46]	Optimal Channel Strategy for a Fresh Produce E-Commerce Supply Chain

[42] Qi Ma, Chi-Cheng Chang, Chin-Tsai Lin, "Detecting the crisis of supply chain management on e-commerce for sustainability using q-technique", *Sustainability (Switzerland)* 13/16 (2021), https://doi.org/10.3390/su13169098.

[43] Wang, Dang, Nguyen, "Outsourcing reverse logistics".

[44] Damla İzmirli, Banu Y. Ekren, Vikas Kumar, Siwarit Pongsakornrungsilp, "Omni-chanel network design towards circular economy under inventory share policies", *Sustainability (Switzerland)* 13/5 (2021), https://doi.org/10.3390/su13052875.

[45] Paulo Renato de Sousa, Marcelo Werneck Barbosa, Leise Kelli de Oliveira, Paulo Tarso Vilela de Resende, Ricardo Ruiz Rodrigues, Myrian Teixeira Moura, Daniel Matoso, "Challenges, opportunities, and lessons learned: Sustainability in Brazilian omnichannel retail", *Sustainability (Switzerland)* 13/2 (2021), https://doi.org/10.3390/su13020666.

[46] Qian Zheng, Manman Wang, Feng Yang, "Optimal channel strategy for a fresh produce e-commerce supply chain", *Sustainability (Switzerland)* 13/11 (2021), https://doi.org/10.3390/su13116057.

Authors	Publication title
Prajapati et al.[47]	Sustainable logistics network design for multi-products delivery operations in B2B e-commerce platform
Jiang et al.[48]	Sustainable Management for Fresh Food E-Commerce Logistics Services
Suryawanshi et al.[49]	Sustainable and resilience planning for the supply chain of online hyperlocal grocery services
Gatta et al.[50]	E-Groceries: A Channel Choice Analysis in Shanghai
Wang, Gao and Wang[51]	Sustainable Supply Chain Decisions under E-Commerce Platform Marketplace with Competition

(continued)

[47] Dhirendra Prajapati, Fuli Zhou, Mengdi Zhang, H. Chelladurai, Saurabh Pratap, "Sustainable logistics network design for multi-products delivery operations in B2B e-commerce platform", *Sadhana—Academy Proceedings in Engineering Sciences* 46/2 (2021), https://doi.org/10.1007/s12046-021-01624-1.

[48] Yi Jiang, Polin Lai, Chia-Hsun Chang, Kum Fai Yuen, Sihang Li, Xinchen Wang, "Sustainable management for fresh food E-commerce logistics services", *Sustainability (Switzerland)* 13/6 (2021), https://doi.org/10.3390/su13063456.

[49] Pravin D. Suryawanshi, Pankaj Dutta, L. Varun, G. Deepak, J. Shailesh, "Sustainable and resilience planning for the supply chain of online hyperlocal grocery services", *Sustainable Production and Consumption* 28 (2021), https://doi.org/10.1016/j.spc.2021.05.001.

[50] Valerio Gatta, Edoardo Marcucci, Ila Maltese, Gabriele Iannaccone, Jiarui Fan, "E-groceries: A channel choice analysis in shanghai", *Sustainability (Switzerland)* 13/7 (2021), https://doi.org/10.3390/su13073625.

[51] Junbin Wang, Xuan Gao, Zhiguo Wang, "Sustainable supply chain decisions under e-commerce platform marketplace with competition", *Sustainability (Switzerland)* 13/8 (2021), https://doi.org/10.3390/su13084162.

Table 3.6 (continued)

Authors	Publication title
Cluster 3—Covid-19	
Kitukutha, Vasa and Oláh[52]	The Impact of COVID-19 on the economy and sustainable e-commerce
Settey et al.[53]	The Growth of E-Commerce Due to COVID-19 and the Need for Urban Logistics Centers Using Electric Vehicles: Bratislava Case Study
Villa and Monzón[54]	Mobility Restrictions and E-Commerce: Holistic Balance in Madrid Centre during COVID-19 Lockdown
Atkinson et al.[55]	'We're in this together': A content analysis of marketing by alcohol brands on Facebook and Instagram during the first UK Lockdown, 2020

[52] Kitukutha, Vasa, Oláh, "The impact of covid-19".

[53] Settey et al., "The growth of e-commerce".

[54] Rafael Villa, Andres Monzón, "Mobility restrictions and e-commerce: Holistic balance in madrid centre during COVID-19 lockdown", *Economies* 9/2 (2021b), https://doi.org/10.3390/economies9020057.

[55] Amanda Marie Atkinson, Harry Sumnall, Beth Meadows, "We're in this together: A content analysis of marketing by alcohol brands on Facebook and Instagram during the first UK Lockdown", *International Journal of Drug Policy* 98 (2021), https://doi.org/10.1016/j.drugpo.2021.103376.

Authors	Publication title
Cluster 4—Last mile logistics	
Bjørgen, Bjerkan and Hjelkrem[56]	E-groceries: Sustainable last mile distribution in city planning
Villa and Monzón[57]	A Metro-Based System as Sustainable Alternative for Urban Logistics in the Era of E-Commerce
Comi and Savchenko[58]	Last-mile delivering: Analysis of environment-friendly transport
Iwan et al.[59]	Efficiency of light electric vehicles in last mile deliveries—Szczecin case study

(continued)

[56] Astrid Bjørgen, Kristin Ystmark Bjerkan, Odd Andre Hjelkrem, "E-groceries: Sustainable last mile distribution in city planning", *Research in Transportation Economics* 87 (2021), https://doi.org/10.1016/j.retrec.2019.100805.

[57] Rafael Villa, Andres Monzón, "A metro-based system as sustainable alternative for urban logistics in the era of e-commerce", *Sustainability (Switzerland)* 13/8 (2021a), https://doi.org/10.3390/su13084479.

[58] Antoni Comi, Lidiia Savchenko, "Last-mile delivering: Analysis of environment-friendly transport", *Sustainable Cities and Society* 74 (2021), https://doi.org/10.1016/j.scs.2021.103213.

[59] Stanisław Iwan, Mariusz Nürnberg, Mariusz Jedliński, Kinga Kijewska, "Efficiency of light electric vehicles in last mile deliveries—Szczecin case study", *Sustainable Cities and Society* 74 (2021), https://doi.org/10.1016/j.scs.2021.103167.

Table 3.6 (continued)

Authors	Publication title
Mommens et al.[60]	Delivery to homes or collection points? A sustainability analysis for urban, urbanized, and rural areas in Belgium
Kiba-Janiak et al.[61]	Sustainable last mile delivery on e-commerce market in cities from the perspective of various stakeholders. Literature review
Serrano-Hernandez, Ballano and Faulin[62]	Selecting Freight Transportation Modes in Last-Mile Urban Distribution in Pamplona (Spain): An Option for Drone Delivery in Smart Cities

60 Koen Mommens, Heleen Buldeo Rai, Tom van Lier, Cathy Macharis, "Delivery to homes or collection points? A sustainability analysis for urban, urbanised and rural areas in Belgium", *Journal of Transport Geography* 94 (2021), https://doi.org/10.1016/j.jtrangeo.2021.103095.

61 Maja Kiba-Janiak, Jakub Marcinkowski, Agnieszka Jagoda, Agnieszka Skowrońska, "Sustainable last mile delivery on e-commerce market in cities from the perspective of various stakeholders: Literature review", *Sustainable Cities and Society* 71 (2021), https://doi.org/10.1016/j.scs.2021.102984.

62 Adrian Serrano-Hernandez, Aitor Ballano, Javier Faulin, "Selecting freight transportation modes in last-mile urban distribution in Pamplona (Spain): An option for drone delivery in smart cities", *Energies* 14/16 (2021), https://doi.org/10.3390/en14164748.

Authors	Publication title
Cluster 5—The impact of e-commerce on sustainability	
Buldeo Rai[63]	The net environmental impact of online shopping, beyond the substitution bias
Tokar et al.[64]	A guide to the seen costs and unseen benefits of e-commerce
D'Adamo et al.[65]	E-Commerce Calls for Cyber-Security and Sustainability: How European Citizens Look for a Trusted Online Environment
Yacob et al.[66]	The importance of E-commerce adoption and entrepreneurship orientation for sustainable micro, small, and medium enterprises in Indonesia

(continued)

[63] Buldeo Rai, "The net environmental impact of online shopping".

[64] Tokar et al., "A guide to the seen costs and unseen benefits".

[65] D'adamo et al., "E-commerce calls for cyber-security and sustainability".

[66] Syahmardi Yacob, Urip Sulistiyo, Erida Erida, Ade Perdana Siregar, "The importance of e-commerce adoption and entrepreneurship orientation for sustainable micro, small, and medium enterprises in Indonesia", *Development Studies Research* 8/1 (2021), https://doi.org/10.1080/21665095.2021.1976657.

Table 3.6 (continued)

Authors	Publication title
Guo et al.[67]	Research on Environmental Issue and Sustainable Consumption of Online Takeout Food—Practice and Enlightenment Based on China's Meituan
Chen, Wu and Zhong[68]	Research on Competitiveness of China's Social Commerce Enterprises Based on Macro- and Micro-Niche
Lamontagne[69]	Coming Soon to a Store—or Doorstep

Source Own study based on Scopus database using MAXQDA software

[67] Meiwen Guo, Liang Wu, Jianping Peng, Chun-Hung Chiu, "Research on environmental issue and sustainable consumption of online takeout food—Practice and enlightenment based on China's Meituan", *Sustainability (Switzerland)* 13/12 (2021), https://doi.org/10.3390/su13126722.

[68] Xu Chen, Yingliang Wu, Rujie Zhong, "Research on competitiveness of China's social commerce enterprises based on macro- and micro-niche", *Sustainability (Switzerland)* 13/1 (2021), https://doi.org/10.3390/su13010422.

[69] Nancy D. Lamontagne, "Coming soon to a store—Or doorstep", *Plastics Engineering* 77/4 (2021), https://doi.org/10.1002/peng.20484.

in a multi-channel supply network to contribute to the concept of the circular economy (CE). The results indicate that with a well-planned inventory management strategy, a multi-channel supply network can deliver reduced maintenance and transportation costs, contributing to the CE concept. The challenges and opportunities of multi-channel are also discussed by de Sousa et al.[70] Articles on the sustainable food industry and problems related to the online supply of fresh products play an important role in the second cluster.[71,72,73,74] The area that should be considered as well when studying the environmental impact of e-commerce is the supply chain of international e-commerce platforms as sustainability is becoming increasingly important for online sales, both in the B2C[75] and the B2B market.[76] In the second cluster, the authors choose mainly mathematical models and quantitative data as a research technique.

Although most of the analyzed articles published in 2021 take into account the conditions related to the Covid-19 pandemic, cluster three contains studies that analyze the direct impact of the pandemic on the area of e-commerce and CSR. Covid-19 pandemic can be treated as an accelerator of sustainable e-commerce. Kitukutha, Vasa and Oláh[77] point to the need that was raised during Covid-19 pandemic to develop information and communication technologies using appropriate policies to support sustainable e-commerce. Settey et al.[78] and Villa and Monzón[79] analyze logistics solutions in cities through simulation and case studies to improve sustainable supply.

[70] de Sousa et al., "Challenges, opportunities, and lessons learned".

[71] Jiang et al., "Sustainable management for fresh food".

[72] Suryawanshi et al., "Sustainable and resilience planning".

[73] Gatta et al., "E-groceries: A channel choice analysis".

[74] Zheng, Wang, Yang, F., "Optimal channel strategy".

[75] Wang, Gao, Wang, "Sustainable supply chain".

[76] Prajapati et al., "Sustainable logistics network design".

[77] Nicodemus Kitukutha, Laszlo Vasa, Judit Oláh, "The impact of covid-19 on the economy and sustainable e-commerce", *Forum Scientiae Oeconomia* 9/2 (2021), https://doi.org/10.23762/FSO_VOL9_NO2_3.

[78] Settey et al., "The growth of e-commerce due to COVID-19".

[79] Villa and Monzón, "Mobility restrictions and e-commerce".

The fourth cluster consists of a group of publications clearly related to the last-mile delivery. The authors emphasize the particular importance of this area in the development of sustainable e-commerce.[80,81] The increasing share of e-commerce, intensified by the Covid-19 pandemic, requires the introduction of effective ecological solutions in this area. In this cluster, the authors choose simulation studies and quantitative data as the main research techniques.

The fifth cluster contains a collection of works on broadly understood CSR relations and sustainable development with e-commerce. Tokar et al.,[82] based on a literature review, analyze both the benefits and costs of e-commerce, including environmental aspects. The environmental impact of online shopping is also studied by Buldeo Rai[83] and Guo et al.[84] Buldeo Rai,[85] based on a review of the literature, points to the lack of a clear picture of the different types of e-consumers with regard to their overall consumption patterns, travel habits and home conditions. D'Adamo et al.[86] identify responsible, sustainable e-commerce and cyber-security as areas of focus in today's society. Furthermore, e-commerce and entrepreneurship orientation is indicated by Yacob et al.[87] as determinants of sustainable micro, small and medium-sized enterprises.

To visualize the research results Fig. 3.6 presents the graph with the main conclusions.

[80] Bjørgen, Bjerkan, Hjelkrem, "E-groceries: Sustainable last mile distribution".
[81] Comi and Savchenko, "Last-mile delivering".
[82] Tokar et al., "A guide to the seen costs and unseen benefits of e-commerce".
[83] Buldeo Rai, "The net environmental impact of online shopping".
[84] Guo et al., "Research on environmental issue and sustainable consumption".
[85] Buldeo Rai, "The net environmental impact of online shopping".
[86] D'adamo et al., "E-commerce calls for cyber-security and sustainability".
[87] Yacob et al., "The importance of E-commerce adoption".

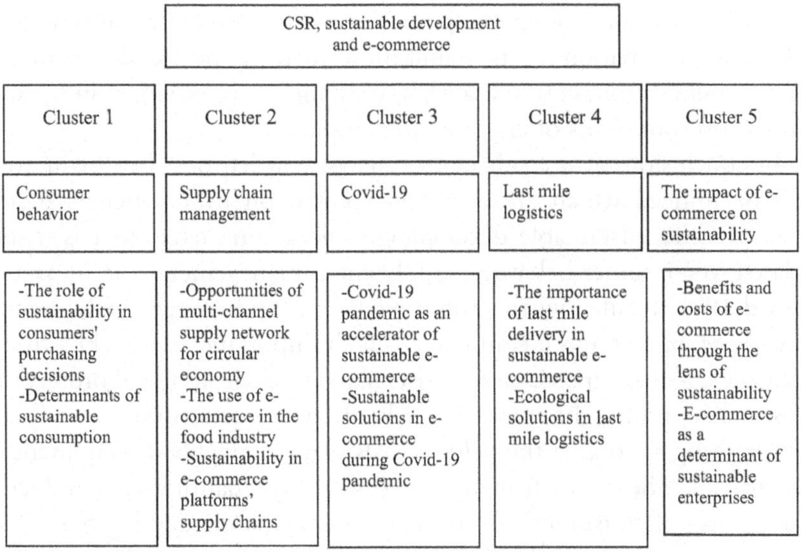

Fig. 3.6 Diversification of research in CSR, sustainable development and e-commerce (*Source* Own elaboration)

3.4 Summary

The area related to corporate social responsibility is widely commented on in the literature, however, the issues within this concept in relation to e-commerce are not yet sufficiently addressed by researchers.

The results of the presented study indicate the state of publication, structure and evolution of various topics in the area of CSR, sustainable development and e-commerce. The SLR, bibliometric analysis and content analysis provided an insight into popular, reputable articles, influential magazines and countries. As a result of the analysis of the content of the latest articles, five research areas in the field of CSR, sustainable development and e-commerce were identified, the current research trend and research directions were indicated. This is the first study of this type to show the diversity of research areas within CSR, sustainable development and e-commerce, combined with bibliometric analysis and SLR. The research questions on the main research directions, research methods, dimensions and activities related to the concept of CSR and sustainable development in e-commerce were answered. In addition, information on the publication trend was provided—including year of publication, country, author, discipline, and the most influential publications in terms of citations were indicated.

In conclusion, as a result of the analysis carried out, five main areas can be noticed which are currently focused on by researchers in the field of CSR, sustainable development and e-commerce, that is, issues related to consumer behavior, supply chain management, the impact of Covid-19, last-mile logistics and the relationship between CSR, sustainable development and e-commerce. Much importance is attached to the influence of e-commerce on the area related to environmental protection. Researchers notice the increasing role of consumer attitudes as a factor determining actions in the field of CSR and sustainable development of enterprises. The research in this area is mostly quantitative, conducted on a group of consumers. As a result of the dynamic development of e-commerce, exacerbated by the Covid-19 pandemic, researchers point to many new challenges in supply chain management and logistics. In the case of e-commerce, the extremely important last-mile logistics attracts the attention of researchers who mainly use mathematical models and simulation studies to indicate the most effective solutions that reduce transport costs and at the same time are sustainable. As part of the research on the relationship of CSR, sustainable development and e-commerce, there are few analyses related to the attitudes of managers toward this phenomenon, and there is also no comprehensive quantitative research on enterprises. Also noteworthy is the gap that appears in the case of comparative studies between solutions used in different countries.

The presented study has some limitations, one of them is the analysis of publications with the use of only one database—the Scopus database. Further research can be supplemented with records of Web of Science and Google Scholar databases. Moreover, the content analysis in the conducted study concerns articles published in 2021. The presented review should be supplemented with the previous years and the content analysis of all 127 publications. Another solution is to analyze the articles with the highest number of citations.

References

Andreopoulou, Zacharoula, Christiana Koliouska, Emilios Galariotis, and Constantin Zopounidis. "Renewable energy sources: Using PROMETHEE II for ranking websites to support market opportunities." *Technological Forecasting and Social Change* 131 (2017): 31–37. https://doi.org/10.1016/j.techfore.2017.06.007.

Archambault, Eric, David Campbell, Yves Gingras, and Vincent Lariviere. "Comparing bibliometric statistics obtained from the Web of science and Scopus." *Journal of the American Society for Information Science and Technology* 60/7 (2009): 1320–1326. https://doi.org/10.1002/asi.21062.

Atkinson, Amanda Marie, Harry Sumnall, and Beth Meadows. "We're in this together': A content analysis of marketing by alcohol brands on Facebook and Instagram during the first UK lockdown." *International Journal of Drug Policy* 98 (2021): 103376. https://doi.org/10.1016/j.drugpo.2021.103376.

Bjørgen, Astrid, Kristin Ystmark Bjerkan, and Odd Andre Hjelkrem. "E-groceries: Sustainable last mile distribution in city planning." *Research in Transportation Economics* 87 (2021): 100805. https://doi.org/10.1016/j.retrec.2019.100805.

Brand, Benedikt, and Theresa Maria Rausch. "Examining sustainability surcharges for outdoor apparel using adaptive choice-based conjoint analysis." *Journal of Cleaner Production* 289 (2021): 125654. https://doi.org/10.1016/j.jclepro.2020.125654.

Buldeo Rai, Heleen. "The net environmental impact of online shopping, beyond the substitution bias." *Journal of Transport Geography* 93 (2021): 103058. https://doi.org/10.1016/j.jtrangeo.2021.103058.

Caspersen, Elise, and Stale Navrud. "The sharing economy and consumer preferences for environmentally sustainable last mile deliveries." *Transportation Research Part D: Transport and Environment* 95 (2021): 102863. https://doi.org/10.1016/j.trd.2021.102863.

Chen, Xu, Yingliang Wu, and Rujie Zhong. "Research on competitiveness of China's social commerce enterprises based on macro- and micro-niche." *Sustainability (Switzerland)* 13/1 (2021): 1–20. https://doi.org/10.3390/su13010422.

Comi, Antoni, and Lidiia Savchenko. "Last-mile delivering: Analysis of environment-friendly transport." *Sustainable Cities and Society* 74 (2021): 103213. https://doi.org/10.1016/j.scs.2021.103213.

D'adamo, Idiano, Rocio González-Sánchez, Maria Sonia Medina-Salgado, and Davide Settembre-Blundo. "E-commerce calls for cyber-security and sustainability: How European citizens look for a trusted online environment." *Sustainability (Switzerland)* 13/12 (2021): 1–17. https://doi.org/10.3390/su13126752.

Dartnell, Lewis R., and Kaitlin Kish. "Do responses to the COVID-19 pandemic anticipate a long-lasting shift towards peer-to-peer production or degrowth?" *Sustainable Production and Consumption* 27 (2021): 2165–2177. https://doi.org/10.1016/j.spc.2021.05.018.

Davies, Ian, Robert Mason, and Chandra Lalwani. "Assessing the impact of ICT on UK general haulage companies." *International Journal of Production Economics* 106/1 (2007): 12–27. https://doi.org/10.1016/j.ijpe.2006.04.007.

Dutta, Pankaj, Anurag Mishra, Sachin Khandelwal, and Ibrachim Katthawala. "A multiobjective optimization model for sustainable reverse logistics in Indian e-commerce market." *Journal of Cleaner Production* 249 (2020): 119348. https://doi.org/10.1016/j.jclepro.2019.119348.

Duque-Uribe, Verónica, William Sarache, and Elena Valentina Gutierrez. "Sustainable supply chain management practices and sustainable performance in hospitals: A systematic review and integrative framework." *Sustainability* 11/21 (2019): 5949. https://doi.org/10.3390/su11215949.

de Sousa, Paulo Renato, Marcelo Werneck Barbosa, Leise Kelli de Oliveira, Paulo Tarso Vilela de Resende, Ricardo Ruiz Rodrigues, Myrian Teixeira Moura, and Daniel Matoso. "Challenges, opportunities, and lessons learned: Sustainability in Brazilian omnichannel retail." *Sustainability (Switzerland)* 13/2 (2021): 1–17. https://doi.org/10.3390/su13020666.

Falagas, Matthew E., Eleni I. Pitsouni, George A. Malietzis, and Georgios Pappas. "Comparison of PubMed, Scopus, web of science, and Google Scholar: Strengths and weaknesses." *The FASEB Journal* 22 (2008): 338–342. https://doi.org/10.1096/fj.07-9492LSF.

García-Jurado, Alejandro, Jose Javier Pérez-Barea, and Francisco Fernández-Navarro. "Towards digital sustainability: Profiles of millennial reviewers, reputation scores and intrinsic motivation matter." *Sustainability (Switzerland)* 13/6 (2021): 1–19. https://doi.org/10.3390/su13063297.

Gatta, Valerio, Edoardo Marcucci, Ila Maltese, Gabriele Iannaccone, and Jiarui Fan. "E-groceries: A channel choice analysis in Shanghai." *Sustainability (Switzerland)* 13/7 (2021): 1–18. https://doi.org/10.3390/su13073625.

Gatta, Valerio, Edoardo Marcucci, Marialisa Nigro, Sergio Maria Patella, and Simone Serafini. "Public transport-based crowdshipping for sustainable city logistics: Assessing economic and environmental impacts." *Sustainability (Switzerland)* 11/1 (2018): 1–14. https://doi.org/10.3390/su11010145.

Guo, Meiwen, Liang Wu, Jianping Peng, and Chun-Hung Chiu. "Research on environmental issue and sustainable consumption of online takeout food—Practice and enlightenment based on china's Meituan." *Sustainability (Switzerland)* 13/12 (2021). https://doi.org/10.3390/su13126722.

Hawlitschek, Florian, Timm Teubner, and Henner Gimpel. "Consumer motives for peer-to-peer sharing." *Journal of Cleaner Production* 204 (2018): 144–157. https://doi.org/10.1016/j.jclepro.2018.08.326.

Iwan, Stanisław, Mariusz Nürnberg, Mariusz Jedliński, and Kinga Kijewska. "Efficiency of light electric vehicles in last mile deliveries—Szczecin case study." *Sustainable Cities and Society* 74 (2021). https://doi.org/10.1016/j.scs.2021.103167.

İzmirli, Damla, Banu Y. Ekren, Vikas Kumar, and Siwarit Pongsakornrungsilp. "Omni-chanel network design towards circular economy under inventory share policies." *Sustainability (Switzerland)* 13/5 (2021): 1–24. https://doi.org/10.3390/su13052875.

Jiang, Yi, Polin Lai, Chia-Hsun Chang, Kum Fai Yuen, Sihang Li, and Xinchen Wang. "Sustainable management for fresh food e-commerce logistics services." *Sustainability (Switzerland)* 13/6 (2021): 3456. https://doi.org/10.3390/su13063456.

Kauffman, Robert John, Ting Li, and Erick Van Heck. "Business network-based value creation in electronic commerce." *International Journal of Electronic Commerce* 15/1 (2010): 113–144. https://doi.org/10.2753/JEC1086-4415150105.

Khudzari, Jauharah Md, Jiby Kurian, Boris Tartakovsky, and G.S. Vijaya Raghavan. "Bibliometric analysis of global research trends on microbial fuel cells using Scopus database." *Biochemical Engineering Journal* 136 (2018): 51–60. https://doi.org/10.1016/j.bej.2018.05.002.

Kiba-Janiak, Maja, Jakub Marcinkowski, Agnieszka Jagoda, and Agnieszka Skowrońska. "Sustainable last mile delivery on e-commerce market in cities from the perspective of various stakeholders: Literature review." *Sustainable Cities and Society* 71 (2021): 102984. https://doi.org/10.1016/j.scs.2021.102984.

Kitukutha, Nicodemus, Laszlo Vasa, and Judit Oláh. "The impact of covid-19 on the economy and sustainable e-commerce." *Forum Scientiae Oeconomia* 9/2 (2021): 47–72. https://doi.org/10.23762/FSO_VOL9_NO2_3.

Lamontagne, Nancy D. "Coming soon to a store—Or doorstep." *Plastics Engineering* 77/4 (2021): 18–23. https://doi.org/10.1002/peng.20484.

Leung, Xi Y., Jie Sun, and Billy Bai. "Bibliometrics of social media research: A co-citation and co-word analysis." *International Journal of Hospitality Management* 66 (2017): 35–45. https://doi.org/10.1016/j.ijhm.2017.06.012.

Li, Peng, and Di Wu. "A multi-echelon network design in a dual-channel reverse supply chain considering consumer preference." *International Journal of Environmental Research and Public Health* 18/9 (2021): 4760. https://doi.org/10.3390/ijerph18094760.

Ma, Qi, Chi-Cheng Chang, and Chin-Tsai Lin. "Detecting the crisis of supply chain management on e-commerce for sustainability using q-technique." *Sustainability (Switzerland)* 13/16 (2021): 9098. https://doi.org/10.3390/su13169098.

Mangiaracina, Riccardo, Gino Marchet, Sara Perotti, Angela Tumino. "A review of the environmental implications of B2C e-commerce: A logistics perspective." *International Journal of Physical Distribution & Logistics Management* 45/6 (2015): 565–591. https://doi.org/10.1108/IJPDLM-06-2014-0133.

Mommens, Koen, Heleen Buldeo Rai, Tom van Lier, and Cathy Macharis. "Delivery to homes or collection points? A sustainability analysis for urban, urbanised and rural areas in Belgium." *Journal of Transport Geography* 94 (2021): 103095. https://doi.org/10.1016/j.jtrangeo.2021.103095.

Nagariya, Ramji, Divesh Kumar, I. Kumar, I. "Service supply chain: From bibliometric analysis to content analysis, current research trends and future research directions." *Benchmarking: An International Journal 28*/1 (2021): 333–369. https://doi.org/10.1108/BIJ-04-2020-0137.

Oliva, Rogelio, John D. Sterman, and Martin Giese. "Limits to growth in the new economy: Exploring the 'get big fast' strategy in e-commerce." *System Dynamics Review* 19/2 (2003): 83–117. https://doi.org/10.1002/sdr.271.

Prajapati, Dhirendra, Fuli Zhou, Mengdi Zhang, H. Chelladurai, and Saurabh Pratap. "Sustainable logistics network design for multi-products delivery operations in B2B e-commerce platform." *Sadhana—Academy Proceedings in Engineering Sciences* 46/2 (2021): 1–13. https://doi.org/10.1007/s12046-021-01624-1.

Qi, Wei, Lefei Li, Sheng Liu, and Zuo-Jun max Shen. "Shared mobility for last-mile delivery: Design, operational prescriptions, and environmental impact." *Manufacturing and Service Operations Management* 20/4 (2018): 737–751. https://doi.org/10.1287/msom.2017.0683.

Rao, Prakash, Sreejith Balasubramanian, Nitin Vihari, Shazi Jabeen, Vinaya Shukla, and Janya Chanchaichujit. "The e-commerce supply chain and environmental sustainability: An empirical investigation on the online retail sector." *Cogent Business and Management* 8/1 (2021). https://doi.org/10.1080/23311975.2021.1938377.

Rausch, Theresa Maria, Daniel Baier, and Stefanie Wening. "Does sustainability really matter to consumers? Assessing the importance of online shop and apparel product attributes." *Journal of Retailing and Consumer Services* 63 (2021): 102681. https://doi.org/10.1016/j.jretconser.2021.102681.

Serrano-Hernandez, Adrian, Aitor Ballano, and Javier Faulin. "Selecting freight transportation modes in last-mile urban distribution in Pamplona (Spain): An option for drone delivery in smart cities." *Energies* 14/16 (2021): 4748. https://doi.org/10.3390/en14164748.

Settey, Tomas, Jozef Gnap, Dominika Beňová, Michal Pavličko, and Ol'ga Blažeková. "The growth of e-commerce due to COVID-19 and the need for urban logistics centers using electric vehicles: Bratislava case study." *Sustainability (Switzerland)* 13/10 (2021): 5357. https://doi.org/10.3390/su13105357.

Sharma, Gajendra, and Wang Lijuan. "The effects of online service quality of e-commerce websites on user satisfaction." *Electronic Library* 33/3 (2015): 468–485. https://doi.org/10.1108/EL-10-2013-0193.

Sivaraman, Deepak, Sergio Pacca, Kimberly Mueller, and Jessica Lin. "Comparative energy, environmental, and economic analysis of traditional and e-commerce DVD rental networks." *Journal of Industrial Ecology* 11/3 (2008): 77–91. https://doi.org/10.1162/jiec.2007.1240.

Suryawanshi, Pravin, Pankaj Dutta, L. Varun, G. Deepak, and J. Shailesh. "Sustainable and resilience planning for the supply chain of online hyperlocal grocery services." *Sustainable Production and Consumption* 28 (2021): 496–518. https://doi.org/10.1016/j.spc.2021.05.001.

Tokar, Travis, Robert Jensen, and Brent D. Williams. "A guide to the seen costs and unseen benefits of e-commerce." *Business Horizons* 64/3 (2021): 323–332. https://doi.org/10.1016/j.bushor.2021.01.002.

Villa, Rafael, and Andres Monzón. "A metro-based system as sustainable alternative for urban logistics in the era of e-commerce." *Sustainability (Switzerland)* 13/8 (2021a): 4479. https://doi.org/10.3390/su13084479.

Villa, Rafael, and Andres Monzón. "Mobility restrictions and e-commerce: Holistic balance in madrid centre during COVID-19 lockdown." *Economies* 9/2 (2021b): 57. https://doi.org/10.3390/economies9020057.

Wang, Chia-Nan, Thanh-Tuan Dang, and Mgoc-Ai-Thy Nguyen. "Outsourcing reverse logistics for e-commerce retailers: A two-stage fuzzy optimization approach." *Axioms* 10/1 (2021): 34. https://doi.org/10.3390/axioms10010034.

Wang, Junbin, Xuan Gao, and Zhiguo Wang. "Sustainable supply chain decisions under e-commerce platform marketplace with competition." *Sustainability (Switzerland)* 13/8 (2021): 1–23. https://doi.org/10.3390/su13084162.

Xie, Guojie, Lijuan Huang, Chrysostomos Apostolidis, Zuqing Huang, Weiwei Cai, Guokai Li. "Assessing consumer preference for overpackaging solutions in e-commerce." *International Journal of Environmental Research and Public Health* 18/15 (2021): 7951. https://doi.org/10.3390/ijerph18157951.

Yacob, Syahmardi, Urip Sulistiyo, Erida Erida, and Ade Perdana Siregar. "The importance of e-commerce adoption and entrepreneurship orientation for sustainable micro, small, and medium enterprises in Indonesia." *Development Studies Research* 8/1 (2021): 244–252. https://doi.org/10.1080/21665095.2021.1976657.

Zheng, Qian, Manman Wang, and Feng Yang. "Optimal channel strategy for a fresh produce e-commerce supply chain." *Sustainability (Switzerland)* 13/11 (2021): 6057. https://doi.org/10.3390/su13116057.

Part II

New Roles for Sustainability, SMEs and Social Entrepreneurship

4

Takeaway Coffee: The Interplay Between Convenience and Sustainability

Maria Sherrington

4.1 Introduction

In our 'on the go' lifestyle, coffee is bought to take away in disposable cups (Novoradovskaya et al. 2020). The cups are symbols of a 'throwaway culture' where consumers are accustomed to disposable packaging convenience (Poortinga and Whitaker 2018, p. 8). Disposable cups represent one of the lesser-known problems of plastic pollution, with approximately 16 billion cups discarded globally every year (Novoradovskaya et al. 2021) and feature among the top marine beach litter items in Europe (Addamo et al. 2017). They contribute to carbon dioxide emissions and interfere with the United Nations Sustainable Development Goals (Keller et al. 2021). In the United Kingdom (UK), 2.5 billion cups are thrown away each year, but fewer than one in 400 (0.25%) are recycled. Around 500,000 cups are littered every day and may function as

M. Sherrington (✉)
University of Central Lancashire, Preston, UK
e-mail: AMSherrington@uclan.ac.uk

© The Author(s), under exclusive license to Springer Nature Switzerland AG 2024

A. Sörensson et al. (eds.), *Creating New Roles for a Sustainable Economy*, Palgrave Studies in Governance, Leadership and Responsibility,
https://doi.org/10.1007/978-3-031-61551-1_4

'beacons of litter', a social norming cue that encourages further littering (House of Commons Environmental Audit Committee 2018). Large-scale cup recycling schemes could reduce the environmental footprint by up to 40%, with reusable cups reducing carbon emissions further still (Foteinis 2020).

To enable progress towards environmental sustainability, progress in government, corporate, and consumer sustainability responsibility is of essence (Varadarajan 2016). For takeaway coffee and disposable cups, this would involve governments creating an environment that discourages disposable cup use, offering specialist recycling infrastructure, and rewarding research and development into sustainable alternatives. Interacting with consumers directly, coffee shops could encourage reusable cup use and facilitate recycling of disposable cups. Consumers' responsibility, in turn, is to preferably use a reusable cup and recycle any disposable cups.

To manage the problem of disposable cups, successful governance and leadership by government and business depends upon insight into consumer values and behaviour relating to takeaway coffee consumption. The purpose of this exploratory study was to investigate how consumer sustainability attitudes and practice transfer to takeaway coffee consumption. This was done by exploring coffee drinkers' perceived value of takeaway coffee. The coffee cup, whether disposable or reusable, was seen as integral to the takeaway coffee experience and the study also sought to explore coffee drinkers' behaviour around cups. Through original research with an international sample of coffee drinkers, further insight into value perception of takeaway coffee and behaviour associated with cups was sought. Such consumer-level insight was sought to uncover what initiatives would assist in tackling the disposable cup challenge outlined above. The study introduces consumer perceived value (Holbrook 1999) as a lens to synthesise the research findings and to determine the impact of consumer value upon sustainability behaviour. Coffee is a low-involvement product with purchasing often habitual in character (De Pelsmacker et al. 2005). Many consumers assume that takeaway coffee cups are recyclable, because they are paper-based and frequently feature a recyclable 'Möbius Loop' symbol (Maye et al. 2019). The consumer solution to the disposable cup problem is simple, developing the habit of carrying a reusable cup. However, pro-environmental behaviours require additional effort/non-monetary sacrifice, such as remembering your reusable cup (Tseng 2016) and in the absence of a tangible reward, it requires an intentional effort to engage in those behaviours (Novoradovskaya et al. 2020). Awareness of coffee shop discounts for bringing a cup is low and consumer uptake of these is only about 1% (Maye et al. 2019). This study responds to the call of Poortinga and Whitaker (2018) to further understand the barriers to using reusable cups.

The chapter begins with a literature review on consumer behaviour towards coffee cups, followed by a description of the research method. The research findings are then presented, followed by a discussion of consumers' value perception of takeaway coffee by mapping the findings onto Holbrook's (1999) typology of consumer value. The conclusion provides recommendations suggesting how government and business can use the findings to inform strategies to increase sustainable takeaway coffee behaviour. Areas for future research associated with decreasing disposable cup use, and embracing reusable cups, are then proposed.

4.2 Literature Review

Academic literature on sustainability and coffee is multi-disciplinary in nature and young, with a surge of publications in the last five years. What follows is a review of consumer behaviour towards takeaway coffee cups.

Consumer Behaviour Towards Takeaway Coffee Cups

Sandhu et al. (2021, p. 9) recognise an urgent need to gain an understanding of environment-friendly takeaway coffee cup use by consumers to develop solutions to address the issue of disposable takeaway coffee cups. Their study found the pervasiveness of takeaway coffee culture with the 'takeaway and throwaway' as the accepted norm to represent a barrier to the use of an environment-friendly cup. Another barrier included the confusion surrounding environment-friendly options, such as how to distinguish a compostable from a regular takeaway cup. Similarly, van Keulen and Kirchherr (2021) refer to disposable coffee cups being an accepted norm and so presenting a barrier to reusable cup use. Sandhu et al. (2021) found graphic illustration of environmental harm of coffee cup waste and the copying of pro-environmental behaviour by significant others to be related to a shift to environment-friendly takeaway cups. They also identified institutional changes that can assist in overcoming barriers, including improved recycling infrastructure. Ertz et al.'s (2017) research found the perception of a reuse-friendly context key to reusable coffee cup behaviour, involving, for instance, active encouragement to consumers to present their reusable cups to the barista.

A charge for a disposable coffee cup is more likely to encourage reusable cup use than the offer of a reward through a discount (Ropret Homar and Cvelbar 2021). This follows from consumers' tendency to be loss averse (Kahneman 2011), that is, unwilling to pay extra for a takeaway cup as opposed to being motivated by gains, such as receiving a discount for bringing a reusable cup. Poortinga and Whitaker (2018) found a disposable coffee cup charge to help promote reusable cup use, whereas a discount lacked effect. They suggest that a charge signals that using your own cup is the default expectation and so acts as a habit disruptor against profligate disposable cup use. Bringing your own cup involves more effort with the 'discount threshold' indicating the smallest price discount needed to induce willingness to carry a reusable coffee cup. In a consumer experiment, Tseng (2016) found a minimum discount of 20% to be appropriate.

Studies have investigated what factors influence the uptake of reusable cups. Novoradovskaya et al. (2020) found that pro-environmental attitudes along with the intention to use a reusable cup significantly predicted use. In a later study, Novoradovskaya et al. (2021) demonstrated the importance of establishing habits. Behaviours that are performed regularly, like buying your coffee in a reusable cup, turn habitual and automatic. Maye et al. (2019) showed how improving consumers' awareness of unintended consequences of using single-use coffee cups is likely to encourage reusable cup uptake. Keller et al.'s (2021) study found increased awareness, responsibility, and negative emotions, complemented by social norms, positive emotions, and goal feasibility, to be associated with an increased intention to change away from disposable coffee cups.

Several studies have explored the role of social norms in promoting avoidance of disposable coffee cups, or the use of reusable cups. Social influence interventions are based on the idea that people align their behaviour to the actions of others. In a process of 'social normalisation', sustainable behaviour can become accepted as standard (Rettie et al. 2013). Social influence is often exerted by means of social norms or social modelling (Dorn and Stöckli 2018). Social norms represent unwritten rules that guide individuals' behaviour based on what others are doing (descriptive norms) and what others approve/disapprove of (injunctive norms) (Borg et al. 2020). Social modelling sees a confederate perform a desirable behaviour anticipating that others will copy it. Social influence interventions are particularly powerful in a social context, such as a takeaway outlet (Dorn and Stöckli 2018). Borg et al. (2020) found perceptions about social norms to be a strong predictor of plastic avoidance behaviours. Terrier et al. (2020) found normative environmental messages to be effective at encouraging using café crockery, rather than taking coffee away in a disposable cup. Loschelder et al. (2019) used dynamic norms to nudge consumers to use café crockery or reusable mugs. Dynamic norms suggest that an increasing number of people are changing their behaviour, emphasising the changing norm over time to elicit (pre-)conformity to this change. Loschelder et al.'s (2019) intervention increased sustainable alternatives being chosen by consumers by 17.3%. Dorn and Stöckli (2018) found evidence of the effect of social modelling with customers likely to choose a reusable takeaway box when they observed others doing so.

Holbrook's (1999) Typology of Consumer Value

To encourage consumers to commit to responsible behaviour, it is necessary to investigate the value that they see in a cup of takeaway coffee. The current study sought to add this insight. Holbrook (1999) claims that the concept of consumer value constitutes the foundation for the marketing concept in the sense that each party to a transaction gives up one thing in return for something else of greater value. Holbrook's (1999) typology reflects three key dimensions of consumer value: (1) extrinsic versus intrinsic, (2) self-oriented versus other-oriented, and (3) active versus reactive. Accordingly, extrinsic value relates to a means-end relationship whereby consumption serves to accomplish some further purpose. Intrinsic value refers to when a consumption experience is appreciated in and of itself. Value is self-oriented when a consumer prizes an aspect of consumption for the effect it has on them, and other-oriented when consumption experiences are valued for the effect it has on others, including the planet. Finally, value is active when it involves a consumer doing something to/with a product and reactive when it results from a consumer responding to an object. Holbrook (1999) combines these three dichotomies into an eight-celled typology of consumer value, where each cell represents a distinct type of value in the consumption experience as detailed in Table 4.1. To the best of the author's knowledge, this is the first study to apply the typology to consumers' perception of takeaway coffee and so this represents a theoretical contribution to the literature, complete with some amendments to the framework to fit the context.

This study sought to shed light on coffee drinkers' perceived consumer value of takeaway coffee. There were three objectives for the research:

Table 4.1 Holbrook's (1999) typology of consumer value

		Extrinsic	Intrinsic
Self-oriented	*Active*	Efficiency (Input/Output, Convenience)	Play (Fun)
	Reactive	Excellence (Quality)	Aesthetics (Beauty)
Other-oriented	*Active*	Status (Success, Impression Management)	Ethics (Virtue, Justice, Morality)
	Reactive	Esteem (Reputation, Materialism, Possessions)	Spirituality (Faith, Ecstasy, Sacredness, Magic)

1. Investigate consumers' value perception of takeaway coffee.
2. Study consumer thoughts around disposable and reusable coffee cups, investigating the interplay between consumer practice, convenience, and sustainability.
3. Explore consumers' perceptions of sustainability in relation to takeaway coffee, including ethical commitments, and the transfer of these to takeaway coffee consumption.

4.3 Method

This study used a qualitative approach to seek in-depth understanding. Individual interviews were conducted with a convenience sample of 13 interviewees resident in Canada, China, Cyprus, Denmark, Finland, Lithuania, the Philippines, Saudi Arabia, Spain, Sweden, and the United Kingdom. The research was exploratory in approach and the choice of countries was arbitrary, with the aim to capture insight from a range of countries throughout the world. Two interviewees were of a different nationality but had lived in their country of residence long enough to be able to report reliably on coffee customs in their new country. Table 4.2 provides details of the interviewees. Appendix 1 provides data about their coffee consumption.

The interviews, 40–90 minutes in duration, were conducted via Microsoft Teams and were audio- and video-recorded. Prospective interviewees received an information leaflet that explained the study purpose, collection of data and participants' rights, including the right to withdraw at any time without offering an explanation. Interviewees opted into the study by completing a consent form. The study had institutional ethics approval.

Once an interviewee had consented to participate and indicated their availability, the researcher sent out a Microsoft Teams invitation. The interviews were semi-structured in approach, allowing in-depth investigation of a real-world phenomenon (drinking takeaway coffee), facilitating the acquisition of both broad and detailed knowledge (Ma et al. 2020). The interview topics were designed to explore

Table 4.2 Interviewee details

	Country of residence	Country of birth	Gender	Age	Highest level of education completed
Interviewee 1	UK	UK	Female	50–59	Master's degree
Interviewee 2	Philippines	Philippines	Male	40–49	Master's degree
Interviewee 3	Denmark	Germany	Female	30–39	Master's degree
Interviewee 4	Sweden	Sweden	Male	30–39	Bachelor's degree
Interviewee 5	Cyprus	Greece	Male	40–49	Ph.D.
Interviewee 6	Spain	Spain	Male	18–29	Bachelor's degree
Interviewee 7	Lithuania	Lithuania	Female	18–29	Bachelor's degree
Interviewee 8	Saudi Arabia	Saudi Arabia	Female	18–29	Master's degree
Interviewee 9	Finland	Finland	Female	40–49	Ph.D.
Interviewee 10	England and Canada	England	Female	60–69	Ph.D.
Interviewee 11	UK	UK	Female	40–49	Ph.D.
Interviewee 12	UK	UK	Male	18–29	Bachelor's degree
Interviewee 13	China	China	Female	30–39	Ph.D.

the research objectives and included: role of takeaway coffee in society, positive takeaway coffee experience, drive-thru use (addressing objective one: investigate consumers' value perception of takeaway coffee), cup littering, reusable cup use, cup recycling (addressing objective two: study consumer thoughts around disposable and reusable coffee cups, investigating the interplay between consumer practice, convenience, and sustainability), corporate social responsibility, and purchase decision-making (addressing objective three: explore consumers' perceptions of sustainability in relation to takeaway coffee, including ethical commitments, and the transfer of these to takeaway coffee consumption). Images relating to each topic were shown, supported by questions to prompt the discussion. The role of the images was to elicit interviewee accounts and interpretations and stimulate dialogue (Saunders et al. 2019). Appendix 2 provides details of images and questions.

In common with Sandhu et al.'s (2021) study of pro-environmental behaviour of takeaway coffee cup use, this study used thematic analysis to analyse the interview data. Thematic analysis involves coding and categorising research data to identify themes or patterns for further analysis related to the research questions (Saunders et al. 2019). Coding was facilitated by repeated listening to the interviews. Units of data (words, expressions, sentences) were labelled with a code to symbolise that extract's meaning. This process found the interview topics listed above appropriate to categorise the data and so these were used as codes. For each code, lists of themes were drawn up. The lists were searched for patterns to distil the themes into a smaller number representative of the data for that code. The themes were then mapped onto Holbrook's (1999) typology of consumer value.

4.4 Findings

The findings were organised according to the codes determined during the data analysis. For each code, the distilled themes are presented in bold text.

The Role of Coffee

Coffee was found to enjoy significant importance in each country, fulfilling the role of a **societal pillar**. In Sweden, coffee is '*the petrol that makes Swedish society go round*'. Indigenous coffee plantations in the Philippines provide an income source. With tea the traditional drink, China is in the process of developing its own coffee culture with coffee a trendy alternative to tea.

There is an important **social element** to coffee. Coffee shops in Cyprus and Greece perform the role the pub might fulfil in the UK, whereas the male British interviewee spoke about coffee shops as '*the* *new pub*', substituting coffee for alcohol. In Finland, coffee is a '*bridge builder*' with a strong social connotation and is associated with work. Coffee carries noteworthy **individual relevance**, offering a break and fuelling work and travel. Coffee can function as a '*performance prop*', with a takeaway cup used as a form of self-expression for a busy executive, as explained by the Swedish interviewee. The Saudi Arabian interviewee recognised coffee's hedonistic properties in that, in the absence of alcohol, '*coffee is literally our drug*'.

All interviewees reported on a vibrant takeaway coffee culture. The male British interviewee spoke about coffee enjoying similar status to craft beer, with a **subculture** of coffee enthusiasts displaying genuine interest in coffee.

Positive Experience of Takeaway Coffee

The respondents from Cyprus, Greece, and Spain reported less general reliance on takeaway coffee, citing a vivacious coffee shop culture where coffee is enjoyed on site. Speaking about what makes a positive takeaway coffee experience, commonality among interviewees' answers crystallised into various themes.

Interviewees referred to **good coffee** with high expectations regarding taste/quality and temperature. Functional demands regarding **transportability** related to mugs, leakproof lids, and sleeves to protect hands from burning. Several interviewees mentioned aspects relating to **product sustainability, Fairtrade sources**, and **organic produce**. For instance, the Danish interviewee stated a preference for the use of recycled materials and the possibility of using your own cup. The Finnish interviewee expressed a dislike for plastic lids and would decline one if offered. The Greek interviewee wanted to be able to recycle the cup in store. The interviewee from China stressed the importance of an '*eco-friendly*' takeaway cup. Takeaway coffee was found to fulfil **self-pampering** needs. For the Spanish interviewee, takeaway coffee was associated with travelling and '*will make the trip better*'. The Finnish interviewee would sip the coffee on the way to work to '*take the edge off a stressful week ahead*'. The Canadian interviewee spoke about the '*buzz of getting the coffee*' from a nearby drive-thru as a break from working from home. **Atmosphere/aesthetics/interaction** for takeaway coffee were important, with an appreciation of friendly staff, skilled to prepare excellent coffee in pleasant surroundings. The availability of **alternative milks** represented a small, yet important theme.

Drive-Thru Coffee

This business model appeared undeveloped in many countries with several interviewees only naming McDonald's as providing this service. In Saudi Arabia, however, the concept is relevant due to the hot climate with consumers preferring to stay in their cars. The Canadian interviewee described the drive-thru model as very well established, suggesting this was due to long distances and a cold winter climate.

Convenience/availability was the most dominant theme, interwoven with that of **time**. The male British respondent spoke about how this delivery model responds to consumers' demand for **instant gratification**, a mindset that expects almost immediate order fulfilment with minimal consumer input. This tends to be centred on **the individual**, and several interviewees associated drive-thru coffee with **travel**; working away or the daily commute, where it is conducive to the development of **rituals/routines**. The Chinese interviewee explained the preference for ordering by an application in China, offering speedy delivery to time-poor office workers, sharpening the concept of convenience further still.

Coffee Cup Littering

An image of a discarded takeaway cup on a beach prompted this discussion. Interviewees frequently blamed **egocentric behaviour** where consumers prioritised perceived lack of time and self-gratification over the environment. Some described a **systems fault** with coffee shops not offering environmentally fit solutions. The Swedish interviewee claimed it is '*unsustainable that consumers should be expected to make smart choices all the time*', suggesting banning non-recyclable cups to remove those choices. Most interviewees favoured **shared stakeholder responsibility** supported by better infrastructure to create '*disposal convenience*' to match purchase convenience. Individual consumers, socialisation agents (parents and schools), brands, coffee shops, governments, and city/town councils were seen to carry responsibility.

Education/awareness creation was the most prominent theme. Only the Finnish interviewee spoke about the cup on the beach in the context of the '*micro plastics problem*'. The male British respondent recognised that many people would probably think that disposable cups will decompose, suggesting that awareness creation might change behaviour. It was proposed that influencers or celebrities feature in campaigns to **normalise** responsible disposal behaviour. Borg et al. (2020) found social norms to be strong predictors of plastic avoidance. Recognising that behaviour change takes time, the Greek interviewee suggested foregrounding '*small things we can all do every day*', rather than '*big messages about saving the planet*'. This chimes with Black and Cherrier's (2010) recommendation to position sustainable practices alongside self-interested notions, for instance positive emotions experienced when living sustainably.

Reusable Coffee Cups

Reusable cups were regarded as an idealist's choice, an emblem of **environmental sensitivity**. The Lithuanian interviewee stated that '*in a perfect world*' everyone would use them. However, they were likened to '***the opposite of takeaway coffee***' and its associated convenience. Consequently, first you need to buy one. '*Extra workload*' then follows with washing it after use and remembering to take it when leaving home. Tseng (2016) describe these extra efforts as 'perceived non-monetary sacrifice'. A process of behaviour change is needed before such use is cemented as **routine/habit**. Novoradovskaya et al. (2020) describe reusable cup use as relatively novel behaviour without the automaticity that reflects the presence of habit. Wanting to be a role model for her children, the Chinese interviewee had developed a habit of having cups in the car and office. The Finnish interviewee recognised that buying takeaway coffee is not necessarily a planned behaviour, but prompted by convenience/availability and so you may not have your cup to hand. Also, consumer reluctance may follow complexity of choice, as the Danish interviewee recognised that it is '*half a science to figure out which one [reusable cup] is good*'.

Implementation barriers external to the consumer were mentioned. Some interviewees reported coffee shops refusing to handle their reusable cups. Further, the Canadian interviewee raised the query of '*How do you do it with a drive-thru? You get to the window, and they have already made your coffee*'. She also suggested habit as posing a barrier in that consumers are '*just used to getting their Starbucks cup, they do it without thinking*'. Ertz et al. (2017) describe abundant availability of disposable cups coupled with perceived awkwardness of asking to have a reusable cup refilled as a 'contextual hindrance'. Issues around **hygiene** were mentioned, especially retailers not accepting reusable cups during the Covid pandemic. A reusable cup was also seen as a **prompt** for communicating with others. This could be as a beacon for the importance of sustainable coffee drinking.

'On the Go' Recycling

An image of an 'on the go' recycling bin for disposable cups in Manchester, UK, prompted this discussion. The interviewees were not aware of similar infrastructure local to them, but considered it a valuable initiative, as only a very sustainability-oriented consumer would carry an empty cup around until the correct disposal opportunity arises.

Education/awareness was the most dominant theme. Several interviewees were unaware that disposable cups commonly are lined with plastic, necessitating specialist recycling technology. One of the female British respondents proposed that awareness creation may spur reusable cup purchases or at least more responsible disposal. It was found that public awareness may be somewhat higher in Lithuania where the statement 'contains plastic' on disposable cups is compulsory. The Canadian interviewee spoke about the frustration of feeling uncertain about whether the cup, lid or both could be recycled, and how frequently both would go in the bin as a result. The Swedish interviewee re-stated that **the cup is at fault** with the need for an environment-friendly cup as default.

Disposable cup use was seen as intertwined with a '**one-use trash mentality**' that places a premium on convenience. It was felt that **shared value in recycling** was needed to move forward. This is likely to be challenging as, realistically, few people give much thought to what they see as litter. The Spanish interviewee reflected that '*people already think that they are doing a good job*' [by placing the cup in cardboard recycling]. The Danish interviewee spoke about how the power of influencers and movies can be harnessed. We see product placement of disposable cups in movies, providing the opportunity to use the storyline to **normalise recycling behaviour**. Again, a theme of **shared responsibility/collaborative effort** emerged, with funds and technology provided by government and business, and consumers committing to using the infrastructure.

Coffee Brands and CSR

To frame these discussions, images and text relating to sustainability on the Starbucks and McDonald's homepages were shown. The logos of Fairtrade and the Rainforest Alliance, third-party sustainability certification schemes, were also featured.

Eco-suspicion/eco-scepticism was the most prominent theme. Interviewees questioned what they saw as general statements and appealing imagery, which in the absence of supporting **evidence** amounted to **greenwashing**. Several interviewees wanted to know the true meaning of claims made. For instance, the Danish interviewee stated '*I really like to get to know about the background – about the land, people, process. One picture doesn't tell us much about the working conditions, the land that was there before, land conflict, biodiversity, et cetera*'. It was proposed that brands' sustainability rhetoric functioned as **conscience easing**, providing reassurance for stressed consumers that their coffee had been responsibly sourced. However, the interviewee from the Philippines stated that few people take notice of such messages, which was also reported by the Saudi Arabian interviewee. The Chinese interviewee explained that Chinese consumers in general are not attuned to sustainability messages, but that this is now changing with children learning about sustainability at school. The Greek interviewee stated that '*these issues are not quite on the radar yet for Cypriot and Greek people*', but that younger consumers are beginning to take note. The Spanish interviewee described the messages as '*nice additional extras that make you feel better*', but due to a lack of trust in them convenience, availability, and price weigh heavier. Some interviewees simply reflected that only sustainably produced coffee should be on offer with **the sustainable choice as the default choice**. This was considered crucial in a buying situation characterised by a lack of time, knowledge, and a long distance to the source. The Finnish interviewee described takeaway coffee as '*enjoyment products*' and that too much elaboration on sustainability would take the enjoyment away.

Compared to coffee brands' own sustainability claims, third-party sustainability certification was in principle seen as more helpful. One of the British female respondents suggested sustainability certification may function as a **seal of quality**. However, whilst most interviewees were familiar with Fairtrade and its general principles, their knowledge of Rainforest Alliance stopped at the visual recognition of the logo. Familiarity was lower in China, the Mediterranean countries, Saudi Arabia, and the Philippines compared to Canada, Scandinavia, and the UK. Overall, **lack of awareness/insight** was matched for many by a **lack of engagement** with sustainability certification.

Coffee Decision-Making

Purchase decisions for coffee are multidimensional with consumers considering several attributes (Lee and Bateman 2021). The interviewees were asked to prioritise *taste, brand, origin of coffee, sustainability certification, price*, and *availability/convenience*.

Commonality was found across interviewees. Taste, convenience/availability, and brand tended to be in the top three, with taste most frequently in first position. Of relevance to work/travel, convenience/availability came second. Brand was in third place. Rather than big coffee brands, this concept related to small independent coffee shops where the shop name was the brand and the coffee itself was seen as un-branded. This is different to home consumption, where coffee brand is key in a routine-buying situation (Lappeman et al. 2019). For a few sustainability-conscious interviewees, certification featured in the top three, but for the majority it was placed in the lower half of the attributes. Research by De Pelsmacker et al. (2005) also found most consumers rated Fairtrade as less important than brand and taste. Takeaway coffee was considered expensive by many, but this tended not to be a deal breaker as price tends to be similar across outlets. The origin of the coffee tended to be placed in the last position with interviewees claiming lack of specialist knowledge.

4.5 Discussion

To remind the reader, the objectives for the study were to investigate (1) consumers' value perception of takeaway coffee and (2) their thoughts regarding disposable/reusable coffee cups to ascertain the linkages between consumer practice, convenience, and sustainability. Further, the study sought to (3) explore consumers' perceptions of sustainability and the implications of these for takeaway coffee consumption.

To address these objectives, this section maps prominent themes reported in the findings onto Holbrook's (1999) typology of consumer value. Holbrook states that the concept of consumer value constitutes the foundation for the marketing concept in the sense that each party to a transaction gives up one thing in return for something else of greater value. In the context of takeaway coffee, the customer trades money in return for coffee, but the transaction involves additional sacrifice, for instance, spending time and effort to acquire the coffee. Holbrook's typology depicts the consumption experience as consisting of different value types. As the analysis will show, the value of takeaway coffee is multi-faceted.

As a reminder, in Holbrook's typology, value is *self-oriented* when a consumer prizes an aspect of consumption for the effect it has on them, and *other-oriented* when consumption experiences are valued for the effect they have on others, including the planet. *Extrinsic value* relates to a means-end relationship whereby consumption serves to accomplish some further purpose, whereas *intrinsic value* refers to when a consumption experience is appreciated in and of itself. Further, value is *active* when it involves a consumer doing something to/with a product and *reactive* when it results from a consumer responding to an object.

Starting with the *self-oriented* part of the typology and the *extrinsic* aspects, the *excellence* element is at the heart of consumers' value perception of takeaway coffee, featuring foremost **taste**. Interviewees spoke about '**good coffee**'. Third-party sustainability certification supports this value element for a niche group for whom certification markings work as a **seal of quality**. Closely linked is the value element of *efficiency*. **Convenience** is *the* buzz word for takeaway coffee, where **availability** serves to provide **instant gratification** in a **time**-efficient manner. These efficiency aspects provide a scaffold to the functional aspects of the coffee by providing a stimulant that **fuels work and travel** and helps to cement **routines**.

In terms of the *self-oriented intrinsic* aspects, Holbrook's value element of *play* did not fit with takeaway coffee as depicted in the interviews. Given its *active* orientation within the typology, this element has been replaced with *self-care* to encompass such aspects as **self-pampering** and having a break. In terms of the value element of *aesthetics,* the **atmosphere** of the coffee shop was of importance and friendly **interaction** with staff was valued even when taking coffee out. Branding and packaging of takeaway coffee attracted interest and enjoyment too.

Addressing the *other-oriented extrinsic* aspects, Holbrook recognises the difficulty of articulating the difference between the elements of *status* and *esteem.* Given the *active* orientation of *status* whereby a consumer does something to/with takeaway coffee, this relates to interviewees' discussion of the function of the cup. If this is a reusable cup, it can be used as a **prompt** to **model** sustainable behaviour to fellow consumers. However, this cup was regarded by many as '**the opposite of takeaway coffee**' as it comes with a workload. This finding chimed with Tseng's (2016) recognition that pro-environmental behaviours require additional effort/non-monetary sacrifice and Novoradovskaya et al.'s

(2020) reference to intentional effort in the absence of a tangible reward. This detracts from the overall value of takeaway coffee, something that Holbrook's typology does not directly accommodate for. Any cup, disposable or reusable, can perform the task of **self-expression** depicting the person as important and busy.

Esteem is *reactive* in nature, resulting from the consumer responding to the concept of takeaway coffee. Remaining with the cup, the environmental promise of reusable cups notwithstanding, some consumers have a range of designer cups perhaps as part of a **conspicuously green consumption** imperative, or simply conventional consumerist tendencies. Whether for reputation management or otherwise, this accumulation of cups misses the true purpose of reusable cups.

In terms of the *other-oriented intrinsic* aspects, the *ethics* element is where consumers can make active choices concerning takeaway coffee to benefit people and the planet. Sustainability aspects permeated the discussion. The interviewees voiced support for sustainability within the coffee industry, but expressed doubt that consumers in general pay much attention to enjoying takeaway coffee sustainably. Several reasons for this emerged, one of which was the very nature of takeaway coffee where a premium is placed on **convenience**. In a society seeking **instant gratification**, time-poor individuals seek effortless access to good coffee. Accepting a disposable coffee cup represents **normalised behaviour** and, in any case, is commensurate with the convenience element. This supports Sandhu et al. (2021) and van Keulen and Kirchherr (2021) in their contention that disposable cups are the accepted norm and as such present a barrier to the adoption of reusable cups. Even in this sample of highly educated individuals, many **lacked awareness** that mainstream disposable cups contain plastic. Those in the know felt hampered by the lack of sustainable, disposable alternatives. Reusable cups had limited take-up, due to the **extra workload** involved, but also due to **retail barriers**, such as limited direct encouragement from coffee shops and a sense that recycling of disposable cups was not widely promoted in stores. This reinforces Ertz et al.'s (2017) call for a reuse-friendly context. In terms of claims to sustainability commitments by coffee brands, interviewees' responses were characterised by **eco-suspicion**. The presence of third-party sustainability certification was regarded positively and for some represented **evidence** that coffee brands were actively working towards implementing sustainability principles. However, insight regarding the Fairtrade and the Rainforest Alliance schemes was varied and few interviewees confirmed taking certifications into account when making takeaway coffee purchase decisions.

The other *intrinsic other-oriented* aspect, *spirituality*, did not apply to takeaway coffee and was replaced by *social value*. As such, a vibrant **takeaway coffee culture** was confirmed with the suggestion that coffee is '**trendy**' and the foundation for a movement similar to craft beer.

In summary, the analysis suggested that takeaway coffee is dominated by self-oriented values. Taste and convenience are valued as the supreme elements driving takeaway coffee consumption. Due to a lack of time and awareness and outside pressure, other-oriented elements such as sustainability receive comparatively low priority. Most consumers did not appreciate the environmental problems associated with disposable cups and uptake of the more labour-intensive and convenience-unfriendly reusable cups is still low. In the interplay between convenience and sustainability, convenience has the upper hand. This follows from takeaway coffee being a low-involvement product (De Pelsmacker et al. 2005) where behaviour is guided by routines and social norms, and where elaboration on sustainability aspects tends to play a small role, if any, in purchase decisions. For the majority of respondents, the pro-environmental attitudes and intentions required for reusable cup use (Novoradovskaya et al. 2020) and the associated habitual behaviour (Novoradovskaya et al. 2021) were missing. This analysis is summarised in an adapted version of Holbrook's typology of consumer value in Table 4.3.

4.6 Conclusion

This study has found takeaway coffee consumption to be more value-driven than values-driven, so self-oriented aspects dominate, with an emphasis upon *efficiency* in the form of convenience and *excellence* relating to taste. Drinking takeaway coffee is an individual, time-constrained pursuit with limited attention paid to *ethics values* such as

Table 4.3 Holbrook's (1999) typology of consumer value applied to takeaway coffee

		Extrinsic	Intrinsic
Self-oriented	*Active*	Efficiency Convenience, availability, instant gratification, fuel	Self-care Self-pampering, time out
	Reactive	Excellence Taste/aroma, sustainability certification	Aesthetics Atmosphere, branding and packaging
Other-oriented	*Active*	Status Cup as self-expression, modelling of sustainability	Ethics Sustainability valued; convenience a priority
	Reactive	Esteem Conspicuously green consumption	Social value Takeaway coffee culture, coffee 'trendy'

sustainability. There are several reasons for the lack of regard for sustainability. On a fundamental level, takeaway coffee is a low-involvement product (De Pelsmacker et al. 2005), so consumers are less likely to elaborate on aspects such as sustainability certification and avoiding disposable cups. Disposable cup use is normalised with reusable cups seen as 'the opposite of takeaway coffee'. These findings apply to all nationalities included in the study. Whilst the mindset regarding takeaway cup use is shared, greater tendency of Cypriot, Greek, and Spanish consumers to enjoy coffee on coffee shop premises suggests lesser reliance on takeaway coffee in those countries.

The study interviewed a sample of highly educated coffee drinkers, many of whom were not aware that disposable cups contain plastic necessitating specialist recycling technology. Even so, consumers may feel that their takeaway cup is one in a billion and so fail to see how individuals can do much to fix the problem. A similar picture was apparent for sustainability certifications, which came far down the list of choice criteria when buying takeaway coffee.

The research has demonstrated a clear need to boost other-oriented, ethics-related aspects of consumer value relating to takeaway coffee. Given that these intrinsic value aspects are *active* in nature and that consumers can make a difference through their choices, the goal must be to empower consumers to make positive choices. This could be achieved if everyone enjoyed their coffee mindfully in a coffee shop using reusable crockery. However, this would not offer a solution to mobile coffee consumers, so three recommendations are offered here:

Consumer awareness and knowledge creation is required, whereby coffee drinkers are informed about the environmental impact of disposable cups and their limited recyclability. The ultimate objective would be to change consumer behaviour, lowering cup use. Campaigns could be led by governments and coffee chains through social media platforms and coffee shops. Based on the principle of social conformity (Rettie et al. 2013), 'ordinary' coffee drinkers could feature in the campaigns and recruiting social media influencers could also be considered.

Tackling cup littering and recycling requires a managed team effort. However, the interview data and the literature both identified that there is no captain—everyone is responsible, but no one takes the lead. Hence, the second aspect relates to the need for ambitious sustainability initiatives led by governments with coffee brand and recycling industry input and for these to be coordinated with other countries via groupings such as the European Union, and crucially overseen by the United Nations in the context of the Sustainable Development Goals. As part of this initiative, governments should lead on what cup materials can be sold. Accordingly, minimum requirements on disposable cups should be that they are fully recyclable or home compostable. Industry-wide use of reusable cups that consumers value and keep should be encouraged and recycling convenience should be assured through ubiquitous infrastructure.

An outright ban on disposable cups might not offer a realistic solution, as they are key to the drive-thru concept and applications offering home delivery. Instead, the third aspect relates to **cutting back on disposable cups**. Given consumers' reluctance to make a financial sacrifice (Kahneman 2011), charging for disposable cups should be considered. This puts a value on disposable cups. Combining this approach with a discount for consumers using their own cups would further reinforce this value proposition. Coffee shops should preferentially accept reusable cups and offer convenient recycling of disposable cups, actively encouraging recycling. UK consumer acceptance of plastic carrier bags charges (Department for Environment, Food and Rural Affairs 2020) may be indicative of consumer willingness to embrace these proposals.

The research findings are limited by the use of a small convenience sample. Future research should conduct surveys with consumers in different countries to establish how receptive consumers are to a disposable cup charge. The research should also ascertain what factors would encourage reusable cup use, including persuasive discount levels.

Appendix 1: Interviewees' Estimated Coffee Consumption

	Level of coffee consumption	Description of coffee consumption	Location of coffee consumption	Proportion of monthly consumption represented by takeaway coffee
Interviewee 1	Several cups a day	I am a moderate coffee drinker	Make coffee at home/work; at a coffee shop; enjoy takeaway coffee on the go	10% or less
Interviewee 2	Several cups a day	I am a moderate coffee drinker	Make coffee at home/work; at a coffee shop; enjoy takeaway coffee on the go	50%
Interviewee 3	Several cups a day	I am a moderate coffee drinker	Make coffee at home/work; at a coffee shop; enjoy takeaway coffee on the go	10% or less
Interviewee 4	Several cups a day	I enjoy coffee frequently	Make coffee at home/work; enjoy takeaway coffee on the go	10% or less
Interviewee 5	Several cups a day	I enjoy coffee frequently	Make coffee at home/work; at a coffee shop; enjoy takeaway coffee on the go	75% or more
Interviewee 6	2–5 cups per fortnight	I enjoy coffee sometimes	At a coffee shop; enjoy takeaway coffee on the go	25%
Interviewee 7	One cup per day	I am a moderate coffee drinker	Make coffee at home/work; at a coffee shop; enjoy takeaway coffee on the go	10% or less
Interviewee 8	Several cups a day	I enjoy coffee frequently	Make coffee at home/work; at a coffee shop; enjoy takeaway coffee on the go	50%
Interviewee 9	Several cups a day	I enjoy coffee frequently	Make coffee at home/work; at a coffee shop; enjoy takeaway coffee on the go	10% or less

(continued)

(continued)

	Level of coffee consumption	Description of coffee consumption	Location of coffee consumption	Proportion of monthly consumption represented by takeaway coffee
Interviewee 10	One cup per day	I am a moderate coffee drinker	At a coffee shop; enjoy takeaway coffee on the go	50% in the UK 75% or more in Canada
Interviewee 11	One cup per day	I enjoy coffee frequently	Make coffee at home/work; at a coffee shop; enjoy takeaway coffee on the go	50%
Interviewee 12	Several cups a day	I enjoy coffee frequently	Make coffee at home/work; at a coffee shop; enjoy takeaway coffee on the go	25%
Interviewee 13	One cup per day	I enjoy coffee frequently	Make coffee at home/work; at a coffee shop; enjoy takeaway coffee on the go	10% or less

Appendix 2: Details of Images and Questions Used in the Interviews

Images that served as discussion prompts:

1. A set of neutral images of takeaway coffee (supported with verbal prompts asking participants to consider the role takeaway coffee fulfils in their lives, etc.).
2. A close-up image of coffee pouring into a cup from a coffee machine.
3. An image of a Costa Drive-Thru (supported with questions to probe lifestyle and opinions around this form distribution).
4. A discarded coffee cup on a beach (introduction of the aspects of sustainability, plastics pollution, one-use packaging littering of the environment).
5. A set of reusable coffee cups (supported with questions to explore the uptake of this approach, attitudes, beliefs, behaviour, etc.).
6. A coffee cup recycling station in Manchester, UK (supported with questions to explore attitudes, beliefs and behaviour towards this type of infrastructure).
7. McDonald's sourcing messages regarding coffee and milk (supported with questions to explore attitudes and beliefs).
8. Starbucks sustainability and ethical sourcing messages (supported with questions to explore attitudes and beliefs). The Rainforest Alliance logo and the Fairtrade logo (to explore awareness, knowledge, uptake, etc.).
9. Verbal list of: Taste, brand, price, convenience/availability, origin of coffee, sustainability certifications.

Discussion prompts for each image:

1	What role does coffee play in contemporary consumer society within your country? What role does takeaway coffee play there?
2	For you, what aspects contribute to a positive experience of takeaway coffee?

(continued)

(continued)

3	The availability of takeaway coffee is such that many of us are never far from a coffee shop, we may not even need to get out of our cars. Convenience and availability are key for many consumers. How important do you perceive that convenience and availability are to consumers within your country? Is the concept of a 'drive-thru' available where you live? Who uses them? How do you perceive the role that they play?
4	Describe your reaction to this image. Is this something that you come across where you live? What can be done about this? Whose responsibility is this?
5	Are reusable coffee cups available where you live? Can you describe the person who carries one of these around? How desirable do you see the use of reusable coffee cups? What is the uptake where you live?
6	This is an 'on the go' recycling station suitable for coffee cups in Manchester, UK. Recycling of one-use drinking vessels requires specialist technology. How important is the possibility of being able to recycle coffee cups? Who should be responsible for providing the technology necessary? What is our responsibility as consumers to use them?
7	How important is it for consumers to be able to access information regarding the sourcing of key ingredients such as coffee and milk? To what extent are the lives of coffee farmers and dairy herds of importance to the enjoyment of our coffee? Are you familiar with these third-party sustainability certifications? Are they prominent within coffee outlets where you live? What role do they play within consumer decision-making regarding takeaway coffee?
8	When buying takeaway coffee, what is the most important factor to you and why? Can you rank order the aspects on the screen?

References

Addamo, AM, Laroche, P, Hanke, G (2017) Top marine beach litter items in Europe. EUR 29249 EN, Luxembourg: Publications Office of the European Union. https://op.europa.eu/en/publication-detail/-/publication/d1d555f4-af6f-11e8-99ee-01aa75ed71a1/language-en. Accessed 17 July 2023

Black, IR, Cherrier, H (2010) Anti-consumption as part of living a sustainable lifestyle: daily practices, contextual motivations and subjective values. Journal of Consumer Behaviour 9(6):437–453

Borg, K, Curtis, J, Lindsay, J (2020) Social norms and plastic avoidance: testing the theory of normative social behaviour on an environmental behaviour. Journal of Consumer Behaviour 19(6):594–607

De Pelsmacker, P, Driesen, L, Rayp, G (2005) Do consumers care about ethics? Willingness to pay for fair-trade coffee. The Journal of Consumer Affairs 39(2):363–385

Department for Environment, Food and Rural Affairs (DEFRA) (2020) Single-use plastic carrier bags charge: data for England 2021 to 2022. https://www.gov.uk/government/publications/carrier-bag-charge-summary-of-data-in-england/single-use-plastic-carrier-bags-charge-data-in-england-for-2019-to-2020. Accessed 17 July 2023

Dorn, M, Stöckli, S (2018) Social influence fosters the use of a reusable takeaway box. Waste Management 79:296–301

Ertz, M, Huang, R, Jo, M-S, Karakas, F, Sarigollü, E (2017) From single-use to multi-use: study of consumers' behavior toward consumption of reusable containers. Journal of Environmental Management 193:34–344

Foteinis, S (2020) How small daily choices play a huge role in climate change: the disposable paper cup environmental bane. Journal of Cleaner Production 255:120294

Holbrook, MB (1999) Introduction to consumer value. In Holbrook, MB (ed) Consumer Value: A Framework for Analysis and Research. Routledge, London, pp 1–28

House of Commons Environmental Audit Committee (2018) Disposable packaging: coffee cups. Second report of session 2017–19. House of Commons, London. https://publications.parliament.uk/pa/cm201719/cmselect/cmenvaud/657/657.pdf. Accessed 17 July 2023

Kahneman, D (2011) Thinking Fast and Slow. Penguin Random House, London

Keller, A, Köhler, JK, Eisen, C, Kleihauer, S, Hanss, D (2021) Why consumers shift from single-use to reusable drink cups: an empirical application of the stage model of self-regulated behavioural change. Sustainable Production and Consumption 27:1672–1687

Lappeman, J, Orpwood, T, Russell, M, Zeller, T, Jansson, J (2019) Personal values and willingness to pay for fair trade coffee in Cape Town, South Africa. Journal of Cleaner Production 239:118012

Lee, Y, Bateman, A (2021) The competitiveness of fair trade and organic versus conventional coffee based on consumer panel data. Ecological Economics 184:106986

Loschelder, DD, Siepelmeyerc, H, Fischer, D, Rubele, JA (2019) Dynamic norms drive sustainable consumption: norm-based nudging helps café customers to avoid disposable to-go-cups. Journal of Economic Psychology 75:102146

Ma, X, Park, C, Moultrie, J (2020) Factors for eliminating plastic in packaging: the European FMCG experts' view. Journal of Cleaner Production 256:120492

Maye, D, Kirwan, J, Brunori, G (2019) Ethics and responsibilisation in agri-food governance: the single-use plastics debate and strategies to introduce reusable coffee cups in UK retail chains. Agriculture and Human Values 36(2):301–312

Novoradovskaya, E, Mullan, B, Hasking, P (2020) Choose to reuse: predictors of using a reusable hot drink cup. Journal of Consumer Behaviour 19(6):608–617

Novoradovskaya, E, Mullan, B, Hasking, P, Velure Uren, H (2021) My cup of tea: behaviour change intervention to promote use of reusable hot drink cups. Journal of Cleaner Production 284:124675

Poortinga, W, Whitaker, L (2018) Promoting the use of reusable coffee cups through environmental messaging, the provision of alternatives and financial incentives. Sustainability 10(3):873

Rettie, R, Burchell, K, Barnham, C (2013) Social normalisation: using marketing to make green normal. Journal of Consumer Behaviour 13(1):9–17

Ropret Homar, A, Cvelbar, LK (2021) The effects of framing on environmental decisions: a systematic literature review. Ecological Economics 183:106950

Sandhu, S, Lodhia, S, Potts, A, Crocker, R (2021) Environment friendly takeaway coffee cup use: individual and institutional enablers and barriers. Journal of Cleaner Production 291:125271

Saunders, M, Lewis, P, Thornhill, A (2019) Research Methods for Business Students. 8th edn. Pearson Education Limited, Harlow

Terrier, L, Varga, P, Scaroni, A, Zizka, L (2020) To go or not to go, that is the question: using social influence to reduce hot beverage cup waste. Journal of Foodservice Business Research 23(4):350–357

Tseng, C-H (2016) The effect of price discounts on green consumerism behavioral intentions. Journal of Consumer Behaviour 15(4):325–334

Van Keulen, M, Kirchherr, J (2021) The implementation of the circular economy: barriers and enablers in the coffee value chain. Journal of Cleaner Production 281:125033

Varadarajan, R (2016) Sustainability and marketing: concurrent pursuit of a smaller environmental footprint and a larger market footprint. In Malholtra, NK (ed) Marketing in and for a Sustainable Society. Emerald Publishing Limited, pp 1–27

5

Unleashing the Power of Social Entrepreneurs for Regional Development: Insights from Jämtland Härjedalen

Konstantin Golpayegani and Ulrich Schmudde

5.1 Introduction

With all the urbanization and industrialization that has occurred over the past few decades, the Swedish countryside has seen migration and depopulation (Jordbruksverket 2012). Many social, economic, and environmental challenges have been created by urbanization. As urbanization grows, there is an opportunity to build on rural resilience and sustainability central to the international policy (Li et al. 2019) and the Sustainable Development Goals (SDGs), herein mentioning sustainable cities and communities. For the countryside to continue to develop and be dynamic, a wide range of stakeholders have a significant contribution including governments, private companies, civil society, and academics. However, the local inhabitants also make a significant contribution to being the municipality's source of revenue while remaining in place for

K. Golpayegani (✉) · U. Schmudde
Business Administration, Mid Sweden University, Östersund, Sweden
e-mail: konstantin.golpayegani@miun.se

© The Author(s), under exclusive license to Springer Nature Switzerland AG 2024

A. Sörensson et al. (eds.), *Creating New Roles for a Sustainable Economy*, Palgrave Studies in Governance, Leadership and Responsibility,
https://doi.org/10.1007/978-3-031-61551-1_5

developing the region (Bois 2014). It is natural for a place to become deserted if the inhabitants tend to move out to the urban areas. Thus, villages and communities in rural areas would fade away when there are no residents who create activities.

Due to Jämtland Härjedalen's low population density, the county experiences difficulties regarding societal, economic, and business access to infrastructure and services, more particularly in the remote areas (Jonsson and Pettersson 2020, p. 23). Jämtland Härjedalen is one of the biggest counties in Sweden and offers a wide variety of famous tourist destinations (Schmudde and Sörensson 2020). The vibrant cultural life in Jämtland Härjedalen offers excellent potential for businesses to grow in the cultural and creative sectors. Due to its cognizance of and close relationships to the rural area and its industry, Östersund (the capital of the county) has been named a member of the UNESCO Creative Cities Network in the category of food (Jonsson and Pettersson 2020). This increases the county's chances for positive and long-lasting social and economic community development which is overlooked. Therefore, the problem lies in the development of the region of Jämtland Härjedalen and the virtue of it by the inter-collaboration of local actors.

The regional community is in the hands of the entrepreneurs and start-ups, which play a pivotal role despite large corporations' importance in revitalizing the economy (Ivanova and Cepel 2018; Zaušková and Madlenák 2012). Entrepreneurs behind start-ups may be distinguished by their high level of innovation, flexibility (Santisteban et al. 2021), ability to expand employment opportunities (Dobeš et al. 2017), and cover market gaps. These respond to regional development and the employment opportunities within such regions (Hudakova 2018).

Current research in regional development emphasizes mostly tourism and its development on such regions (Ollivaud and Haxton 2019). The majority of the studies have also concentrated on the contributions of entrepreneurship in regional development among others (Głodowska 2017; Pietrzak et al. 2017; Yay et al. 2018) which includes different geographical contexts. Thus, it is noteworthy to mention that entrepreneurs contribute to production, employment, and regional development (Hudakova 2018). However, due to the rich socio-cultural characteristics of the region in focus, both tourists' and entrepreneurs' interests are attracted to the municipalities. One of the most efficient ways to preserve the regional and rural areas is to promote social entrepreneurship (Von Friedrichs et al. 2014) as the goal is to see and create opportunities at the regional level as well as to develop the regional area and make it more appealing to the residents. According to Revko (2017), social entrepreneurs can actively prevent the issue of depopulation by taking on development projects that make the region more active. With that said, the research of social entrepreneurship within regional development has been limitedly explored (Christmann 2014; Friedman and Desivilya 2010) herein focusing on other factors such as the point of contention between entrepreneurs and the regional development as well as focusing on other geographical locations.

Since the municipality of Jämtland Härjedalen has seen a great opportunity and has therefore invested in innovation, research, and competency development (Jonsson and Pettersson 2020) with the aim of developing the region by involving a wide variety of actors (Härjedalen 2015). The purpose of this study is to address the research gaps concerning the contributions of social entrepreneurs in regional development in rural areas, using the region of Jämtland Härjedalen as a study area thus seeking to answer the questions of:

Q1: How can social entrepreneurs be attracted to the region?

Q2: How can social entrepreneurs' contributions impact regional development?

Q3: How to stimulate the already established social entrepreneurs?

This research article aims to bridge the gap in understanding regional development in rural areas by examining it through the lens of social entrepreneurship. By filling this gap in the literature, the study contributes to the existing literature and offers practical implications for stakeholders involved in regional development within the region of Jämtland Härjedalen. The findings could inform policymakers, community organizations, and other relevant stakeholders on strategies and collaborations that can effectively leverage the potential of social entrepreneurship to drive sustainable regional development in rural areas.

5.2 Literature Review

Social Entrepreneurs

With the aim of getting a better understanding of the concept "social entrepreneurship" in its popular usage requires considering both its social as well as its entrepreneurial aspects. Disparities between the two points are highlighted by matters such as what are considered to be the most prominent features of entrepreneurship also within the framework of social purposes. There have been many attempts to define entrepreneurship but a consensus on a definition of the area is unlikely. One of the earliest definitions of entrepreneurship was provided by Schumpeter (1934), who characterized entrepreneurs as innovators. Mueller et al. (2012), on the other hand, defined it as follows: "*The entrepreneur is the primary actor in the formation of a new enterprise*". Startup businesses are often innovation- and technology-based and usually entrepreneurs focus heavily on the product/service and the monetary aspects of it. Nevertheless, entrepreneurship's definition has seriously hindered attempts to develop a conceptual framework (Shane and Venkataraman 2000). In this regard, the fundamental elements of entrepreneurship are opportunity and the individual, according to Venkataraman (1997). Therefore, it can be said that entrepreneurship includes examining opportunity sources, assessing opportunities, exploiting them, as well as the people who find, assess, and take advantage of them. The opportunity for profitability may exist for entrepreneurs, but they must understand the potential of this possibility in order to take advantage of it (Shane and Venkataraman 2000).

Similar to the concept of entrepreneurship, social entrepreneurship has become popular both in academia and in industrial practice but lacks a clear definition (Peredo and McLean 2006). One of the clearest definitions of social entrepreneurship was by Johnson (2000) "*social entrepreneurship is emerging as an innovative approach for dealing with complex social needs*". On the other hand, Mort et al. (2003) came up with a definition of social entrepreneurship which may be considered the most elaborate; in terms of social entrepreneurship, a number of defining characteristics are intertwined, resulting in a multidimensional construct that is deeply rooted in an organization's mission and its desire for sustainability, besides being highly influenced and shaped by environmental factors. In this sense, social entrepreneurship was not just about making money for one's own company, but it should also work towards generating societal values and contributing to local development (Von Friedrichs et al. 2014).

In order for a social entrepreneur to encounter and act upon opportunities where others see a problem (Politis 2022), promoting regional policies thus stimulating rural economic growth and job creation, green growth, innovation, technological development, resource efficiency, and competition will be emphasized upon (Andersson and Grundel 2021). A large-scale societal transformation can also be viewed as a shift towards a production system based on renewable materials which includes waste and processed biomaterials. In reference to this, "bio-economy" is seen as a social entrepreneurial opportunity that can promote regional development and generally refers to industrial products manufactured or processed using biomass. One of the highlighted examples outside the focal region is the collaboration between the local authorities, wood building company Martinson, and Luleå Technical University for the development of Scandinavia's longest wooden cable-stayed bridge in Skellefteå (Andersson and Grundel 2021). However, the contributions of social entrepreneurship in regional development have not had much focus; thus, García-González and Ramírez-Montoya (2019) emphasized the knowledge transfer within the Quadruple Helix Model by accentuating co-construction in open innovation. On the other hand, Iqbal et al. (2018) added to the literature the importance of the characteristics of an entrepreneur towards the development of creating solutions to socio-economic issues.

Ultimately, with Sweden's booming start-up scene, Sweden now ranks second on the Global Innovation Index in both technology and sustainability, behind Switzerland (Organization 2021). Research on the developing Swedish entrepreneurial ecosystem is lacking, which is concerning given that the Swedish government wants to promote innovation to address social issues on a global scale, increase competitiveness, and improve welfare. The promotion of enhancing innovation tends to diminish the economic imbalance between the urban and rural integration (Atkinson et al. 2019). However, there is still a deficiency of research on social entrepreneurs' contribution to the regional development, especially in Jämtland Härjedalen region.

Value Propositions

It is crucial for firms to be aware of the perceptions of tourists and visitors, at the destination of Jämtland Härjedalen, concerning their experience absorption. This leads to the marketing discipline, or more precisely, to value proposition. The value proposition is a part of the value process within contemporary literature, initially emphasizing the monetary measurement of consumers' advantages (Backhaus 2006). In general, a value proposition is a concept in which products (including goods and services) and experiences result in value (Kotler and Armstrong 2010, p. 9). Individuals, places, ideas, and social entrepreneurs may also fall into this category. It means that more emphasis is placed on the product itself in relation to the benefits and experiences that the product provides, corresponding to value creation. Companies must understand that they are selling an experience as opposed to products (Ulaga and Reinartz 2011). Exemplifying by showcasing the experience of seeing the production of chocolate at a confectionery like "Åre Chokladfabrik" (Åre Chocolate factory), local production of cheese on-site at the farm even experiencing local gastronomy. All these companies contribute to social values in the region, since they increase the job supply for locals, contribute to economic development, and nevertheless motivate locals to stay within the destination impacting the attraction of tourists as well as visitors to the destination (Fang 2020).

Stakeholders

Considering the importance of institutions in interpreting and meditating on the broader economic context, their contributions are suggestively important to both local and regional development (Mincyte and

Dobernig 2016). Therefore, a wide range of stakeholders have a significant contribution in improving entrepreneurial conditions, including governments, private companies, civil society, and academics (Siegel and Wright 2015). It is through the way these stakeholders shape and coordinate the investment and enterprise landscape, as well as mobilize other stakeholders around local and regional development agendas (Zhan 2021). Consecutively, policymakers together with the academics are becoming increasingly interested in how institutions contribute to economic and regional development (Berman 2012). The promotion of policy continuity and the facilitation of dialogue among key stakeholders through informal and formal institutions are essential components of the development process (Pike et al. 2017). National policymakers should focus on regulatory reforms that will facilitate the registration and operation of new businesses, as well as on ways in which the public sector can provide effective structures to support and mentor potential and existing entrepreneurs (Morris and Jones 1999). However, the current literature finds a challenging gap, being in developing organizations that support connections between the business, public, and educational sectors that reinforce the region's voice (Vossenberg 2013).

This leads to the argument that the economic development of a country stands on the foundation of four interdependent pillars: university, industry, government, and civil society—known as the Quadruple Helix model (Iqbal et al. 2018). In this theory, the impact of these four factors on the economy of a nation is explained by inter-collaboration. It is noteworthy to mention that innovation and knowledge are the true engines of economic growth in cities and regions and an integrated innovation ecosystem can be established through a strong combination of universities, industries, and technological infrastructure (ibid). In this model, the government provides access to financial support as well as a structure for the innovation activities, while the society creates a never-ending market for innovative goods and services (Afonso et al. 2012). On the other hand, as civil society contributes to regional development in terms of emerging recreational rural activities, therefore it is important that people remain in the regions (Torre 2016). Alternatively, the purpose of educational institutions is to provide individuals with the skills they need to succeed to become entrepreneurs (Bogren et al. 2013).

Ultimately, this collaboration within the Quadruple Helix Model might result in reduced business costs, improved market access, improved access to information, and the prominence of innovation (Islam et al. 2021; Kolehmainen et al. 2015).

5.3 Data Collection and Analysis

The study area in focus is Jämtland Härjedalen, a county in central Sweden. Jämtland Härjedalen borders Norway on the west, Västerbotten on the north, Gävleborg on the south-east, Västernorrland on the east, and Dalarna in the south (Turism 2022). Jämtland Härjedalen covers 12% of Sweden's land area, but it is home to only 1.5% of the country's population (ibid.). The County, with the exception of Gotland, is Sweden's least industrialized county, with only 15% of the population actively working in industry. The county's capital is Östersund, a Swedish university city of about 51,000 people in the town, which has its own governmental entities. The municipality as a whole has approximately 64,600 inhabitants and a district surface area of 2517 km^2 (Kommun, 2022). It is located near Sweden's fifth largest lake, Storsjön. Östersund is known as the "Winter City", with events such as the biathlon sprint and, in the summer, the "Storsjöyran", Sweden's oldest music festival (Oestersund 2022).

The selection of respondents in our study was carefully designed to ensure a comprehensive understanding of the contributions of social entrepreneurs to regional development in rural areas. We conducted 20 semi-structured interviews, involving a diverse range of stakeholders from various sectors. The inclusion of municipal representatives in the study is crucial as they play a key role in regional development policies and decision-making processes. Their insights provide valuable perspectives on the broader regional context and the contributions of social entrepreneurs within it. Destination marketing organizations (DMOs) bring expertise in promoting and attracting tourists to the region, making their input essential in understanding the potential impact of social entrepreneurship on the tourism sector. The involvement of infrastructure companies is important as they are responsible for providing essential services and facilities that enable social entrepreneurs to operate and thrive. Their perspectives shed light on the infrastructure requirements and challenges faced by social entrepreneurs in rural areas. Engaging with tourist companies allows us to examine the relationship between social entrepreneurship and the tourism industry, exploring how social entrepreneurs contribute to the development of unique and authentic tourism experiences. Including entrepreneurs themselves provides firsthand insights into their experiences, motivations, and challenges in driving regional development through their entrepreneurial endeavors. Lastly, involving university actors such as students brings academic expertise and a fresh perspective to the study and the students' perspective of the regional development. Universities often serve as catalysts for innovation and collaboration, and understanding their role in supporting and nurturing social entrepreneurs can offer valuable insights for fostering a conducive ecosystem for regional development.

By including a diverse range of stakeholders, our study ensures a comprehensive and multifaceted understanding of the contributions of social entrepreneurs to regional development in rural areas. The insights gained from these interviews provide a rich and nuanced exploration of the contributions of social entrepreneurship and its potential for sustainable and inclusive regional growth in the specific context of Jämtland Härjedalen.

In addition to primary data, secondary data was gathered from websites and various reports. Interpretive analysis was performed on the data, which included developing themes. The following themes were taken into consideration: (1) social entrepreneurs, (2) value proposition, and (3) stakeholders (Table 5.1).

The study was conducted in a qualitative format (Järvensivu and Törnroos 2010) and we found that several topics in the available research have been omitted and under-researched, indicating a need to expand the research. Therefore, an abductive technique for theory creation has been applied in order to strengthen the existing theory in regional development. Thus, the gap-spotting theory of Sandberg and Alvesson (2011) supported providing a new perspective and a more comprehensive understanding thus identifying the under-researched topic of social entrepreneurship within the literature.

Table 5.1 Thematic analysis

Themes	Extract examples of interview questions
Social entrepreneurs	What is your interpretation of social entrepreneurship especially in Jämtland Härjedalen? How can Jämtland Härjedalen be developed by social entrepreneurs? Are there incentives that give you/your business encouragement to stay/move to the peripheries?
Value proposition	To what extent does it play a role to be aware of tourists' and visitors' needs and wants to the destination? Which experiences do you sell to your consumers? Which impact do you have on locals by running your business at the rural place?
Stakeholders	What do you think if different actors (e.g. locals, universities, industries, and the public) are involved in regional development? How important are innovations and knowledge for regional development? Are you collaborating with others, (if yes, which ones), and which collaborative potential do you see?

The primary aim of this research was to delve into the intricate role of social entrepreneurs in nurturing regional development within rural areas, with a specific focus on the captivating study area of Jämtland Härjedalen. To accomplish this objective, the study employed a meticulous thematic analysis method, skillfully utilizing a preselected set of codes tailored to address the research questions and align with the existing research framework. These codes revolved around two key domains: (1) exploring the characteristics and contributions of social entrepreneurship and (2) unraveling the dynamics of regional development. The data analysis offered a profound interpretation of the identified themes and patterns, allowing for a nuanced understanding of the research topic at hand. The data analysis procedure followed a well-defined coding protocol consisting of several steps inspired by Braun and Clarke (2006). Initially, the transcripts of the semi-structured interviews were thoroughly reviewed to develop a comprehensive understanding of the data. Initial codes were then generated to capture the essence of the data in relation to the research questions and key themes. These initial codes served as broad categories encompassing the overall meaning and relevance of the data. Subsequently, the data was revisited, and additional codes were refined and introduced to capture more specific themes and patterns. These emergent codes were carefully aligned with the research questions and key themes, including social entrepreneurship contributions, stakeholder roles, destination value propositions, inter-collaboration dynamics, and the intriguing Quadruple Helix Model. For a deeper analysis of the connections and patterns between the codes, the codes were grouped together based on their similarities and differences, ultimately revealing overarching themes that emerged from the data. Inspired by the insights of Braun and Clarke (2006, p. 79), this thematic analysis framework facilitated the identification, interpretation, and reporting of the patterns and themes within the data, adding clarity and transparency to the analytical process. The chosen approach guaranteed the rigor and replicability of the analysis, instilling confidence in the research findings.

5.4 Discussion of Findings

The purpose of this study is to explore regional development within Jämtland Härjedalen and doing so by uncovering the research gaps in the contributions of social entrepreneurs in it.

To have a better understanding of the contributions of social entrepreneurs in regional development, the matter of a theoretical standpoint of social entrepreneurship definition is necessary. According to the findings and the literature review, there is a general lack of agreement about what constitutes entrepreneurship and social entrepreneurship. However, it was pointed out through the findings that what distinguishes them are the contributions to the market which further defined their purpose. Even though the lines that define them are not that clear, entrepreneurship is mainly defined as the construct that involves the discovery, evaluation, and exploitation of opportunities resulting in innovative products (entailing both goods and services) and/or experiences. On the other hand, the definition of social entrepreneurship only added that it uses innovative approaches to deal with social needs and issues.

The region Jämtland Härjedalen is a sparsely populated area that has invested in innovation, research, and competency development since these are crucial for the development of the region. Attractions can be in different facets, but one attraction is the natural place of interest of Jämtland Härjedalen. According to the findings, the entrepreneurs come to the region to get inspiration and thus deliver values to the overall society by using innovation and creativity in their business model. This is supported by the literature of value proposition as being inspired and becoming creative is the antecedent of being innovative. Therefore, in order to attract social entrepreneurs to the region, a sense of inspiration, such as cultural-heritage or socio-cultural conception should be easy to exploit. Therefore, it is crucial for the companies to know about what consumers need and want in order to achieve long-term relationship in terms of product and experience.

In line with that, it is crucially important to take into consideration the opportunities and possibilities that social entrepreneurs have in Jämtland Härjedalen compared to the developed bigger cities in Sweden. However, the smaller cities and rural areas offer a greater deal of culture-heritage activities which might appeal to the inhabitants as well as the potential inhabitants than larger cities, herein the case of Jämtland Härjedalen offers a welcoming rural experience in terms of gastronomy and outdoor activities that are unique. The findings have supported and corroborated that in order to attract social entrepreneurs to the region is by offering an inspirational sense of motive that can encourage the local inhabitants to remain in the region with the aim of impacting the attraction of tourists and visitors. The inspirational sense of motive can be within the possibility bounds of stimulating the cultural-heritage transitive, local gastronomy, and outdoor activities. Furthermore, this approach also concerns the stimulation of the already established social entrepreneurs within the region. Consistent with the findings, the establishment of social entrepreneurs first-movers will promote a chain reaction of an induced inspirations which triggers the stimulation of the already established social entrepreneurs.

On the other hand, Jämtland Härjedalen is seeking competency development from outside of the region (Jonsson and Pettersson 2020) which also includes a connection to the research development by involving Mid

Sweden University within the Quadruple Helix Model. In line with the collected data, Mid Sweden University benefits a considerable amount of knowledge and cultural diversity from Erasmus students mainly from Germany, but also from other European countries, among others, such as the Netherlands, France, Italy, Poland, and Finland.

Mid Sweden University has two campuses: one in Sundsvall in the county of Västernorrland, and one in Östersund, the capital of the county of Jämtland. The university offers in a total of 480 courses, 60 educational programs at bachelor level, 37 educational programs at master-, and a one-year master level (MIUN 2022). Overall Mid Sweden University has 24,500 students, where of 6000 are on campuses (ca. 3000 at each campus) (ibid.). Since Mid Sweden University accounts for half of the addition of newly qualified graduates in Jämtland Härjedalen and Västernorrland counties (ibid.), we think it is useful to take the students and their origin into consideration in this analysis. According to Mid Sweden University's latest annual report 2021, it is obvious that both, outgoing and incoming students, have decreased significantly during the pandemic years as compared to until 2019 (Sörensen 2021). This can be explained by the significant insecurity that has been ongoing since the pandemic started. By interviewing the international students, it was identified that they would like to stay longer but the possibilities that stimulate them to stay are limited. In reference to a respondent, "*what I am going to do tomorrow!?*".

On the other hand, the numbers also show that tourists from Germany and the Netherlands have a positive impression of central Sweden and desire to stay longer in undisturbed nature in sparsely populated areas, where livability can be practiced by connecting hosts and visitors. Considering the year 2021, the county of Jämtland Härjedalen received 11.3 million guest nights, where 3.1 million were business travelers (Turism 2022). Under usual conditions (before the Covid-19 pandemic and the war in Ukraine), it is a fact that Germany is the largest group of foreign business travelers (61,769 guest nights) to Jämtland Härjedalen after the neighboring country of Norway (306,115 guest nights) based on 2019 data (Turism 2022). However, a considerable amount of German or Dutch students have become attracted by the region during their education program which resulted in a longer stay for them than initially planned.

Moreover, the aforementioned target group could support the development of the socio-cultural industry in Jämtland Härjedalen by stimulating their capability and creativity into praxis. On the other hand, the already existing socio-cultural ideas and creativity might stimulate and promote "foreign" social entrepreneurs to act on potential ideas and creativity, which in turn might contribute the regional development in the sense of creating a more attracting and welcoming destination with unmatched local experiences.

By developing the prominence of the various stakeholders such as MIUN innovation, university students including Erasmus students, but also local civils in Jämtland Härjedalen, could encourage the development of socio-cultural ideas which in turn could lead to innovative products and/or experiences. Furthermore, the role of government authorities such as municipalities is crucial in terms of policymaking and creating frameworks to support entrepreneurs and their activities. Furthermore, in line with the study by Iqbal et al. (2018) which has examined, among others, the collaboration among the Quadruple Helix sectors that encourage social entrepreneurial ventures in Pakistan, where social entrepreneurship has not been explored to its fullest potential in terms of research and understanding. Their study discovered that the development of entrepreneurial-related factors (human capital, social capital, and motivational factors), as well as the ultimate development of sustainable social initiatives, depends on the interdependency of the university, government, industry, and civil society. Thus, their study concludes that the collaboration within the Quadruple Helix Model aids in the creation of long-term social entrepreneurship.

Consequently, the study works as an inspiration that a similar thorough study can be conducted within the context of Jämtland Härjedalen with the intention of increasing the contributions of social entrepreneurship in the region supporting the problematization of regional development as mentioned earlier. Having said that, the factors that play a crucial role in determining entrepreneurship in a given economy include the availability of funding, the entrepreneurship education, the regulatory environment, access to markets, and political commitment that enhances the innovative and entrepreneurial capacity (Herrington and Kew 2017). According to the findings, the Quadruple Helix Model fosters regional development by intricating a joined collaboration that can stimulate the contributions of social entrepreneurs in the regional development.

5.5 Conclusion

The growth of regional social entrepreneurship can, in the first place, be influenced by regional as well as local policymakers and as a result, the policymakers should place more of an emphasis on information accessibility that can help entrepreneurs obtain better information about business registration as well as operation. As it was already noted, the region of Jämtland Härjedalen faces challenges in terms of sociological, economic, and commercial access to both infrastructure and services. Therefore, a more specialized focus should be paid to recognizing the requirements of start-ups and expanding businesses based on their industry, size, as well as other operational factors. Consequently, there will be a greater interest in and demand for starting companies by improving the support systems, ideally developed by among others the trade and industry sector, for stimulating social entrepreneurship. Furthermore, the (social) entrepreneurs may benefit from the provided mentorship networks as they embark on their journeys by providing inspiration, guidance, and support. A follow-up step would be for the start-up culture in the region to develop incubators and accelerators that could support (social) entrepreneurs in their business ventures, even though mentioning the already established MIUN innovation, as an incubator. The creation of clusters and business hubs that integrate (social) entrepreneurs, commercial partners, and professionals is essential in order to assist start-up companies in a more protected and supportive environment. Ergo, this is crucial, since specifically rural and semi-rural areas lack adequate infrastructure, which is a major development hindrance for entrepreneurship.

However, the presence of a collaboration within the Quadruple Helix Model promotes the development of the entrepreneurial landscape in the region as the inter-collaboration between stakeholders plays a significant role. This is in the virtue of that there will be a focus on key issues such as the limited support for entrepreneurs such as financial access, socio-cultural opportunities, and the motivation towards youth entrepreneurs. Since the collaboration within the Quadruple Helix Model facilitates the contributions of all the stakeholders, it can be said that from the educational perspective, there is a wide gap between industry and the knowledge/know-how that educational institutions provide which further motivates the reasoning that a collaboration within the Quadruple Helix Model is needed. The implication of this particular study can contribute to the development of competencies and skills for potential entrepreneurs as well as inducing on the challenging gap mentioned before, being: developing organizations that support connections between the business, public, and educational sectors that reinforce the region's voice. This leads to the potentiality of future research on the implementation and implications of the agent-based theory among the stakeholders. We also strive to contribute to the current literature of regional development by highlighting the uncovered topic of social entrepreneurship and its contribution to the regional growth of rural areas. And that within the context of Jämtland Härjedalen which is considered one of the most distinguished tourist destinations in Sweden.

References

Afonso, O., Monteiro, S., & Riberio Thompson, M. J. (2012). A growth model for the quadruple helix. *Journal of Business Economics and Management, 13*(5).

Andersson, I., & Grundel, I. (2021). Regional policy mobilities: Shaping and reshaping bioeconomy policies in Värmland and Västerbotten, Sweden. *Geoforum, 121*, 142–151.

Atkinson, R. D., Muro, M., & Whiton, J. (2019). *The case for growth centers: How to spread tech innovation across America*. B. Institution.

Backhaus, K. (2006). Vom Kundenvorteil über die value proposition zum KKV. *Marketing Review St. Gallen, 23*(3), 7–10. https://doi.org/10.1007/BF03249115.

Berman, E. P. (2012). *Creating the market university: How academic science became an economic engine*. Princeton University Press.
Bogren, M., von Friedrichs, Y., Rennemo, Ø., & Widding, L. Ø. (2013). Networking women entrepreneurs: Fruitful for business growth. *International Journal of Gender and Entrepreneurship, 5*(1), 60–77. https://doi.org/10.1108/17566261311305210.
Bois, L. (2014). Lokala Företagare som Bygdens Utvecklare. In Y. Von Friedrichs, M. Gawell, & J. Wincent (Eds.), *Samhällsentreprenörskap - Samverkande för lokal utveckling*. Mid Sweden University.
Braun, V., & Clarke, V. (2006). Using thematic analysis in psychology. *Qualitative Research in Psychology, 3*, 77–101. https://doi.org/10.1191/1478088706qp063oa.
Christmann, G. B. (2014). Social entrepreneurs on the periphery: Uncovering emerging pioneers of regional development. *DisP—The Planning Review, 50*(1), 43–55. https://doi.org/10.1080/02513625.2014.926725.
Dobeš, K., Kot, S., Kramolis, J., & Sopkova, G. (2017). The perception of governmental support in the context of competitiveness of SMEs in the Czech Republic. *Journal of Competitiveness, 9*, 34–50. https://doi.org/10.7441/joc.2017.03.03.
Fang, W.-T. (2020). Rural tourism. In W.-T. Fang (Ed.), *Tourism in emerging economies: The way we green, sustainable, and healthy* (pp. 103–129). Springer Singapore. https://doi.org/10.1007/978-981-15-2463-9_5.
Friedman, V. J., & Desivilya, H. (2010). Integrating social entrepreneurship and conflict engagement for regional development in divided societies. *Entrepreneurship & Regional Development, 22*(6), 495–514. https://doi.org/10.1080/08985626.2010.488400.
García-González, A., & Ramírez-Montoya, M.-S. (2019). *Higher education for social entrepreneurship in the quadruple helix framework: Co-construction in open innovation.* https://doi.org/10.1145/3362789.3362794.
Głodowska, A. (2017). Business environment and economic growth in the European Union countries: What can be explained for the convergence? *Entrepreneurial Business and Economics Review, 5*(4), 189–204. https://EconPapers.repec.org/RePEc:krk:eberjl:v:5:y:2017:i:4:p:189-204.
Herrington, M., & Kew, P. (2017). *GEM 2016 / 2017 GLOBAL REPORT*.
Hudakova, J. (2018). *Innovation potential of the regions in the Slovak Republic*.
Härjedalen, R. J. (2015). *Regional utveckling inom region Jämtland Härjedalen*.
Iqbal, J., Kousar, S., & Ul Hameed, W. (2018). Antecedents of sustainable social entrepreneurship initiatives in Pakistan and outcomes: Collaboration

between quadruple helix sectors. *Sustainability, 10*(12), 4539. https://www.mdpi.com/2071-1050/10/12/4539.

Islam, A., Jerin, I., Hafiz, N., Tali Nimfa, D., & Abdul Wahab, S. (2021). Configuring a blueprint for Malaysian SMEs to survive through the COVID-19 crisis: The reinforcement of Quadruple Helix Innovation Model. *Journal of Entrepreneurship, Business and Economics, 9*(1), 50. http://scientificia.com/index.php/JEBE/article/view?path.

Ivanova, E., & Cepel, M. (2018). The impact of innovation performance on the competitiveness of the Visegrad 4 countries. *Journal of Competitiveness, 10*, 54–72. https://doi.org/10.7441/joc.2018.01.04.

Johnson, S. (2000). *Literature review on social entrepreneurship*. Canadian Centre for Social Entrepreneurship.

Jonsson, A., & Pettersson, R. (2020). *Besöksnäringens roll för regional utveckling: Ett nedslag i Jämtland Härjedalen*. Mid Sweden University.

Jordbruksverket. (2012). *Arbete och liv på landsbygden: Landsbygdens förutsättningar i kunskapsekonomin*.

Järvensivu, T., & Törnroos, J.-Å. (2010). Case study research with moderate constructionism: Conceptualization and practical illustration. *Industrial marketing management, 39*, 100–108. https://doi.org/10.1016/j.indmarman.2008.05.005.

Kolehmainen, J., Irvine, J., Stewart, L., Karacsonyi, Z., Szabó, T., Alarinta, J., & Norberg, A. (2015). Quadruple helix, innovation and the knowledge-based development: Lessons from remote, rural and less-favoured regions. *Journal of the Knowledge Economy, 7*, 23–42. https://doi.org/10.1007/s13132-015-0289-9.

Kommun, Ö. (2022). *Kommunfakta*. Retrieved December from https://www.ostersund.se/kommun-och-politik/kommunfakta.html.

Kotler, P., & Armstrong, G. (2010). *Principles of marketing*. Pearson Education Limited.

Li, Y., Westlund, H., & Liu, Y. (2019). Why some rural areas decline while some others not: An overview of rural evolution in the world. *Journal of Rural Studies, 68*, 135–143. https://doi.org/10.1016/j.jrurstud.2019.03.003.

Mincyte, D., & Dobernig, K. (2016). Urban farming in the North American metropolis: Rethinking work and distance in alternative food networks. *Environment and Planning A: Economy and Space, 48*(9), 1767–1786. https://doi.org/10.1177/0308518x16651444.

MIUN. (2022). *Detta är Mittuniversitetet*. https://www.miun.se/mot-mittuniversitetet/universitetet/.

Morris, M. H., & Jones, F. F. (1999). Entrepreneurship in established organizations: The case of the public sector. *Entrepreneurship Theory and Practice, 24*(1), 71–91. https://doi.org/10.1177/104225879902400105.

Mort, G. S., Weerawardena, J., & Carnegie, K. (2003). Social entrepreneurship: Towards conceptualisation. *International Journal of Nonprofit and Voluntary Sector Marketing, 8*(1).

Mueller, S., Volery, T., & von Siemens, B. (2012). What do entrepreneurs actually do? An observational study of entrepreneurs' everyday behavior in the start-up and growth stages. *Entrepreneurship Theory and Practice, 36*(5), 995–1017. https://doi.org/10.1111/j.1540-6520.2012.00538.x.

Oestersund, D. (2022). https://destinationostersund.se/.

Ollivaud, P., & Haxton, P. (2019). *Making the most of tourism in Indonesia to promote sustainable regional development*. https://doi.org/10.1787/c73325d9-en.

Organization, W. I. P. (2021). *Global Innovation Index 2021*. WIPO.

Peredo, A. M., & McLean, M. (2006). Social entrepreneurship: A critical review of the concept. *Journal of World Business*, 56–65.

Pietrzak, M., Balcerzak, A., Gajdos, A., & Arendt, L. (2017). Entrepreneurial environment at regional level: The case of Polish path towards sustainable socio-economic development. *Entrepreneurship and Sustainability Issues, 5*, 190–203. https://doi.org/10.9770/jesi.2017.5.2(2).

Pike, A., Rodriguez-Pose, A., & Tomaney, J. (2017). *Local and regional development* (2nd ed.). Routledge.

Politis, D. (2022). *Därför ska sjuksköterskor lära sig entreprenörskap* [Interview]. Institutet för entreprenörskaps- och småföretagsforksning (ESBRI).

Revko, A. M. (2017). Social entrepreneurship as the main resource for the regional development. *Marketing and Management of Innovations*.

Sandberg, J., & Alvesson, M. (2011). Ways of constructing research questions: Gap-spotting or problematization? *Organization, 18*(1), 23–44. https://doi.org/10.1177/1350508410372151.

Santisteban, J., Mauricio, D., & Cachay, O. (2021). Critical success factors for technology-based startups. *International Journal of Entrepreneurship and Small Business, 42*(4), 397–421.

Schmudde, U., & Sörensson, A. (2020). Tourism development in rural areas in Sweden—In the shadow of a well-established destination. *Athens Journal of Tourism, 7*(1), 55–74.

Schumpeter, J. (1934). *The theory of economic development*. Harvard University Press.

Shane, S., & Venkataraman, S. (2000). The promise of entrepreneurship as a field of research. *The Academy of Management Review, 25*(1), 217–226. https://doi.org/10.2307/259271.

Siegel, D. S., & Wright, M. (2015). Academic entrepreneurship: Time for a rethink? *British Journal of Management, 26*(4), 582–595. https://doi.org/10.1111/1467-8551.12116.

Sörensen, E. S. (2021). *Årsredovisning 2021.* M. å.

Torre, A., & Wallet, F. (2016). *Regional development in rural areas: Analytical tools and public policies* (p. 110). Springer briefs in regional science, Springer. https://doi.org/10.1007/978-3-319-02372-4.

Turism, J. H. (2022). *Fakta om turismen: Samlad statistik från Jämland Härjedalen.* JHT.

Ulaga, W., & Reinartz, W. J. (2011). Hybrid offerings: How manufacturing firms combine goods and services successfully. *Journal of Marketing, 75*(6), 5–23. https://doi.org/10.1509/jm.09.0395.

Venkataraman, S. (1997). The distinctive domain of entrepreneurship research. In *Advances in entrepreneurship, firm emergence, and growth* (pp. 119–138). JAI Press.

Von Friedrichs, Y., Gawell, M., & Wincent, J. (2014). Samhällsentreprenörskap - kontexter, organisering och perspektiv för hållbar utveckling. In Y. Von Friedrichs, M. Gawell, & J. Wincent (Eds.), *Samhällsentreprenörskap - Samverkande för lokal utveckling*. Mid Sweden University.

Vossenberg, S. (2013). *Women entrepreneurship promotion in developing countries: What explains the gender gap in entrepreneurship and how to close it?* Maastricht School of Management.

Yay, T., Yay, G. G., & Aksoy, T. (2018). Impact of institutions on entrepreneurship: A panel data analysis. *Eurasian Economic Review, 8*(1), 131–160. https://doi.org/10.1007/s40822-017-0082-0.

Zaušková, A., & Madlenák, A. (2012). The application of the open innovation concept in the furniture industry. Wood and Furniture Industry in Times of Change—New trends and challenges, WoodEMA 2012, Trnava, Slovakia.

Zhan, J. X. (2021). GVC transformation and a new investment landscape in the 2020s: Driving forces, directions, and a forward-looking research and policy agenda. *Journal of International Business Policy, 4*(2), 206–220. https://doi.org/10.1057/s42214-020-00088-0.

6

Corporate Social Responsibility Approach by SMEs' Managing Directors in the Hungarian City of Győr—Empirical Evidence

Adrienn Reisinger

6.1 Introduction

Corporate Social Responsibility (CSR) is a widely known topic among academics and corporate professionals, too. The concept of CSR dates back to the beginning of the twentieth century, but the term itself was coined by Bowen.[1] According to the initial concept, large companies (mainly multinational ones) with their economic power strongly influence their environment; as a result, they should also concentrate on how to protect their social, economic, and physical environment through

[1] Bowen, Howard R. *Social Responsibilities of the Businessman*. No. 3. New York: Harper & Brothers, 1953.

A. Reisinger (✉)
Széchenyi István University, Győr, Hungary
e-mail: reisinger.adrienn@ga.sze.hu

© The Author(s), under exclusive license to Springer Nature Switzerland AG 2024

A. Sörensson et al. (eds.), *Creating New Roles for a Sustainable Economy*, Palgrave Studies in Governance, Leadership and Responsibility,
https://doi.org/10.1007/978-3-031-61551-1_6

responsible behavior.[2] Thus, in the beginning, large companies were in the focus of attention indicated by the word corporate. However, around the turn of the millennium papers were also published about the role of CSR in smaller companies.[3] First, papers focused on the comparison of SMEs' CSR with that of large companies in general,[4] later, over the past 10–15 years research about national characteristics was also available.[5]

While a large number of papers deal with SMEs' CSR at an international level, in Hungary only a few papers have focused on this topic over the past 15 years.[6] According to the literature, disregarding the

---

[2] Davis, Keith. "Can Business Afford to Ignore Social Responsibilities?" *California Management Review* 2, no. 3 (1960): 70–76.

Carroll, Archie B. "A Three-Dimensional Conceptual Model of Corporate Social Performance." *Academy of Management Review* 4 (1979): 497–505.

Carroll, Archie B., and Kareem M. Shabana. "The Business Case for Corporate Social Responsibility: A Review of Concepts, Research and Practice." *International Journal of Management Reviews* 12, no. 1 (2010): 85–105.

[3] Spence, Laura J. "Does Size Matter? The State of the Art in Small Business Ethics." *Business Ethics: A European Review* 8, no. 3 (1999): 163–174.

Tilley, Fiona. "Small Firm Environmental Ethics: How Deep Do They Go?" *Business Ethics: the Environment & Responsibility* 9, no. 1 (2000): 31–41.

Jenkins, Heledd. "A Critique of Conventional CSR Theory: An SME Perspective." *Journal of General Management* 29, no. 4 (2004): 55–75.

[4] Jenkins, Heledd. "A Critique of Conventional CSR Theory: An SME Perspective." *Journal of General Management* 29, no. 4 (2004): 55–75.

Jamali, Dima, Mona Zanhour, and Tamar Keshishian. "Peculiar Strengths and Relational Attributes of SMEs in the Context of CSR." *Journal of Business Ethics* 87 (2009): 355–377.

[5] E.g.: Campopiano, Giovanna, Alfredo De Massis, and Lucio Cassia. "Corporate Social Responsibility: A Survey Among SMEs in Bergamo." *Procedia—Social and Behavioral Sciences* 62 (2012): 325–341.

Pastrana, Nathaly A., and Krishnamurthy Sriramesh. "Corporate Social Responsibility: Perceptions and Practices Among SMEs in Colombia." *Public Relations Review* 40, no. 1 (2014): 14–24.

Youn, Hyewon, Nan Hua, and Seoki Lee. "Does Size Matter? Corporate Social Responsibility and Firm Performance in The Restaurant Industry." *International Journal of Hospitality Management* 51 (2015): 127–134.

Zastempowski, Maciej, and Szymon Cyfert. "Social Responsibility of SMEs from the Perspective of Their Innovativeness: Evidence from Poland." *Journal of Cleaner Production* 3, no. 17 (2021): 128400.

[6] Petheő, Attila, György Pataki, and Réka Matolay. "Corporate Social Responsibility (CSR) Practices by Small- and Medium-Sized Enterprises (SMEs) in Hungary." In *Erdei Ferenc IV. Tudományos Konferencia*, edited by Ferencz, Árpád, 460–463. Kecskemét: Kecskeméti Főiskola, 2007.

general description of SMEs' CSR or its comparison with that of large companies or its analysis with a special topic (e.g. marketing, communication), no research has been conducted yet on how SMEs' CSR is interpreted by their leaders. Csáfor[7] points out that the problem with SMEs' CSR is mainly due to the fact that managing directors do not know the term, or if yes, they are not aware of its meaning. Nevertheless, companies often implement CSR activities in some way being unaware of it. As detailed research about SMEs' CSR approach is still a research gap in Hungary, SMEs' managing directors were enquired about their CSR awareness and approach. An interview survey was carried out with 50 SMEs in the Hungarian city of Győr between August 2021 and September 2022 as part of a scholarship research on the social factors of firms' competitiveness. This chapter seeks to find an answer to the following questions:

Have SMEs' managing directors heard of the term CSR?
Are SMEs' managing directors' aware of the term CSR?
Do SMEs' managing directors use the term?

Csáfor, Hajnalka. "A magyar vállalatok társadalmi felelősségvállalásának sajátosságai." *Acta Academiae Paedagogicae Agriensis Nova Series: Acta Oeconomica* 34 (2007): 169–189.

Csáfor, Hajnalka. "Corporate Social Responsibility as a Managerial Competency for SME in Countries of the Carpathian Euroregion." In *Ankara University International Conference: Marketing and Entrepreneurship AUMEC 2009*, edited by Kocak, Akin, Temi Abimbola, Alper Özer, and Lorraine Watkins-Mathys, 448–458. Ankara: Ankara University the Faculty of Political Sciences, 2009.

Szigeti, Cecília. "KKV-CSR (Corporate Social Responsibility) tevékenysége." In *Vállalkozások ökonómiája: IX. Nemzetközi Tudományos Napok*, edited by Magda, Sándor, and László Dinya, 269–276. Gyöngyös: Károly Róbert Főiskola, 2008.

Benedek, Andrea, István Takács, and Katalin Takácsné György. "The Examination of the CSR Attitudes of the CEOs Among Hungarian SMEs." *Wspolczesne Zarzadzanie: Kwartalnik Srodowisk Naukowych I Liderow Biznesu* 3, no. 31 (2015): 283–297.

Benedek, Andrea, Katalin Takács-György, and István Takács. "The Appearance of CSR at SMEs—Results of a Corporate Survey." In *The International Conference Small and Medium Sized Enterprises in a Globalized World: 6th edition*, edited by Pop, Cornelia, and Oana Gica, 7–17. Cluj-Napoca: Babes-Bolyai University, 2013.

Gasparetz, András, and Balázs Szentes, "CSR tevékenység kommunikációja a KKV marketingben." *Vállalati kommunikációmenedzsment*, edited by Borgulya, Ágnes, and Márta Konczosné Szombathelyi, 260–265. Budapest: L'Harmattan Kiadó, Károli Gáspár Református Egyetem, 2017.

[7] Csáfor, Hajnalka. "A magyar vállalatok társadalmi felelősségvállalásának sajátosságai." *Acta Academiae Paedagogicae Agriensis Nova Series: Acta Oeconomica* 34 (2007): 169–189.

Do SMEs implement any kind of CSR activity?
Is there any relation between a firm's size (small or medium) and its age (i.e. establishment before or after the turn of the millennium)?

6.2 CSR in SMEs—Does Size Matter?

The basic concept of CSR was evolved by Carroll (1979, 1991), who described the levels of CSR in his pyramid model (Fig. 6.1).

The four levels comprise economic, legal, ethical, and philanthropic responsibility. Although this approach was mainly developed for large companies, even today it seems to be an initial point to understand CSR. Over the past decades several approaches and definitions have been created, but still, there is no general definition of the term CSR.[8]

Fig. 6.1 Carroll's pyramid model for CSR (*Source* Compiled by the author based on Carroll, Archie B. "The Pyramid of Corporate Social Responsibility: Toward the Moral Management of Organizational Stakeholders." *Business Horizons* 34, no. 4 [1991]: 39–48)

[8] Russo, Angeloantonio, and Francesco Perrini. "Investigating Stakeholder Theory and Social Capital: CSR in Large Firms and SMEs." *Journal of Business Ethics* 91, no. 2 (2010): 207–221.

According to the European Commission,[9] CSR is "the responsibility of enterprises for their impacts on society." This is an approach with a wide perspective indicating that CSR covers "social, environmental, ethical, human rights, and consumer concerns."

Nowadays CSR is a more complex phenomenon because it could be referred to all types of companies from micro to large ones. The first papers drawing attention to CSR in SMEs were published around 2000. At first, it was important to differentiate SMEs' CSR from that of large companies. The basic idea was that SMEs are not the mini-versions of large companies, and their cultural, economic, and social environment is different from large ones.[10] Based on this approach, Jenkins collected the main differences between large and smaller firms' CSR (Table 6.1).

In SMEs, the owner and the manager are often one person[11]; it means that the characteristics and attitudes of owner-managers are important.[12] This fact indicates that the owner-managers' awareness of CSR is a crucial topic. Information on their knowledge of CSR could be important; however, the literature is more likely to focus on attitudes and perceptions.[13] This is the reason why SMEs tend to have a social capital-based approach instead of stakeholder theory.[14] Smaller firms do not

---

9 European Commission. "Commission Recommendation of 6 May 2003 Concerning the Definition of Micro, Small and Medium-Sized Enterprises." (C(2003) 1422), Brussels, 2003, 6.

10 Jenkins, Heledd. "A Critique of Conventional CSR Theory: An SME Perspective." *Journal of General Management* 29, no. 4 (2004): 55–75.

11 Spence, Laura J. "Does Size Matter? The State of the Art in Small Business Ethics." *Business Ethics. A European Review* 8, no. 3 (1999): 163–174.

12 Jenkins, Heledd. "A Critique of Conventional CSR Theory: An SME Perspective." *Journal of General Management* 29, no. 4 (2004): 55–75.

Jenkins, Heledd. "Small Business Champions for Corporate Social Responsibility." *Journal of Business Ethics* 67 (2006): 241–256.

13 Benedek, Andrea, István Takács, and Katalin Takácsné György. "The Examination of the CSR Attitudes of the CEOs Among Hungarian SMEs." *Wspolczesne Zarzadzanie: Kwartalnik Srodowisk Naukowych I Liderow Biznesu* 3, no. 31 (2015): 283–297.

Fassin, Yves, Annick van Rossem, and Marc Buelens. "Small-Business Owner-Managers' Perceptions of Business Ethics and CSR-Related Concepts." *Journal of Business Ethics* 98 no. 3 (2011): 425–453.

14 Perrini, Francesco. "SMEs and CSR Theory: Evidence and Implications from an Italian Perspective." *Journal of Business Ethics* 67 (2006): 305–316. https://doi.org/10.1007/s10551-006-9186-2.

Table 6.1 Comparison of large and small business CSR based on Jenkins

Corporate CSR	Small Business CSR
Who	**Who**
Responsible to a wide range of stakeholders	Responsible to fewer and/or different stakeholders
Perceived responsibility to society at large	Perceived responsibility to the local community
Importance of shareholders	SMEs often don't have stakeholders
Why	**Why**
Protection of brand image and reputation	Protection of customer business
Pressure from consumers	Pressure from business customers down the supply chain
Shareholders' pressure, Socially Responsible Investing (SRI) movement	Pressure from creditors? Unaffected by SRI movement
The business case	Proven business case lacking
How	**How**
Based on "corporate values"	Based on principles of "owner-manager"
Formal strategic planning for CSR	Informally planned CSR strategies
Emphasis on standards and indices	Emphasis on intuition and ad hoc processes
Key involvement for CSR professionals	No dedicated personnel for CSR programs
Mitigation of risk	Avoidance of risk
What	**What**
Prominent campaigns e.g. Cause Related Marketing	Small-scale activities such as sponsorship of local football team
Publicity linked to CSR activities	Activities often unrecognized as CSR related

Source Jenkins, Heledd. "A Critique of Conventional CSR Theory: An SME Perspective." *Journal of General Management* 29, no. 4 (2004): 55–75, 5

often label their socially responsible activities with the term CSR because their owner-managers are often unaware of it.[15]

[15] Jenkins, Heledd. "A Critique of Conventional CSR Theory: An SME Perspective." *Journal of General Management* 29, no. 4 (2004): 55–75.

Perrini, Francesco. "SMEs and CSR Theory: Evidence and Implications from an Italian Perspective." *Journal of Business Ethics* 67 (2006): 305–316.

Zastempowski, Maciej, and Szymon Cyfert. "Social Responsibility of SMEs from the Perspective of Their Innovativeness: Evidence from Poland." *Journal of Cleaner Production* 3, no. 17 (2021): 128400.

6.3 Research Methodology

This chapter is based on a qualitative method including a semi-structured interview with SMEs as it could provide detailed information about firms highlighting their views. Being granted a scholarship[16] for the period 2020–2023 about the social approaches of firms' competitiveness, my research is focused on companies' CSR approaches and activities, especially those of Hungarian SMEs due to the limited number of research in this field.

The Hungarian city of Győr located in the north-west part of Hungary with a population of around 130,000 inhabitants was chosen as a research field. Being very prosperous in the country with a low unemployment rate and a high-quality industrial and service sector these days, Győr is traditionally an industrial settlement, with companies playing a significant role in the construction and manufacturing industries. The social and cultural life in the city is also vibrant; therefore, companies in Győr have an excellent social environment. The economic and social setting enables companies to provide high-quality goods and services.

The interviews were conducted with 50 SMEs in Győr between August 2021 and October 2022. The sample was based on two criteria: (1) the headquarters should be located in Győr and (2) based on the number of employees in 2021/2022, they should be classified as small- or medium-sized firms.[17] The sample was not further narrowed based on activity or other factors as the intention was to include a diversity of companies. The Opten database[18] served as a basis for searching SMEs in Győr. The database included 600 SMEs in Győr in 2021; the interview survey could reach 8.33 percent of them. The interviews were conducted with the managing directors, but there were four firms, where also other colleagues were present. The interviews were mainly carried

[16] János Bolyai Research Scholarship of the Hungarian Academy of Sciences.

[17] According to the EU Recommendation (C(2003) 1422), a small enterprise employs 10–49 persons and has a maximum of 10 million EUR annual turnover and/or annual balance sheet. Medium-sized companies have employees between 50 and 249, the turnover is under 50 million EUR, and the annual balance sheet does not exceed 43 million EUR.

[18] A database in Hungary with general and financial information on firms based on their annual reports.

Table 6.2 Characteristics of the sample, $n = 50$

Firm size	
Small	39
Medium	11
Year of establishment	
Before 2000	29
2000 or later	21
Legal form	
Ltd	46
Plc	4
Sector	
Industry	26
Service	23
Agriculture	1

Source Compiled by the author based on the interview survey

out in person, but in eight cases, due to the pandemic situation or other reasons, they were on-line or by phone.

Table 6.2 introduces the sample with 50 SMEs. The ratio of small- and medium-sized companies in the sample is almost the same as in the population based on the Opten database in 2021 (the ratio of small firms is 84 percent in the population and 78 percent in the sample). The number of firms established before 2000 is higher and almost all of them operate in the form of a Ltd.

6.4 Results

Table 6.3 provides information about the results.

Question 1 focused on whether companies included in the sample have ever heard of the term Corporate Social Responsibility (CSR). About two-thirds of the sample answered yes. The figures indicate that the term is more widely known among medium-sized companies. Except for one, all managing directors have heard of this term, while 41 percent of directors in small firms have not heard of it. Companies established after 2000 were more familiar with the term CSR than those set up before 2000. Despite the fact that one-third of companies have not heard

Table 6.3 CSR in SMEs based on firm size and age

		Firm size		Establishment	
	Sample, $n = 50$	Small, $n = 39$	Medium, $n = 11$	Before 2000, $n = 29$	2000 and after, $n = 21$
Have SMEs ever heard of the term CSR?					
Yes	33	23	**10**	17	**16**
No	17	16	**1**	12	**5**
Are SMEs aware of the meaning of CSR?					
Yes	32	22	**10**	17	15
Only the content	16	15	**1**	11	5
No	2	2	0	1	1
Do SMEs use the term?					
Yes	25	16	**9**	14	11
No	25	23	**2**	15	10
Do SMEs implement any kind of CSR activity?					
Yes	47	36	11	27	20
No, and they do not want to	2	2	0	1	1
No, but they want to	1	1	0	1	0

(continued)

Table 6.3 (continued)

		Firm size		Establishment	
	Sample, $n = 50$	Small, $n = 39$	Medium, $n = 11$	Before 2000, $n = 29$	2000 and after, $n = 21$
Activity levels[19]					
1	3	3	0	2	1
2	9	7	2	8	**1**
3	29	23	6	16	13
4	7	5	2	2	**5**
5	2	1	1	1	1

Source Compiled by the author based on interviews. Strong relations are highlighted in bold

[19] Companies behave ethically, they care about their good economic performance and consider their employer role very important: they are responsible for the employees' and their families' wellbeing.

Employees are affected by the company management in the way what managing directors regard as a responsible behavior as they could serve as a good example for them and can teach them to be more conscious. Employers also can support employees if they need help or understanding.

Companies donate and support people and civil organizations who need help mainly at local level, to the best of their ability.

Companies take part in civil and social life, they are active in chambers, give presentations at schools or for other companies, etc.

Companies are active in discussing their ideas and opinions about current and local issues, they feel that through their activity they are able to form the environment.

of the term, almost all of them could describe it in some way. Thirty-two companies were clearly aware of the term; however, in the case of sixteen companies managing directors did not seem to hear of the term CSR, but when they were given some explanation on the topic, they could share their thoughts and provide information on their activities. Managing directors at medium-sized companies who have already heard the term were also aware of its meaning. There were only two small firms for which social responsibility was unfamiliar.

It seems to be interesting that although companies are likely to have some information on social responsibility, half of them do not use the term CSR, among them not only companies which are "only" familiar with the content but also those which are aware of the term CSR. The reason for this is that they do not consider labeling their activity; for them, it is more important to take action without using a term for it. Compared with small firms, medium-sized companies label their CSR activity in a higher proportion.

There are only three companies which do not implement any kind of CSR activities. Two of them (small firms) have no intention of doing it as they are unfamiliar with the term and the concept behind it, such kind of activities are not relevant for them.[20] They do not intend to deal with social problems because they are not crucial to their activity. There is one company where the managing director is aware of CSR, but they are not allowed to implement any CSR activities by their parent company. In this case, the managing director admitted the importance of CSR and expressed his wish to support the local environment if they had the opportunity.

Based on the interviews, the following five levels were set up for CSR approaches:

a. Companies behave ethically; they care about their good economic performance and consider their employer role very important: they are responsible for the employees' and their families' well-being.

---

[20] How do they know that it is not important when they are unfamiliar with it? During the interview, the managing director was briefly given some explanation of the term CSR; however, it was considered unimportant for the firm.

b. Employees are affected by the company management in the way what managing directors regard as a responsible behavior as they could serve as a good example for them and can teach them to be more conscious. Employers also can support employees if they need help or understanding.
c. Companies donate and support people and civil organizations who need help mainly at the local level, to the best of their ability.
d. Companies take part in civil and social life, they are active in chambers, give presentations at schools or for other companies, etc.
e. Companies are active in discussing their ideas and opinions about current and local issues, they feel that through their activity they are able to shape the environment.

If a company is at the second level, it means that it is active in the first two; if a company is at the third level, it means that it is active in the first three levels, and so on. The first level refers to all firms, every managing director characterized the company where responsibility for the employees and their families is crucial. They give competitive salaries indicating their huge responsibility for a lot of people.

Most companies can be found at the third level with different kinds of philanthropic activities.[21] For these firms, CSR means the philanthropic behavior at the local level. For them, supporting local actors is of high importance, they feel that they can give back something to the local community in this way.

The highest two levels refer to companies which are active in the local civil and social life. This level includes nine companies, two of them are at the top, and they behave as an opinion-former. One of them is a small-sized company with an active philanthropic life implementing activities with which they can shape their environment through events, meetings where they can contribute to local decision-making, and have relations with prominent local actors. The other company is a medium-sized one with more than forty years of history, but their socially responsible activities became important after the generational change ten years ago. Since then, the company has been very active in the field of CSR. In addition

[21] Providing information about detailed CSR activities is beyond the scope of this study.

to regularly communicating their activities, they are embedded in the local community; as a result, smaller firms may regard them as a good example.

There was no relation with the size of the companies, but firms which were established after 2000 were more likely to be at the fourth level.

6.5 Discussion and Conclusions

This research aimed to highlight SMEs' approach to Corporate Social Responsibility in Győr, Hungary by conducting a semi-structured interview with their managing directors. About two-thirds of them have already heard of the term being aware of its meaning. In case the term happened to be unknown before the interview, the term was translated into Hungarian and its meaning was described. Although they were aware of the concept, they did not know the term for it. There were only two companies with managing directors being unaware of the concept denoted by the term.

Fifty percent of the responding companies apply the term CSR, while the rest do not think that it is important to label such kinds of activities. For example, in the view of a managing director in a small firm, being socially responsible is something that comes from instinct, being an unconscious activity. The managing directors of medium-sized companies are more likely to be aware of the CSR concept; as a result, they also apply it more frequently. This is also reflected by the literature indicating a correlation between the size of the company and its more conscious attitude to CSR.[22] It was also revealed that the managing directors of younger firms (established in 2000 or later) were more likely to hear of the term CSR. This might be explained by the relatively young age and their studies where CSR was already a part of the curricula. Another reason might be the increasing importance of social responsibility over the past two decades, which coincided with the establishment of these companies.

[22] E.g.: Jenkins, Heledd. "A Critique of Conventional CSR Theory: An SME Perspective." *Journal of General Management* 29, no. 4 (2004): 55–75.

Carroll[23] in his pyramid model indicates that there are four levels of corporate social responsibility. When companies were asked about how they define and interpret CSR, almost all of them described it as an activity for the local community through donation. They did not mention the economic, legal, or ethical approach, but they described it in a different context, namely in terms of responsible behavior as not being part of CSR. It reveals that they care about their good economic performance and consider their employer's role as an important behavior by being responsible for the employees' and their families' well-being. This is regarded as the first level of the CSR approach. The second level also refers to similar responsibilities but with a higher level of employees' support. These activities coincide with the first three levels of Carroll's pyramid; thus based on the theory, the first two levels in this research may be considered CSR activities, but most companies were unaware of it and did not label these activities as CSR. Companies described these activities as managing directors' responsible attitude but not as CSR. CSR begins with the fourth also the highest level in Carroll's pyramid.

Based on the interviews, two more levels were added with reference to such activities beyond donations serving the local community. This approach is closer to the EU's CSR definition with a comprehensive approach to the topic focusing not only on philanthropic responsibility but also on the social relations of companies. Only a few companies could reach this level, two-thirds of them are small-sized firms. While bigger companies answered yes to the first three questions (Have SMEs' managing directors heard of the term CSR? Are SMEs' managing directors' aware of the term CSR? Do SMEs' managing directors use the term?), small companies were more active in complex CSR activities in my sample. Although small firms are more likely to belong to the first two levels, the results indicate that small firms also seem to be active in CSR at a higher level. I believe that small firms' attitude to CSR could be as important as that of big companies but in a different way with a different kind of approach.

[23] Carroll, Archie B. "A Three-Dimensional Conceptual Model of Corporate Social Performance." *Academy of Management Review* 4 (1979): 497–505.

According to the findings, company size matters when CSR awareness and its use are in the focus, while the correlation between the activity level and firm size is not clear. The firm age has an effect only on the fact whether managing directors have ever heard of the term, but the correlation is the opposite as there is more likelihood that younger firms' leaders have heard of the term. The results may depend on several factors, which is the reason why more research in different social and economic environments is required to have clear information about the topic.

It is known from the literature that SMEs' CSR is different from that of large companies, but the reason behind it is not always clear. SMEs are characterized by personal decision-making by the owner-managers. It means that the owner and the manager are often the same person and they are responsible for every decision about the firm including CSR. Therefore, collecting information about managing directors' CSR awareness is crucial for further research.

This chapter aimed to provide an overview of managing directors' awareness and approaches to corporate social responsibility in the case of SMEs. Although there is a wider scope of research at the international level about SMEs' CSR, but in Hungary this topic is given only little attention.

According to the findings, about two-thirds of the managing directors have already heard of the term CSR, and almost all of them could give an explanation about it. But there were companies which did not immediately recognize the meaning of CSR but after being explained the meaning of the term in Hungarian, they could become aware of the concept. Being familiar with the term and the concept behind does not mean its application. In addition, there are companies where managing directors do not find it important to label the socially responsible activities. They were also asked about the type of their firms' CSR activity.

This chapter did not provide information about detailed activities as the focus was laid on the meaning of the term, managers' opinion on CSR, as well as the level of CSR activities. Of the five levels, the first two refer to the level of internal CSR with a focus on employees. The third level describes the level of support in terms of the local community and the top two indicate a complex activity beyond donation. Consequently, companies are active in social life and shaping their environment by giving ideas, taking part in decision-making, etc.

It is also noteworthy that smaller companies are more likely to belong to the fourth level, which may prove that also small-sized firms can be active in CSR. Small companies were often shy about their activities but the point is that they do not have to compare themselves with large companies. Big companies' activity represents a different dimension; however, also smaller firms can provide beneficial actions for their employees and their local community.

The limitation of the research is that SMEs investigated are located in one settlement, in Győr. The economic and social performance of the city is prosperous in Hungary, but companies in other parts of the country could have different results. The sample does not describe the population, so my results can be used in a limited way as they are only related to 50 SMEs. In conclusion, the findings may convey some generalized message about the view of SMEs' leaders on CSR.

Future research might focus on detailed activities of SMEs with more information about the motivating factors behind CSR activities. Conducting research in different parts of the country or in a specific industry may also provide more exact information about the topic.

The chapter demonstrates some guidance for researchers and practitioners by introducing detailed information about how SMEs are related to CSR and it also adds some new approaches related to SMEs' CSR activities to the literature. Detailed information on this topic may also contribute to more conscious further research.

Acknowledgements This chapter was supported by the János Bolyai Research Scholarship of the Hungarian Academy of Sciences.

References

Benedek, Andrea, István Takács, and Katalin Takácsné György. "The Examination of the CSR Attitudes of the CEOs Among Hungarian SMEs." *Wspolczesne Zarzadzanie: Kwartalnik Srodowisk Naukowych I Liderow Biznesu* 3, no. 31 (2015): 283–297.

Benedek, Andrea, Katalin Takács-György, and István Takács. "The Appearance of CSR at SMEs—Results of a Corporate Survey." In *The International Conference Small and Medium Sized Enterprises in a Globalized World: 6th edition*, edited by Pop, Cornelia, and Oana Gica, 7–17. Cluj-Napoca: Babes-Bolyai University, 2013.

Bowen, Howard R. *Social Responsibilities of the Businessman*. No. 3. New York: Harper & Brothers, 1953.

Campopiano, Giovanna, Alfredo De Massis, and Lucio Cassia. "Corporate Social Responsibility: A Survey Among SMEs in Bergamo." *Procedia—Social and Behavioral Sciences* 62 (2012): 325–341.

Carroll, Archie B. "A Three-Dimensional Conceptual Model of Corporate Social Performance." *Academy of Management Review* 4 (1979): 497–505.

Carroll, Archie B. "The Pyramid of Corporate Social Responsibility: Toward the Moral Management of Organizational Stakeholders." *Business Horizons* 34, no. 4 (1991): 39–48.

Carroll, Archie B., and Kareem M. Shabana. "The Business Case for Corporate Social Responsibility: A Review of Concepts, Research and Practice." *International Journal of Management Reviews* 12, no. 1 (2010): 85–105.

Çera, Gentjan, Jaroslav Belas, Josef Marousek, and Edmond Çera. "Do Size and Age of Small and Medium-Sized Enterprises Matter in Corporate Social Responsibility?" *Economics and Sociology* 13, no. 2 (2020): 86–99.

Csáfor, Hajnalka. "A magyar vállalatok társadalmi felelősségvállalásának sajátosságai." *Acta Academiae Paedagogicae Agriensis Nova Series: Acta Oeconomica* 34 (2007): 169–189.

Csáfor, Hajnalka. "Corporate Social Responsibility as a Managerial Competency for SME in Countries of the Carpathian Euroregion." In *Ankara University International Conference: Marketing and Entrepreneurship AUMEC 2009*, edited by Kocak, Akin, Temi Abimbola, Alper Özer, and Lorraine Watkins-Mathys, 448–458. Ankara: Ankara University the Faculty of Political Sciences, 2009.

Davis, Keith. "Can Business Afford to Ignore Social Responsibilities?" *California Management Review* 2, no. 3 (1960): 70–76.
European Commission. *Commission Recommendation of 6 May 2003 Concerning the Definition of Micro, Small and Medium-Sized Enterprises.* (C(2003) 1422), Brussels, 2003.
European Commission. *A Renewed EU Strategy 2011–14 for Corporate Social Responsibility*. Brussels, 2011.
Fassin, Yves, Annick van Rossem, and Marc Buelens. "Small-Business Owner-Managers' Perceptions of Business Ethics and CSR-Related Concepts." *Journal of Business Ethics* 98 no. 3 (2011): 425–453.
Gasparetz, András, and Balázs Szentes. "CSR tevékenység kommunikációja a KKV marketingben." In *Vállalati kommunikációmenedzsment*, edited by Borgulya, Ágnes, and Márta Konczosné Szombathelyi, 260–265. Budapest: L'Harmattan Kiadó, Károli Gáspár Református Egyetem, 2017.
Jamali, Dima, Mona Zanhour, and Tamar Keshishian. "Peculiar Strengths and Relational Attributes of SMEs in the Context of CSR." *Journal of Business Ethics* 87 (2009): 355–377.
Jenkins, Heledd. "A Critique of Conventional CSR Theory: An SME Perspective." *Journal of General Management* 29, no. 4 (2004): 55–75.
Jenkins, Heledd. "Small Business Champions for Corporate Social Responsibility." *Journal of Business Ethics* 67 (2006): 241–256.
Pastrana, Nathaly A., and Krishnamurthy Sriramesh. "Corporate Social Responsibility: Perceptions and Practices Among SMEs in Colombia." *Public Relations Review* 40, no. 1 (2014): 14–24.
Perrini, Francesco. "SMEs and CSR Theory: Evidence and Implications from an Italian Perspective." *Journal of Business Ethics* 67 (2006): 305–316.
Petheő, Attila, György Pataki, and Réka Matolay. "Corporate Social Responsibility (CSR) Practices by Small- and Medium-Sized Enterprises (SMEs) in Hungary." In *Erdei Ferenc IV. Tudományos Konferencia*, edited by Ferencz, Árpád, 460–463. Kecskemét: Kecskeméti Főiskola, 2007.
Russo, Angeloantonio, and Francesco Perrini. "Investigating Stakeholder Theory and Social Capital: CSR in Large Firms and SMEs." *Journal of Business Ethics* 91, no. 2 (2010): 207–221.
Spence, Laura J. "Does Size Matter? The State of the Art in Small Business Ethics." *Business Ethics: A European Review* 8, no. 3 (1999): 163–174.
Szigeti, Cecília. "KKV-CSR (Corporate Social Responsibility) tevékenysége." In *Vállalkozások ökonómiája: IX. Nemzetközi Tudományos Napok*, edited by Magda, Sándor, and László Dinya, 269–276. Gyöngyös: Károly Róbert Főiskola, 2008.

Tilley, Fiona. "Small Firm Environmental Ethics: How Deep Do They Go?" *Business Ethics: The Environment & Responsibility* 9, no. 1 (2000): 31–41.

Youn, Hyewon, Nan Hua, and Seoki Lee. "Does Size Matter? Corporate Social Responsibility and Firm Performance in the Restaurant Industry." *International Journal of Hospitality Management* 51 (2015): 127–134.

Zastempowski, Maciej, and Szymon Cyfert. "Social Responsibility of SMEs from the Perspective of Their Innovativeness: Evidence from Poland." *Journal of Cleaner Production* 3, no. 17 (2021): 128400

Part III

Key Organizational Challenges for Sustainable Development

7

The Systematic Sustainable Business Model (SBM) Approach—A Flexible Organizational Tool

Åsa Devine and Michaela Sandell

7.1 Introduction

Sustainability is an all-pervasive topic in society. It is discussed on all levels from international agencies to individuals. This gives both a push and pull effect for organizations[1] to implement a clear sustainability strategy demonstrating a well-composed range of sustainability activities. Needless to say, this can be challenging and the nebulous definitions

[1] In this chapter organization is consistently used as an encompassing term for entities such as firm, business, company, corporation, civic organization, trade union, universities, government organizations, NGOs (see Comin et al.'s 2020 comment on the complexity of SBM and need for inclusive approach) without making a distinction between profit and non-profit organizations, private and public organization. In line with Bocken et al. (2013), the presented Systematic Sustainable Business Model approach is aimed to all organizations.

Å. Devine (✉) · M. Sandell
School of Business and Economics, Linnaeus University, Växjö, Sweden
e-mail: asa.devine@lnu.se

© The Author(s), under exclusive license to Springer Nature Switzerland AG 2024

A. Sörensson et al. (eds.), *Creating New Roles for a Sustainable Economy*, Palgrave Studies in Governance, Leadership and Responsibility,
https://doi.org/10.1007/978-3-031-61551-1_7

in the area of sustainability make it even more difficult to formulate a strategy which can also be followed up and acted on. An organization's activities can be perceived as the DNA of its strategy (Porter, 1996). Thus, while the connection between the organization's activities and strategy at a quick glance may appear obvious, the problem emerges when executing the move from the abstract concept of strategy to the precise concept of activity (Richardson, 2008). It is in this intersection between strategy and execution that the business model (BM) framework comes to play an important role, or to use Richardson's (2008) words for what a business model entails:

> it is a conceptual framework that helps to link the firm's strategy, or theory of how to compete, to its activities, or execution of the strategy. The business model framework can help to think strategically about the details of the way the firm does business. (Richardson, 2008, p. 5).

Richardson (2008) concludes that the BM framework encompasses "a consistent logical picture" (p. 19) of how the implementation of activities together forms the strategy of the organization. Thus, the BM can be of value for organizations as an assessment and implementation tool. However, in the seminal article by Teece (2010) it is argued that the theoretical foundation underpinning the business model concept essentially is missing. This lack, or neglect as Teece puts it, spans across the vast research areas of economics, organization, marketing, and strategy alike (Teece, 2010) and up until recently, this research area has commonly been described as fragmented and ambiguous (Ritter and Lettl, 2018). More recently, research on novel BMs has however started to reap a growing interest among both researchers (Ritter and Lettl, 2018) and practitioners (Schaltegger et al., 2016) and with that has come consensus in particular areas. One agreed-on aspect, or common feature, from the BM research (see, e.g. Teece, 2010; Richardson, 2008) is the importance of value.

Still, the status of the BM as an organizational tool appears to be largely developing, and up until recently, it has been far from a ready-to-use state. This appears to be particularly unfortunate given the current environmental and societal changes that more than ever warrant a closer look at every aspect of an organization's activities (Bocken et al., 2014) with emphasis on sustainability management (Bocken et al., 2015). The sustainable business model (SBM), also referred to as the business model for sustainability (Short et al., 2014), can be seen as a contemporary offspring of the general BM. As a descendant of the growing BM field, the SBM can be thought of as any natural offspring in that it depends on its parent (i.e. BM), but develops to be someone that goes beyond the capacity and scope of its parent (Lüdeke-Freud and Dembek, 2017).

Given the broad and emerging (Comin et al., 2020), even referred to as infant (Dentchev et al., 2018), nature of the SBM literature, much effort remains to be made. One of these efforts includes the development of a practical tool to be used by organizations (Lüdeke-Freud and Dembek, 2017) in their efforts to implement an SBM (Goni et al., 2021). This is supported by Comin et al. (2020) and Nosratabadi et al. (2019) who point out the need for research on *how* to apply and implement the abstract SBM concept, and hence bridging conceptualization and empirical work. The few tools that are available to organizations are found to be complicated to use, which may coincide with their conceptual nature (Baldassarre et al., 2017) and lack of operationalization. At the same time, and seemingly contradictory to what Baldassarre et al. (2017) claim, SBM are described as lacking in conceptualization (Dentchev et al., 2018). The available SBM tools have also been described as less useful due to being highly specialized and therefore not offering general support to decision-makers (Baldassarre et al., 2017). Dentchev et al. (2018) emphasize the fruitfulness of developing rigorous SBM models or tools for investigating SBM. Anchored in the above discussion, the purpose of this chapter is to develop the Systematic Sustainable Business Model (SBM) approach.

7.2 Literature Review SBM

In order to assess the status of the SBM literature, a literature review was undertaken. This literature review was inspired by the three stages of a systematic literature review described by Tranfield et al. (2003). The first stage of the literature review was the planning phase. The approach taken was to be receptive and open to what has been published within the general scope of "Sustainable Business Model." The justification for this approach was to depict the status of the broader research domain prior to narrowing the scope down further. This phase was managed in the later months of 2022. The databases used for this purpose were Business Source Ultimate and Emerald Journals, with additional cross-references being conducted using Google Scholar. The criteria used for assessment of the articles found were that they had to be scientific articles or conference proceedings published in English in academic journals and relevant to the topic of SBM. The date of publication of the articles was not an issue given the recency of the topic.

During the second stage of the literature review, the articles found were placed into three separate groups based on their various foci. These three groups were referred to as the SBM literature review group, the group of SBM archetypes and the group of SBM tools. In total, 31 scientific articles were found relevant to this topic. The three groups of articles can be described as interdependent but were initially managed as discrete. More exactly, the insight from the assessment of the articles placed in the SBM literature review group allowed deciphering of the core characteristics of SBM. Such an understanding of the core characteristics became the basis for evaluating and understanding the status of the research on SBM tools. The articles placed in the group of SBM archetypes were infused into the systematic SBM tool developed to bridge the gap seen in the status of research on SBM tools.

The final stage of the literature review can consequently be separated in terms of two sets of findings. The first set of findings related to the core characteristics of the SBM. Consolidating the discussions in contemporary research reviews indeed reveals that the SBM is different from the BM when it comes to a range of characteristics. These characteristics are further understood to encompass the core of SBM:

- Focus is on sustainability, e.g. the triple bottom line (Ferlito and Faraci, 2022; Ferreira et al., 2022; Comin et al., 2020; Shakeel et al., 2020; Nosratabadi et al., 2019; Geissdoerfer et al., 2018; Lüdeke-Freud and Dembek, 2017)

- There is a generous view on value, value creation, and consequently success (Lüdeke-Freud and Dembek, 2017) including the creation of monetary and non-monetary value (Shakeel et al., 2020; Dentchev et al., 2018; Geissdoerfer et al., 2018) also referred to as "inclusive value" (Comin et al., 2020, p. 2039).
- Value capture is not limited to the organization and its shareholders (Lüdeke-Freud and Dembek, 2017), but the generated value can benefit a broad range of stakeholders (Goni et al., 2021; Geissdoerfer et al., 2018), i.e. multi-stakeholders (Shakeel et al., 2020). An inclusive understanding of stakeholders (Lüdeke-Freud and Dembek, 2017) is taken, including also society and the natural environment (Goni et al., 2021).
- Innately related to this idea of inclusiveness is the collaborative perspective (Comin et al., 2020), i.e. stakeholder involvement, spanning across any value dimensions and value networks. Terminologies such as collaboration, co-creation, and co-growth (Comin et al., 2020) are frequent concepts appearing in the SBM literature which aligns with the principle of a system approach rather than a single firm focus (Dembek and York, 2022). It is within value networks systemic sustainability is possible (Breuer and Lüdeke-Freud, 2014).

The second set of findings relates to the status of the SBM tools. No claims are made to assert that the selected articles and their approaches encompass an exhaustive list of relevant articles published on SBM tools. However, the rigor of the approach is believed adequate to suggest that the extent to which the articles build on, and consistently integrate, the core characteristics of SBM varies. The literature review points to the opportunity for contributing to the SBM research field by offering organizations a systematic SBM tool. This work has already begun, but the extent to which these initiatives ensure actual focus on the sustainable business model as compared to, e.g. general business models, varies. Inspired by the expression of Bonfanti et al. (2022), an SBM can be thought of as an intricate system of sustainable activities, and at the center of such system may the core characteristics of the SBM reside. A SBM that embodies the said core characteristics can, based on this logic, be perceived to have a solid core, while a SBM that do not may consist of a comparably empty shell without a solid core. In fact, if a BM do not incorporate the core characteristics one might question if it is a SBM or a BM of a different nature. The SBM core characteristics are consequently deemed suitable as criteria for assessing SBM explicit focus. This approach generally coincides with the approach and conclusions put forward by Dembek and York (2022). For a compilation of an illustrative sample of SBM research developing SBM tools or models, see Table 7.1.

The article assessment indicates that SBM tools, i.e. SBM models, tend to integrate some of the SBM core characteristics. This may indicate that a consensus among SBM researchers is underway with regards to the core characteristics. However, how and to what extent these researchers take a stance on the core characteristics varies. Some explicitly use the core characteristics as a foundation, while others more implicitly and vaguely have references to what may be understood to be such characteristics. Still, close to all seem to leave out one or more of the core characteristics altogether, which opens for criticism in terms of building unbalanced SBM tools. It is particularly unfortunate when sustainability and sustainable conduct in terms of activities are managed on a high level of abstraction (Dembek et al., 2022; Franca et al., 2017; Bocken et al., 2013) or not explicitly embedded into the presented models (Attanasio et al., 2022; Dembek et al., 2022; Ferlito and Faraci, 2022; Bocken et al., 2015; Bocken et al., 2013). Considering how value is managed, it appears clear that value is an integral part of the assessed SBM tools and that it is generously managed. What is interesting however is that different researchers include different value dimensions. There is an indication that particularly value delivery is overlooked (Pies and Schultz, 2023; Dembek and York, 2022; Bocken et al., 2015; Bocken et al., 2013) or treated as inseparable from value creation (Ferlito and Faraci, 2022; Méndez-León et al., 2022). Regarding taking a generous view of stakeholders capturing value, this is the case judging from the assessed articles. This means that any member of a particular value network (Pies and Schultz, 2023) or value system (Bonfanti et al., 2022), including the natural environment, animals, society, and employees (Attanasio et al.,

Table 7.1 A literature review resulted in 14 scientific articles focused on developing SBM tools

Sources	Core characteristics				
	Sustainability focus e.g. tripple bottom line	Generous view of value e.g. non-monetary value	Generous view of stakeholders capturing value, i.e. other than the organization and shareholders	Inclusive understanding of stakholders involvement e.g. collaboration and network	Modeling approach
Pies and Schultz (2023)	*Yes*	*Value proposition, value creation and value capture. "value creation is best conveived as overcoming social dilemmas". Not mentioning value delivery*	*Shareholders and stakeholders interests should be simultaneously acknowledged "for the sake of sustainable development." All members of the value network can capture value*	*Yes. "Value creation beyond the organizational boundary of the firm". Value network as compared to focus on how a corporation aspire to be sustainable*	Ordonomic approach to governance of SBMI. Present a tool for governance of SBMI
Attanasio et al. (2022)	Yes, but somewhat implicit. Sustainab. form the boundary due to choice of case companies. Not explicit in their model	*Value intention, value proposition, value creation, value delivery, value capture*	*Yes, including the natural environment, society, animals, and employees*	*Yes, stakeholder groups including employees, suppliers, partners, customers, government and media all contribute*	Stakeholder value flow model of SBM

(continued)

Table 7.1 (continued)

Sources	Core characteristics Sustainability focus e.g. tripple bottom line	Generous view of value e.g. non-monetary value	Generous view of stakeholders capturing value, i.e. other than the organization and shareholders	Inclusive understanding of stakholders involvement e.g. collaboration and network	Modeling approach
Bonfanti et al. (2022)	*Yes*	*Value proposition, value creation, delivery, capture and value exchanged are considered Sustainable value in particular*	*A broad range of stakeholders are considered. Their results show that contribution to the SDGs "depend not on the individual company but rather on each actor in the stakeholder ecosystem"*	*Yes, "value exchanged between a company and a wide range of stakeholders belonging to the organization´s value constellation"*	Operationalization of SBM and map onto SDGs. Conclude achievement of SDGs of the SBMs
Dembek et al. (2022)	No. SBM is only mentioned. No sign of sustainability in the their model	*Inclusive, but somewhat vague: Value is subjectively managed as perceived by a stakeholder*	*Yes, they include value captured by business partners, customers, beneficiaries, and other stakeholders in thier model, but also the broader socio-economic and environmental systems*	*Yes. Direct and indirect stakeholders are recipients and co-creators of value*	Activity system framework including value, outcome and impact

Sources	Core characteristics				
	Sustainability focus e.g. tripple bottom line	Generous view of value e.g. non-monetary value	Generous view of stakeholders capturing value, i.e. other than the organization and shareholders	Inclusive understanding of stakholders involvement e.g. collaboration and network	Modeling approach
Dembek and York (2022)	Rather implicit, but sustainability form the boundary due to choice of case company	*Very inclusive including indirect value e.g. company trust and creation of identity. Mututal value, value creation and capture. Economic value, environmental value and social value*	*Yes. Multiple stakeholders including the environment and community members*	*Yes*	Matrix with a set of SBM characteristics mapped against BM content, structure, governance and value outcome. SBM lens for BoP context
De Oliveira Paula and Van Aduard De Macadeo-Soares (2022)	*Yes. Take a stance in TBL, but in their data set they only include the social and environmental pillars*	Value is not part of their model	Not part of their model, but mentioned in the article	*Alliances of various types are considered and integrated in their model*	Innovation barriers, aliance portfolio diversity, absorptive capacity and SBMI included in their model

(continued)

Table 7.1 (continued)

Sources	Core characteristics				
	Sustainability focus e.g. tripple bottom line	Generous view of value e.g. non-monetary value	Generous view of stakeholders capturing value, i.e. other than the organization and shareholders	Inclusive understanding of stakholders involvement e.g. collaboration and network	Modeling approach
Ferlito and Faraci (2022)	Yes, they say they do, but in the description of their model it is hard to decipher what sustainability actually entail on operational level	*Somewhat. Mention value proposition, value creation & delivery and value capture*	No. "the firm´s results and their measurement". "in the value capture process, firms aim at monetizing the outputs of their activities". "value captured by the firm"	No	Implementation of SBIP aligned with SDGs. To change into SBM
Méndez-León et al. (2022)	*Yes. Anchor their results in the TBL*	*Sustainable value. Positive and negative value. Value creation as a process. Value proposition compents, value creation and delivery component, value capture component.* *Negative value = value destroyed* *Shared value = sutainable value*	*Yes*	"A complex system of multi-stakeholder activities". Stakeholders are not explicitly depicted in their model however	Constructs a framework which takes a holistic view of value and also includes stakeholder activities

Sources	Core characteristics				
	Sustainability focus e.g. tripple bottom line	Generous view of value e.g. non-monetary value	Generous view of stakeholders capturing value, i.e. other than the organization and shareholders	Inclusive understanding of stakholders involvement e.g. collaboration and network	Modeling approach
Baldassarre et al. (2017)	They use representatives for the TBL, but their proxy representatives can be questioned. E. g an office worker is a proxy for "society". In their result they are more abstract referring to "sustainability problem"	*Economic, societal and environmental values. Creating "shared value for all stake-holders" in the "extended stakeholder network". "deliver the intended value across the extended network of stakeholders". Delivery of "superior value for multiple stakeholders"*	Value capture not clearly managed, the focal point was development of value propositions	*Yes. "Focus is on how the value proposition evolves and improves through different practices". The different practices involve various stakeholder (user) groups*	Combines SBMI and principles from user-driven innovation
Franca et al. (2017)	Non-precise management but refers to "sustainability lens", and "sustainability principles"	Social and environmental values are mentioned, profit is in focus. Value proposition mentioned, but not elaborated down to value creation, delivery and capture	Vague mentioning of "larger groups of stakeholders" and "wider partnership", but not related to value capture	Vague mentioning of multi- stakeholder collaboration	A FSSD framework inform BMC Presents a model

(continued)

Table 7.1 (continued)

Sources	Core characteristics				
	Sustainability focus e.g. tripple bottom line	Generous view of value e.g. non-monetary value	Generous view of stakeholders capturing value, i.e. other than the organization and shareholders	Inclusive understanding of stakholders involvement e.g. collaboration and network	Modeling approach
Morioka et al. (2016)	Mention TBL, but do not elaborate	*Value proposition, value creation, delivery and capture mentioned, and the idea is that "economic results are not enough to ensure sustainable value capture"*	Internal and external stakeholders considered, but not elaborated in their conceptual model. Value capture cannot be idenfied in applied models, but multi-stakeholders are shown	Firm performance is related to stakeholders other than "customers and sharehoders"	Sustainable value proposition, creation, delivery and capture are mapped against performance dimension. Presents a model
Bocken et al. (2015)	Yes, but not explicitly anchored in their model	*Opportunity for new value creation, value destroyed, value missed, and value captured*	*"shared value creation for all stakeholders including the environment and society." "Value captured represents the positive benefits delivered to stakeholders". "postitive outcomes for all stakeholders"*	*Yes*	Value mapping as a tool

Sources	Core characteristics: Sustainability focus e.g. tripple bottom line	Generous view of value e.g. non-monetary value	Generous view of stakeholders capturing value, i.e. other than the organization and shareholders	Inclusive understanding of stakholders involvement e.g. collaboration and network	Modeling approach
Breuer and Lüdeke-Freud (2014)	Few examples related to energy systems	Values missed or destroyed, ideal values, new values, core values are mentioned but not operationalized	Not in focus	*Value network, system approach. "value emerge from the distributed activities of different actors". "exchange of resources and know-how" is mentioned*	Value innovation, BMI and components are integrated in their innovation management model
Bocken et al. (2013)	Refer casually to sustainability in relation to their models. In the intro they refer to "industrial sustainability"	*Yes. Positive and negative value creation. Opportunity for new value creation, value destroyed, value missed, and value captured Value exchange between network actors. Do not consider value creation and delivery*	*Yes. "value creation for all stakeholders" including environment and society as "recipients of value", a broad range network actors and custiners*	*Yes. Value network as compared to focus on a firm generating value*	Presents a tool that allows firms to assess to what extent they embedded sustainability into their BM

Note The extent to which these articles embed the core characteristics of SBM varies. Italic indicates the integration of core characteristics

2022) can capture the value generated from the sustainability activities. The same goes for the inclusive understanding of stakeholders involvement, where a broad group of stakeholders within and outside the organizational boundaries contributes to value being generated (Pies and Schultz, 2023; Attanasio et al., 2022; Bonfanti et al., 2022; Baldassarre et al., 2017; Breuer and Lüdeke-Freud, 2014; Bocken et al., 2013).

In sum, the work that has been initiated as far as developing SBM tools for organization offers inspiration and direction, but there appears to be room for strengthening the embeddedness of the SBM core characteristics included in SBM tools. In order to contribute to this area, the conceptual building blocks of SBM archetypes and activities; value frame; and stakeholders are further elaborated and combined into an SBM tool.

7.3 Sustainable Business Model

A systematic literature review carried out by Ferreira et al. (2022) reveals that the most cited article in the SBM field until the year 2019 is the article by Bocken et al. (2014). Bocken et al.'s article from 2014 continues to be cited also in more recent articles (e.g. Pies and Schultz, 2023; Attanasio et al., 2022; Dembek and York, 2022; De Oliveira Paula and Van Aduard De Macadeo-Soares, 2022; Ferlito and Faraci, 2022; Méndez-León, Reyes-Carillo, and Díaz-Pichardo, 2022). Consequently, and given the ambition of consolidating existing research, it appears logical to anchor the SBM tool in such an authoritative article. The Systematic SBM approach described in this chapter is therefore taking an overall stance in Bocken et al.'s (2014) eight seminal SBM archetypes. To add rigor, Bocken et al.'s work has been complimented by Ritala et al.'s (2018) nine revised SBM archetypes; Lüdeke-Freud et al.'s (2018) SBM pattern taxonomy consisting of 11 SBM pattern groups; and Evans et al. (2017) sustainable value framework. A synthesis of the research findings from these articles reveals an opportunity for consolidation due to the alignment of research findings, e.g. "Cooperative patterns" discussed by Lüdeke-Freud et al. (2018) was consolidated with the "Alternative ownership" exemplified as cooperative ownership, mutual ownership, and collectives mentioned by Bocken et al.'s (2014). Due to complimentary but differentiating research findings, there was also a need to extend the SBM archetype frame, e.g. inclusion of the archetype "Giving" as proposed by Lüdeke-Freud et al. (2018). The chapter continues with a description of the ten archetypes found and explication of related sustainability activities. Thereafter the value framework and multi-stakeholders are described, which together with the ten archetypes come to encompass the Systematic SBM approach.

Archetypes and Activities

The proceeding SBM archetype and activity discussion is structured based on the three sustainability pillars: environmental, social, and economic. Each pillar contains several archetypes, i.e. sustainability approaches. Ritter and Lettl (2018) give an account of different business model perspectives and make a point of treating business model activities as primarily a separate perspective, but with some overlaps compared to business model archetypes. The understanding here however is that archetypes are generic approaches, or "*underlying mechanism for delivering sustainability*" (Short et al., 2014, p. 604), to how an organization operates, and it is further assumed that such generic approaches can congregate a variety of sustainability activities. That said, each archetype is elaborated in terms of specific activities, also referred to as components.

Environmental Sustainability Archetypes

The environmental sustainability pillar encompasses the three archetypes: Maximization of material and energy efficiency; Closing resource loops; and Substitute with renewable and natural processes.

Archetype 1: Maximization of material and energy efficiency. Defined as the optimal use of resources (Ritala et al., 2018) and minimizing waste. This can be identified in product design, product process, and supply chain (Lüdeke-Freud et al., 2018). See Table 7.2.

Archetype 2: Closing resource loops. Defined as reusing materials and energy through industry clusters in which resource symbiosis exists

Table 7.2 Maximize material and energy efficiency—Archetype 1

Environmental	Definitions		Components	References
Maximize material & energy efficiency Archetype 1	"Optimizing the resources used" (Ritala et al., 2018, p. 219)	Product design (Lüdeke-Freud et al., 2018)	De-materialization (of products and packaging) Increased functionality	Bocken et al. (2014)
	"Do more with fewer resources, generating less waste, emissions and polutions" (Bocken et al., 2014, p. 48)	Production processes	(to reduce total number of products required) Lean manufacturing Continuous improvement	Ritala et al. (2018) Bocken et al. (2014)
	Key is to reduce waste to a minimum (Bocken et al., (2014)	Supply chain (Lüdeke-Freud et al., 2018)	Low emissions/Zero emission Physical to virtual Produce on demand	Bocken et al. (2014) Evans et al. (2017) Lüdeke-Freud et al. (2018)

(Bocken et al., 2014). This can be done through reuse, recycling, remanufacturing, take-back management, repair, co-product generation, online waste exchange platform, and upgrading (Lüdeke-Freud et al., 2018). See Table 7.3.

Archetype 3: Substitute with renewable and natural processes. Defined as reduced "environmental impact through choice and innovation of renewable resources and production systems" (Bocken et al., 2014, p. 50). This can be accomplished by moving from non-renewable resources (Bocken et al., 2014) to solar and wind-power-based energy innovations (Bocken et al., 2014; Ritala et al., 2018). See Table 7.4.

Social Sustainability Archetypes

The social sustainability pillar is managed through four archetypes. These archetypes are Delivery of functionality rather than ownership; Adoption of a stewardship role; Encouragement of sufficiency; and finally, Giving.

Archetype 4: Delivery of functionality rather than ownership. Defined as use without ownership (Bocken et al., 2014). This can be done through product-oriented product-service systems (PSS), e.g. maintenance and extended warranties (Bocken et al., 2014); use-oriented PSS, e.g. rental, leasing, sharing; and result-oriented PSS, e.g. pay per use (Lüdeke-Freud et al., 2018). See Table 7.5.

Archetype 5: Adoption of a stewardship role. Defined as engaging with stakeholders to promote well-being and health (Bocken et al., 2014). This can be managed by treating the natural environment as a stakeholder (see, e.g. Ritala et al., 2018), the employees (including suppliers' employees) as stakeholders (see, e.g. Bocken et al., 2014), the surrounding society/community as stakeholders (Evans et al., 2017), and customers as stakeholders (see, e.g. Ritala et al., 2018). See Table 7.6.

Archetype 6: Encouragement of sufficiency. Defined as encouraging the reduction of production and consumption (Bocken et al., 2014). This can be done through consumer education and communication to raise awareness, adherence to product longevity ideals, adherence to frugal business ideals, responsible product distribution, and responsible product promotion (Bocken et al., 2014). See Table 7.7.

Table 7.3 Closing resource loops—Archetype 2

Environmental	Definitions	Components	References
*Closing resource loops Archetype 2**	Eliminate what traditionally is thought of as waste "by turning waste streams into useful and valuable input to other production and making better use of under-utilised capacity" (Bocken et al., 2014, p. 49)	Industry cluster in which resource symbiosis exist	Bocken et al. (2014)
		Reuse	Lüdeke-Freud et al. (2018)
		Recycle	
		Re-manufacture/next life sales	
		Take back management/ extended producer responsibility	
		Repair	Lüdeke-Freud et al. (2018)
	"Patterns that help integrate the idea of circular material and energy flows (…) i.e. how materials and energy flow into, out of, and return to a company" (Lüdeke-Freud et al., 2018, p. 153)	Co-product generation	
		Online waste exchange platform	
		Upgrading	

*Including circular economy and cradle-to-cradle (Bocken et al., 2014)

Table 7.4 Substitute with renewables and natural processes—Archetype 3

Environmental	Definition	Components	References
Substitute with renewables and natural processes Archetype 3	"Reduce environmental impact and increase business resilience by addressing resource constraints (...) associated with non-renewable resources and current production systems" (Bocken et al., 2014, p. 50)	Move from non-renewable energy sources	Bocken et al. (2014)
		Solar & wind-power based energy innovations	Ritala et al. (2018) Bocken et al. (2014)

Table 7.5 Deliver functionality rather than ownership—Archetype 4

Social	Definition	Components	References
Deliver functionality rather than ownership Archetype 4	"Provide services that satisfy user's needs without having to own physical products" (Bocken et al., 2014, p. 50)	Product oriented PSS, e.g. maintenance, extended warrantees	Bocken et al. (2014)
		Use oriented PSS, (Deals with through-life and end-of-life issues as manufacturer retain ownership) e.g. rental, leasing, sharing	Lüdeke-Freud et al. (2018)
		Result oriented PSS, pay per use	

Archetype 7: Giving. Defined as giving products or services to those in need. This can be managed by "buy one, give one" offers and donations of products (Lüdeke-Freud et al., 2018). See Table 7.8.

Economic Sustainability Archetypes

For economic sustainability three archetypes are included: Repurpose for society/environment, Inclusive value creation, and Develop sustainable scale-up solutions.

Table 7.6 Adopt a stewardship role—Archetype 5

Social	Definition		Components	References
Adopt a stewardship role *Archetype 5*	"Proactively engaging with all stakeholders to ensure their long-term health and well-being" (Bocken et al., 2014, p. 51)	The natural environment as a stakeholder	Improve physical environment	Ritala et al. (2018)
			Promote nature preservation projects	
			Sustainable growing and harvesting of crops	Bocken et al. (2014)
			Biodiversity protection and regeneration	Bocken et al. (2014) Evans et al. (2017)
		The employees (incl. suppliers employees) as stakeholders	Ethical trade (fair trade), e.g. employee welfare, living wages, labour standards	Bocken et al. (2014) Evans et al. (2017)
			Equality and diversity	
			Empowerment	Lüdeke-Freud et al. (2018)

Social	Definition	Components	References
		Inclusive sourcing	
	The surrounding society/community as a stakeholder	Community development, e.g. education, health	Evans et al. (2017)
	The customers as stakeholders	Downstrem stewardship, care for consumers e.g. health and well-being	Bocken et al. (2014) Evans et al. (2017)
		Choice editing by retailers (bad/ unethical offers removed)	Ritala et al. (2018) Bocken et al. (2014)

Table 7.7 Encourage sufficiency—Archetype 6

Social	Definition	Components	References
Encourage sufficiency Archetype 6	"Solutions that actively seek to reduce consumption and production" (Bocken et al., 2014, p. 52)	Consumer education and communication to raise awareness	Bocken et al. (2014)
		Adherance to product longevity (i.e. slow-down replacement) ideals*	
		Adherance to frugal business ideals, e.g. functional not "flashy" offers	
		Responsible product distribution, e.g. market place for second hand	
		Responsible product promotion, e.g. sales of only what is needed	Bocken et al. (2014), Ritala et al. (2018)

Table 7.8 Giving—Archetype 7

Social	Definition	Components	References
Giving Archetype 7	"Patterns that help donate products or services to target groups in need, i.e how costs are coverered and social target groups are reached." (Lüdeke-Freud et al., 2018, p. 153)	Buy one, give one	Lüdeke-Freud et al. (2018)
		Donating products	

Archetype 8: Repurpose for society/environment. Defined as the integration of stakeholders as co-owners and co-managers (Lüdeke-Freud et al., 2018). This can be done through a not-for-profit, hybrid business/ social enterprise (for profit) (Bocken et al., 2014), alternative ownership,

no dividends (Lüdeke-Freud et al., 2018), and localization, including shorter supply chains (see, e.g. Bocken et al., 2014). See Table 7.9

Archetype 9: Inclusive value creation. Defined as sharing resources, knowledge, and wealth creation (Ritala et al., 2018). This can be done through sharing resources/assets, sharing knowledge, and sharing wealth creation (Ritala et al., 2018). See Table 7.10.

Archetype 10: Develop sustainable scale-up solutions. Defined as maximizing benefits for society and the environment through large-scale sustainable solutions (Bocken et al., 2014). This can be done through microfinancing (Lüdeke-Freud et al., 2018), sustainability incubators (see, e.g. Ritala et al., 2018), patient/slow capital collaborations, licensing, franchising (Bocken et al., 2014), and crowdfunding (see, e.g. Ritala et al., 2018). See Table 7.11.

Table 7.9 Repurpose for society/environment—Archetype 8

Economic	Definitions	Components	References
Repurpose for society/ environment Archetype 8	"Patterns that integrate a broad range of stakeholders as co-owners and co-managers, how partners are defined and how the organisation is governed" (Lüdeke-Freud et al., 2018, p. 153)	Not for profit	Bocken et al. (2014)
		Hybrid businesses/ social enterprise (for profit)	Bocken et al. (2014) Lüdeke-Freud et al. (2018)
		Alternative ownership: cooperative, mutual, collective e.g. peer-to-peer product-sharing platforms	Ritala et al. (2018), Bocken et al. (2014)
		No dividends (i.e. profit is not distributed to the shareholders)	Lüdeke-Freud et al. (2018)
		Localization incl shorter supply chains	Bocken et al. (2014) Lüdeke-Freud et al. (2018)

Table 7.10 Inclusive value creation—Archetype 9

Economic	Definition	Components	References
Inclusive value creation Archetype 9	"sharing resources, knowledge, (...) and wealth creation" (Ritala et al., 2018, p. 219)	Sharing resources/ assets (e.g. innovative product financing)	Ritala et al. (2018) Bocken et al. (2014) Lüdeke-Freud et al. (2018)
		Sharing knowledge (innovation at the bottom of pyramid)	Ritala et al. (2018)
		Sharing wealth creation (create value for previously under-addressed group) (e.g. through micro distributiono and retail)	Ritala et al. (2018) Lüdeke-Freud et al. (2018)

7.4 Value Frame and Stakeholders

The value frame included in this research incorporates value creation, value delivery, and value capture. This is largely anchored in research by Richardson (2008) and Teece (2010) as well as more recent research by Evans et al. (2017), Teece and Linden (2017), and Nosratabadi et al. (2019). A comment is warranted here in relation to the research by Bonfanti et al. (2022) and their inclusion of value exchange. The difference taken by Bonfanti et al. (2022) compared to the stance taken in the chapter is based on the understanding that one would expect that the organization can co-operate and work collectively also in the phases of creation, delivery, and capture. Thus, there appears to be little advantage to separate out value exchange, not least given that exchange only indicates that value is given and taken, no indication is made in connection to which of the value dimensions this exchange happens.

Each of the three value dimensions is further elaborated down to a set of multi-stakeholders as proposed by Geissdoerfer et al. (2018), that is, value as derived from a particular sustainability activity is explicated

Table 7.11 Develop sustainable scale-up solutions—Archetype 10

Economic	Definition		Components	References
Develop sustainable scale-up solutions Archetype 10	"Delivering sustainable solutions at a large scale to maximize benefits for society and the environment" (Bocken et al., 2014, p. 53)	Entrepreneurial support models (Bocken et al., 2014)	Microfinancing	Lüdeke-Freud et al. (2018)
			Sustainability incubators	Ritala et al. (2018) Bocken et al. (2014)
			"Patient/slow capital" collaborations	Bocken et al. (2014)
			Licensing, franchising	
			Crowdfunding	Ritala et al. (2018) Bocken et al. (2014) Lüdeke-Freud et al. (2018)

down to the type of stakeholder. This said value is generously managed in line with Comin et al. (2020) who include economic value, social value, environmental value, inclusive value, and even value relevant to more than one stakeholder—as long as such value derives from a sustainability activity (Nosratabadi et al., 2019). This is at first glance contrary to, e.g. Méndez-León et al.'s (2022), focus on sustainable value, but there is of course nothing preventing these two perspectives from coinciding in that sustainable activities create sustainable value.

Thus, value creation is defined in terms of how value is created through sustainable activities initiated by actors within a value-creation network (Richardson, 2008). Assessing value creation can imply determining who is involved in value creation as an initiator of a particular sustainability activity. It can be assumed that the stakeholder group that has the most to gain in terms of a solved problem, also is the group that initiates and participates in the value creation, much in line with the reasoning behind drivers of innovation (von Hippel, 1995). This said, the narrow "single-actor perspective" criticized by Breuer and Lüdeke-Freud (2014) appears obsolete. A contemporary view on value creation stipulates that an organization is not "*an isolated entity. It is embedded in markets and works together with numerous actors—suppliers, workers, customers* etc.—*in order to create value*" (Pies and Schultz, 2023, p. 3).

Value delivery relates to how value is delivered through activities undertaken (Richardson, 2008) to maintain long-term relationships with various stakeholders (Payne et al., 2005). To accomplish a meaningful differentiation of what value creation involves, in comparison to value delivery, the following divide appears appropriate: value creation is the initiation of a sustainability activity which creates, or has the potential to create value, while value delivery is referred to as the management of activities that deliver value. This means that value creation should not in itself be understood as a process which incorporates both value initiation and value delivery as suggested by Pies and Schultz (2023). The pertinence of differentiating between value creation and value delivery lies in that value clearly can be created but never delivered. Further, referring to the SBM core characteristics of inclusive understanding of stakeholder involvement (Comin et al., 2020), separating value creation initiation from value delivery gives an additional nuance and clarity to the Systematic SBM approach. To give an example, if not separating value creation initiation from value delivery it would not be possible to decipher if the organization is the initiator of value creation, while the value delivery may be a collaborative effort between the organization and suppliers in the value system. Consequently, without separating value creation initiation from value delivery the idea of systemic sustainability (Breuer and Lüdeke-Freud, 2014) within a network of actors (Dembek and York, 2022) would be complicated, if not impossible, to pinpoint.

Value capture correspondingly describes how value is captured or harvested (Evans et al., 2017) not only in terms of revenue and profit (Richardson, 2008; Bowman and Ambrosini, 2000) but also how value is captured through alternative "*means of exchange*" (Richardson, 2008, p. 140). Bowman and Ambrosini (2000) define value capture as "*the realization of exchange value by (firms, customers, resource suppliers, and employees)*" (p. 15). This inclusive grip is further strengthened in the statement "*value creation for all stakeholders*" (Antikainen and Valkokari, 2016, p. 10), which makes multi-stakeholder value capture an innate part of organization's sustainability activities. This further suggests that multi-stakeholders can concurrently capture part of the total value each (Teece and Linden, 2017), the so-called co-capture of value.

Since the priority of this chapter clearly is not to decipher what exactly defines value in relation to any one stakeholder at any given time, value is generously managed as perceived by the stakeholder. This approach is overall in line with how Bowman and Ambrosini (2000, p. 2) discuss "*use value*" as being subjectively determined as perceived while diverging from Bowman and Ambrosini's (2000) narrow take on stakeholder, i.e. customer, defined by classical economists. The approach taken in this chapter is, as previously discussed, instead largely agreeing with the general idea that "*a stakeholder is any group or individual that can affect or be affected by the realization of an organization's purpose*" (Freeman et al., 2010, p. 26), within reasonable[2] limits. This approach is in line with the normative core of stakeholder theory as proposed in Donaldson and

[2] For this inclusive grip of stakeholders to be meaningful it should not be excessive and include, for example, competitors (Donaldson and Preston, 1995).

Preston (1995, p. 67, bold as in original): "*Stakeholders are identified by* ***their*** *interests in the corporation, whether the corporation has any corresponding functional interest in* ***them****. (...) each group of stakeholders merits consideration for its own sake and not merely because of its ability to further the interests of some other group, such as the shareowners.*"

More exactly, the stakeholder is managed in line with the relationship-based approach broadly depicted by Payne et al. (2005) in which connectivity, mutual value, and commitment help determine who an organization's stakeholder is. Of the six stakeholder groups proposed by Payne et al. (2005), the customer markets, supplier and alliance markets, and influence markets are further incorporated in the assessment of value creation, delivery, and capture. Alliance markets are referred to as "external organizations" incorporating all external organizations, agencies, and businesses such as NGOs and governmental bodies. Influence market is managed in the concept of "society at large" entailing marginalized groups, local organizations, and communities, and the natural environment including animals, water, solid, forest, and air. Attanasio et al. (2022) offer a compelling list of 10 stakeholder groups, some more or less elaborate compared to the list of Payne et al. (2005). Attanasio et al. (2022) explicate, e.g. universities and research institutions in their list, while such stakeholders are included in the category of external organizations in this chapter.

7.5 The Systematic SBM Approach—A Flexible Tool for Organizations

A Systematic SBM approach has been developed in order to counteract the weaknesses of existing SBM tools. The development has been directed by the following four core characteristics of a SBM: absolute focus on sustainability, generous view of value, generous view of stakeholders, and inclusive understanding of stakeholder involvement. More explicitly, the Systematic SBM approach has a clear focus on all three pillars of sustainability, economic, environmental, and social through the Archetypes as called for by various researchers (Ferlito and Faraci, 2022; Ferreira et al., 2022; Comin et al., 2020; Shakeel et al., 2020; Nosratabadi et al., 2019; Geissdoerfer et al., 2018; Lüdeke-Freud and Dembek, 2017). The value created, delivered, and captured can be both monetary and non-monetary and is very much up to the organization and its stakeholders to define. Thus, the presented Systematic Sustainable Business Model approach (See Table 7.12) takes a generous and inclusive view of value called for by, i.e. Lüdeke-Freud and Dembek (2017). As proposed by Comin et al. (2020), Dembek and York (2022), and Breuer and Lüdeke-Freud (2014), the value process can be shared in all stages showing the collaborative nature of sustainability and value. What stakeholder group to be included in the Systematic SBM approach is flexible as determined by each organization in order to be able to acknowledge the most important stakeholders in their context. This holds even more true for the aspect of value capture which is not limited to the organization itself and its shareholders but is captured widely by many stakeholders just as suggested by Lüdeke-Freud and Dembek (2017), Goni et al. (2021), Geissdoerfer et al. (2018), and Shakeel et al. (2020).

The Systematic SBM approach is complex enough to manage, and give insight into, the actions the organization takes in relation to sustainable business practices. This can form the basis for evaluation of the organizations sustainable business strategies as well as guide the adjustment of the organization's future strategies. The flexibility ensures that the model can be adapted to the organization's current circumstances in their time and industry so that the model becomes a relevant and useful tool rather than a box-ticking checklist.

Applying the Systematic SBM approach can help organizations formulate and follow up their sustainability strategies. Clarifying what sustainability activities the organization is involved in can also make the organizations' more mindful regarding these activities and might also encourage involvement in more sustainability activities. The Systematic SBM can also be a basis for communication of how organizations approach the important work in relation to sustainability, e.g. as a sole initiator and/or implementor or in collaboration with others. It

Table 7.12 The systematic sustainable business model (SBM) approach integrating the core characteristics of SBM

	Environmental			Social				Economic		
SBM archetypes:	Archet. 1	Archet. 2	Archet. 3	Archet. 4	Archet. 5	Archet. 6	Archet. 7	Archet. 8	Archet. 9	Archet. 10
# measuring points:										
Value **creation** initiated										
by the company										
by the customer										
by suppliers										
by external organization[a]										
by the society at large[b]										
Value **delivery** managed										
by the company										
by the customer										
by suppliers										
by external organization[a]										
by the society at large[b]										
Value **captured**										
by the company										
by the customer										
by suppliers										
by external organization[a]										
by the society at large[b]										

Note The tool incorporates ten sustainability archetypes, or generic sustainability approaches connected to the triple bottom line (TBL) dimensions. Value is included in terms of value creation being initiated, value delivery being managed, and value being captured. Stakeholders are connected to each of the three value dimensions allowing for any stakeholder to be part of value creation initiation, delivery and capture

[a] include all external organizations, agencies, and businesses e.g. NGOs, governmental bodies

[b] include marginalized groups, local organizations and communities, natural environment including animals, water, soil, forest and air

also allows for detecting overlooked sustainability activities as opportunities for improvement. This systematic approach should in addition lead to increased transparency alleviating the growing mistrust among consumers when it comes to organizations' proclaimed sustainability efforts.

References

Antikainen, M., & Valkokari, K. (2016). A framework for sustainable circular business model innovation. Technology Innovation Management Review, 6:1, 5–12.

Attanasio, G., Preghenella, N., & De Toni, A.F. (2022). Stakeholder engagement in business models for sustainability: The stakeholder value flow model for sustainable development. Business Strategy Environment, 31, 860–874.

Baldassarre, B., Calabretta, G., Bocken, N.M.P., & Jaskiewicz, T. (2017). Bridging sustainable business model innovation and user-driven innovation: A process for sustainable value proposition design. Journal of Cleaner Production, 147, 175–186.

Bocken, N.M.P., Rana, P., & Short, S.W. (2015). Value mapping for sustainable business thinking. Journal of Industrial and Production Engineering, 32:1, 67–81.

Bocken, N.M.P., Short, S.W., Rana, P., & Evans, S. (2014). A literature and practice review to develop sustainable business model archetypes. Journal of Cleaner Production, 65, 42–56.

Bocken, N.M.P., Short, S., Rana, P., & Evans, S. (2013). A value mapping tool for sustainable business modelling. Corporate Governance, 13:5, 482–497.

Bonfanti, A., Mion, G., Brunetti, F., & Vargas-Sánchez, A. (2022). The contribution of manufacturing companies to the achievement of sustainable development goals: An empirical analysis of the operationalization of sustainable business models. Business Strategy Environment, 1–19.

Bowman, C., & Ambrosini, V. (2000). Value creation versus value capture: Towards a coherent definition of value in strategy. British Journal of Management, 11, 1–15.

Breuer, H., & Lüdeke-Freud, F. (2014). Normative innovation for sustainable business models in value networks. The XXV ISPIM conference—Innovation for sustainable economy & society, Dublin, Ireland, 1–17.

Comin, L.C., Aguiar, C.C., Sehnem, S., Yusliza, M.-Y., Cazella, C.F., & Julkovsko, D.J. (2020). Sustainable business models: A literature review. Benchmarking: An International Journal, 27:7, 2028–2047.

Dembek, K., Lüdeke-Freud, F., Rosati, F., & Froese, T. (2022). Untangling business model outcomes, impact and value. Business Strategy Environment, 1–16.

Dembek, K., & York, J. (2022). Applying a sustainable business model lens to mutual value creation with base of the pyramid suppliers. Business & Society, 61:8, 2156–2191.

Dentchev, N., Rauter, R., Jóhannsdóttir, L., Snihur, Y., Rosano, M., Baumgartner, R., Nyberg, T., Tang, X., van Hoof, B., & Jonker, J. (2018). Embracing the variety of sustainable business models: A profilic field of research and a future research agenda, Journal of Cleaner Production, 194, 695–703.

De Oliveira Paula, F., & Van Aduard De Macadeo-Soares, T.D. (2022). The role of firm alliance portfolio diversity to leverage sustainable business model innovation. International Journal of Innovation Management, 26:6, 2250041 (1–34).

Donaldson, T. & Preston, L.E. (1995) The stakeholder theory of the corporation: Concepts, evidence, and implication. Academy of Management Review, 20:1, 65–91.

Evans, S., Vladimirova, D., Holgado, M., Van Fossen, K., Yang, M., Silva, E., & Barlow, C. (2017). Business model innovation for sustainability: Towards a unified perspective for creation of sustainable business models. Business Strategy and the Environment, 26, 597–608.

Ferlito, R., & Faraci, R. (2022). Business model innovation for sustainability: A new framework. Innovation & Management Review, 19:3, 222–236.

Ferreira, J.J., Fernandes, C.I., Veiga, P.M., & Hughes, M. (2022). Prevailing theoretical approaches predicting sustainable business models: A systematic review. International Journal of Productivity and Performance Management, 71:3, 790–813.

Franca, C.L., Broman, G., Robert, K-H., Basile, G., & Trygg, L. (2017). An approach to business model innovation and design for strategic sustainable development. Journal of Cleaner Production, 140, 155–166.

Freeman, R.E., Harrison, J., Wicks, A.C., Parmar, B.L., & De Colle, S. (2010). Stakeholder theory: The state of the art. Cambridge: Cambridge University Press.

Geissdoerfer, M., Vladimirova, D., & Evans, S. (2018). Sustainable business model innovation: A review. Journal of Cleaner Production, 198, 401–416.

Goni, F.A., Chofreh, A.A., Orakani, Z.E., Klemes, J.J., Davoudi, M., & Mardani, A. (2021). Sustainable business model: A review and framework development. Clean Technologies and Environmental Policy, 23, 889–897.

Lüdeke-Freud, F., Carroux, S., Joyce, A., & Massa, L. (2018). The sustainable business model pattern taxonomy—45 patterns to support sustainability-oriented business model innovation. Sustainable Production and Consumption, 15, 145–162.

Lüdeke-Freud, F., & Dembek, K. (2017). Sustainable business model research and practice: Emerging field or passing fancy? Journal of Cleaner Production, 168, 1668–1678.

Méndez-León, E., Reyes-Carillo, T., & Díaz-Pichardo, R. (2022). Towards a holistic framework for sustainable value analysis in business models: A tool for sustainable development. Business Strategy Environment, 31: 15–31.

Morioka, S.N., Evans, S., & Monteiro de Carvalho, M. (2016) Sustainable business model innovation: Exploring evidences in sustainability reporting. Procedia CIRP, 40, 659–667.

Nosratabadi, S., Mosavi, A., Shamshirband, S., Zavadskas, E.K., Rakotonirainy, A., & Chau K.W. (2019). Sustainable business models: A review. Sustainability, 11:1663, 1–30.

Payne, A., Ballantyne, D., & Christopher, M. (2005). A stakeholder approach to relationship marketing strategy: The development and use of the "six markets" model. Relationship Marketing Strategy, 39:7/8, 855–871.

Pies, I., & Schultz, F.C. (2023). The governance of sustainable business model innovation—An ordonomic approach. Scandinavian Journal of Management, 39, 1–12.

Porter, M.E. (1996). What is strategy? Harvard Business Review, 74, 61–78.

Richardson, J. (2008). The business model: An integrative framework for strategy execution. Strategic Change, 17, 133–144.

Ritala, P., Huotari, P., Bocken, N., Albareda, L., & Puumalainen, K. (2018). Sustainable business model adoption among S&P 500 firms: A longitudinal content analysis study. Journal of Cleaner Production, 170, 216–226.

Ritter, T. & Lettl, C. (2018). The wider implications of business-model research. Long Range Planning, 51, 1–8.

Schaltegger, S., Hansen, E.G., & Lüdeke-Freud, F. (2016). Business models for sustainability: Origins, present research, and future avenues. Organization & Environment, 29:1, 3–10.

Shakeel, J., Mardani, A., Chofrey, A.G., Goni, F.A., & Klemes, J.J. (2020). Anatomy of sustainable business model innovation. Journal of Cleaner Production, 261, 1–14.

Short, S.W., Bocken, N.M.P., Barlow, C.Y., & Chertow, M.R. (2014). From refining sugar to growing tomatoes—Industrial ecology and business model evolution. Journal of Industrial Ecology, 18:5, 603–618

Teece, D. (2010). Business models, business strategy and innovation. Long Range Planning, 43, 172–194.

Teece, D., & Linden, G. (2017). Business models, value capture, and the digital enterprise. Journal of Organizational Design, 6:8, 1–14.

Tranfield, D., Denyer, D. & Smart, P. (2003). Towards a methodology for developing evidence-informed management knowledge by means of systematic review, British Journal of Management, 14:3, 207–222.

Von Hippel, E. (1995). The Sources of Innovation. Oxford: Oxford University Press.

8

Citizens' Engagement in the Co-Creation of Smart City—An Empirical Study

Małgorzata Wiścicka-Fernando

8.1 Introduction

Contemporary cities are faced with an increasing challenge of achieving sustainable development, therefore, efforts and strategies are being implemented to create technologically advanced and sustainable cities. Combining those two areas allows for sustainable, but also the modern operation of a city defined as a smart city. Achieving such objectives requires the engagement of city administrators, companies operating within the city, and research institutions. However, although the citizens are deemed to be beneficiaries (clients) (Kresin et al., 2016) of the services provided by the city, their engagement in the creation of smart cities is limited. It is important to recognize that the citizens can also be initiators and co-creators of actions that contribute to the development of their city. This is particularly evident in grassroots efforts, where city

M. Wiścicka-Fernando (✉)
Department of Marketing, University of Szczecin, Szczecin, Poland
e-mail: malgorzata.wiscicka-fernando@usz.edu.pl

© The Author(s), under exclusive license to Springer Nature Switzerland AG 2024

A. Sörensson et al. (eds.), *Creating New Roles for a Sustainable Economy*, Palgrave Studies in Governance, Leadership and Responsibility,
https://doi.org/10.1007/978-3-031-61551-1_8

residents organize themselves to influence city authorities and implement ideas. Therefore, it can be assumed that residents have multiple roles: beneficiaries, initiators, and co-creators.

The individuals involved in the creation and initiation are particularly intriguing. These two attitudes of citizens give rise to the interest in the role city inhabitants play in smart city creation. Consequently, research is needed to explore the extent of residents' involvement and their role in creating a smart city. Addressing this research problem is crucial.

To the best of the author's knowledge, no research has been conducted on the Polish market that provides insights into the involvement of city inhabitants in the creation of a smart city.

A review of literature databases has yielded limited records, indicating a research gap that needs to be filled. The main objective of the research is to *analyze the relationship between citizens' engagement in smart city creation and their demographic factors, such as gender, age, and level of education.*

The presented results concern the first stage of the study—a pilot study that was conducted in the two largest cities of the Western Pomeranian Region in Poland.

The pilot study aimed to explore the phenomena and utilized descriptive statistics and non-parametric statistics.

The upcoming sections of this paper present a literature review concerning smart cities and the attributes of co-creation. The research results are also presented, accompanied by a discussion of the findings.

Building Smarter Cities: Decoding Technology and Empowering Citizens

The concept of a smart city, in its basic form, is understood as the introduction of new technologies, such as new information and communication technologies (ICT) as well as further progress towards databases and communication (Freestone & Favaro, 2022; Townsend, 2013). However, nowadays a smart city is also linked to sustainable development goals (Aurigi & Odendaal, 2021; Mappiasse, 2015; Marsal-Llacuna, 2016;

Monfaredzadeh & Krueger, 2015) and is an answer to a neoliberal[1] form of city development (Sager, 2011). This can become a new way towards changing a city's social, environmental, and economic needs resulting from the necessity to take into consideration an increasing number of city inhabitants. Therefore, it is not possible to state unequivocally what constitutes a smart city, as there are several different categories of smart city development, including service innovation, urban intelligence, urban sustainability, urban openness, infrastructure integration, urban innovation, collaborative partnership, and smart city governance (Lai & Cole, 2022).

The degree of understanding and implementation of a smart city concept depends on the development of a given region. For instance, in post-communist countries, smart cities are tied to architectural, urban, and technological changes.

Nowadays, it is assumed that the sphere of a smart city encompasses: a smart economy, smart mobility, smart environment, smart people, smart living, and smart governance (Noga, 2015). A smart city may be defined based on two major characteristics: integration of various systems for better city governance and the creation of a new, better reality.

With the shift to citizen-centric smart cities, citizen engagement gains importance. However, concerns arise about feasibility due to citizens' limited time in today's competitive society. To achieve a citizen-driven smart city, an incentivization system and diverse civic engagement channels need further development (Noga, 2015).

An important attribute of smart cities allows real-time operation, which facilitates and improves the quality of life of city dwellers. Defining what a smart city is, remains problematic—typically it arises connotations with either technology or people. The word 'smart' is currently associated with all high-tech and smart solutions (Kitchin, 2014; Söderström et al., 2020). The concept of a smart city is oriented towards people and social capital (Freestone & Favaro, 2022; Albino et al., 2015; Bakıcı et al., 2013; Caragliu et al., 2011; Fernandez-Anez et al., 2018; Giffinger et al., 2007; Hollands 2015; Kourtit & Nijkamp,

[1] The subject concerns the divergent perceptions of the city's interests among businesses, residents, and city officials.

2012; Lombardi et al., 2012; Washburn et al., 2009). The different perceptions of the smart city definition are also shown in Table 8.1.

The definition of a smart city is contingent upon the consideration of specific categories or stages of development. The evolution of smart cities can be delineated into distinct phases, encompassing:

Technology-Centric Stage
Efficiency and Infrastructure Stage

Table 8.1 Selected definitions of a smart city

Source	Definition
Harrison et al. (2010)	'Connecting the physical infrastructure, the IT infrastructure, the social infrastructure, and the business infrastructure to leverage the collective intelligence of the city'
Bakıcı et al. (2013)	'A concept that encompasses most of the areas where local governments operate: transportation, civic entrepreneurship, democratic transparency, clean energy, and services provision'
Mohanty et al. (2016)	'A place where traditional networks and services are made more flexible, efficient, and sustainable with the use of information, digital and telecommunication technologies, to improve its operations for the benefit of its inhabitants'
Park et al. (2019)	'A concept has gained substantial attention over the last few years, as it applies advances in the Internet of Things (IoT) technology to enhance the quality and efficiency of services and resources'
Wang et al. (2021)	'The idea...is to use information technology to drive the operation of the city, which includes monitoring, forecasting, and real-time management. The combination of IoT and AI can replace the traditional means of managers in the past'
Lazaroiu and Roscia (2012)	'The large and small districts are proposing a new city model, called the smart city, which represents a community of average technology size, interconnected and sustainable, comfortable, attractive and secure'

Source Zamponi and Barbierato (2022)

Data-Driven Decision-Making Stage
Citizen-Centric Stage
Inclusivity and Social Equity Stage
Integration and Collaboration Stage
Resilient and Future-Proofing Stage

Each stage represents a significant milestone in the progression towards smarter urban environments, with increasing emphasis on diverse aspects of urban planning, citizen engagement, sustainability, and technological integration.

It is important to understand that this development is not linear. This means that a city can have different levels of progress in each stage or focus on a few of them simultaneously. There is no predetermined order for which stage should come first; the decision is taken by the city itself.

The statement highlights a simplified division of smart city development into two stages. Smart City 1.0 is associated with hard infrastructure and technology-driven solutions, while Smart City 2.0 utilizes technology but also places a strong emphasis on citizen engagement (Kresin et al., 2016).

In practice, some indexes rate cities based on selected categories. The IESE Cities in Motion Index and Smart City Index (see Table 8.2) are among the most well-known smart city rankings. However, their results differ significantly due to the distinct areas of analysis. CIMI is based on 9 dimensions, while SCI categories are derived from the UN Human Development Index (HDI).

Table 8.2 Examples of two smart city rankings

The IESE cities in motion index			Smart city index	
Ranking position	Cities in motion indicators	Name of the city	Ranking position	Name of the city
1	A	London—United Kingdom	1	Singapore
2	A	New York—USA	2	Zurich—Switzerland
3	A	Paris—France	3	Oslo—Norway

Source https://media.iese.edu/research/pdfs/ST-0633-E.pdf; https://www.quantumesco.it/en/2021-global-smart-city-index/

It should also be stressed that awareness of smart city concepts can vary widely depending on geographical location, level of urbanization, access to information, and local initiatives promoting smart city concepts. People's perceptions of the concept can range from associating it mainly with technology-based infrastructure to understanding its broader implications for sustainability, citizen engagement, and quality of life.

The smart city concept also has its drawbacks, as it can abuse ethical aspects of life such as privacy or data protection, exclusion of people who do not use digital technology, and also create dependence on technology (Schuch de Azambuja, 2021).

In many cases, implemented smart city concepts face criticism for being decided by city managers without sufficient consideration for residents' input. As a result, there is a growing emphasis on involving residents actively in smart city development. Engaging citizens in the planning and implementation process is seen as crucial for creating citizen-centric smart cities that align with their needs and aspirations. This participatory approach fosters transparency, social equity, and stronger social bonds between citizens and cities. Residents' contributions, local knowledge, and innovative ideas complement the expertise of city managers and enhance adaptability to urban challenges. Emphasizing inclusivity lays the groundwork for transformative smart city initiatives that genuinely serve the collective interests of communities (Mark & Anya, 2019).

Understanding the issues related to a smart city is of enormous importance since it drives subsequent changes and directions of city development. Additionally, a smart city is defined as connections of a network nature (Cretu, 2012; Yigitcanlar, 2015) and it is acknowledged that social innovations constitute a material factor of a developing smart city in which people are important (Castelnovo et al., 2016; Tochterman, 2012), as is learning and knowledge (Nam & Pardo, 2011; Misiak-Kwit, 2020). However, as shown earlier, these issues are still neglected and marginalized (Monfaredzadeh & Krueger, 2015; Colding & Barthel, 2017). A new approach to a smart city emphasizes a significant role played by city residents who have expectations of their own towards city development while having a growing awareness of a smart city (El hilali & Azougagh, 2021). According to the United Nations, half of the global population lives in cities, and by 2030, urban populations are projected to reach over 5 billion citizens (United Nations, 2018). This means that the role of citizens will be gaining importance It is the citizens who hold a crucial role in creating and adapting new technologies (Kummitha, 2018) and their engagement can form spheres for co-creation (Paskaleva, 2011).

A study conducted in the UK demonstrated that only four percent of city residents know what actions their city undertakes within the framework of a smart city. It shows that the degree of citizens' engagement in the creation of a smart city is low, as it fails to notice their role in identifying and solving smart city problems (Kresin et al., 2016). Consequently, by cooperating and building relations with stakeholders, the government creates mutual benefits rather than formulating a classic orientation towards the fulfillment of its goals (Misiak-Kwit et al., 2021). It needs to be further noted that a citizen as a client has also evolved in their role from a market recipient to its co-creator; A citizen is aware, educated, self-assured, and seeks new experiences (Prahalad & Ramaswamy, 2004b; Ramaswamy, 2011; Ramaswamy & Ozcan, 2014). Including citizens in the co-creation of a smart city will form a new level of development from a smart city 1.0 to a smart city 2.0.

In addition to the discussed definitions, the term 'co-creation' encompasses various other interpretations, including social, communicative, me-too, relational, or marketing aspects (Ind & Coates, 2013). In this project, co-creation is regarded as a relational process wherein the government (the company) engages stakeholders (citizens) to collaboratively find solutions to the pursued objectives. The creation of the value between those two entities is the primary focus of this joint endeavor (Prahalad & Ramaswamy, 2004a, 2004b; Prahalad & Ramaswamy, 2000). The concept of co-creation is substantially acknowledged and studied in the fields of public administration and e-government (Cordella and Paletti, 2019; Osborne, 2018; Uppström and Lönn, 2017), it is also recognized as a new paradigm of innovation. Engaged customers demonstrate greater awareness and knowledge, consequently making more responsible choices, reducing consumption, and developing a sense of responsibility for the environment (McColl-Kennedy et al., 2012). Through the co-creation approach, city governance recognizes that citizens are not only recipients of smart city services but active creators of the urban ecosystem.

The key aspects of smart city co-creation that can be distinguished include seeking residents' opinions through various channels such as public consultations, forums, and surveys. Leveraging residents' knowledge and experiences to design smart solutions is another vital component. Emphasizing open data access ensures transparency, allowing citizens to have a clearer understanding of the decision-making process. Additionally, iterative processes enable continuous improvement of products and initiatives based on user feedback, fostering a more citizen-centric approach. Inclusivity and equity are promoted when all citizens have a voice and are actively involved in shaping their city's development, empowering them in the process.

Co-creation assumes a strategic role in the smart city 2.0 concept, as it hinges on meaningful involvement and collaboration. Involving different stakeholders is essential. However, it is crucial to recognize that the acceptance of new solutions by residents is paramount for the successful development of smart cities. Without the support and participation of the residents, the realization of smart city initiatives would be challenging, if not impossible. Therefore, co-creation serves as a foundation for building more inclusive, innovative, and citizen-centric smart cities that cater to the actual needs and preferences of the local community.

8.2 The Framework of the Study

The researcher developed the conceptual framework of the study with two dependent variables and four independent variables. Accordingly, gender, level of education, marital status, and generation are the independent variables of the study. Willingness to co-create a smart city and experience in the co-creation of a smart city are the two dependent variables of the study. The first variable pertains solely to willingness—the openness to participate in the smart city process. The second variable focuses on experience—involvement in previous smart city projects.

Asking citizens about their willingness to co-create and their experience in co-creation provides valuable data that helps in developing more citizen-centric and effective smart city initiatives, ultimately leading to more sustainable and inclusive urban development.

The research focuses on two cities from the West Pomeranian Voivodeship in Poland, namely Szczecin and Koszalin, were part of the study. These cities were selected due to their significance and representation of the region.

Szczecin, located on the Oder River, is a major seaport and serves as an important economic and cultural center in the region. With a rich history and a diverse population, Szczecin is known for its architectural landmarks, vibrant arts scene, and proximity to natural attractions.

Koszalin, situated on the central coast of the Baltic Sea, is a growing city with a focus on education, healthcare, and various industries. It offers a blend of modern amenities and green spaces, making it an attractive destination for residents and visitors alike (Fig. 1).

Based on the research objectives and the conceptual framework, the formulated hypotheses are:

H_{01}: Gender and willingness to co-create the smart city are independent.
H_{a1}: Gender and willingness to co-create the smart city are not independent.

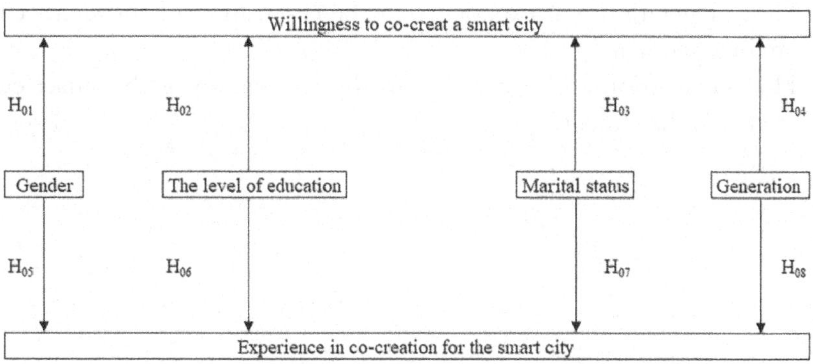

Fig. 8.1 The conceptual framework of the study

H_{02}: The level of education and willingness to co-create the smart city is independent.
H_{a2}: The level of education and willingness to co-create the smart city are not independent.
H_{03}: Marital status and willingness to co-create the smart city are independent.
H_{a3}: Marital status and willingness to co-create the smart city are not independent.
H_{04}: Generation and willingness to co-create the smart city are independent.
H_{a4}: Generation and willingness to co-create the smart city are not independent.
H_{05}: Gender and experience in the co-creation of the smart city are independent.
H_{a5}: Gender and experience in the co-creation of the smart city are not independent.
H_{06}: The level of education and experience in the co-creation of the smart city is independent.
H_{a6}: The level of education and experience in the co-creation of the smart city are not independent.
H_{07}: Marital status and experience in the co-creation of the smart city are independent.
H_{a7}: Marital status and experience in the co-creation of the smart city are not independent.
H_{08}: Generation and experience in the co-creation of the smart city are independent.
H_{a8}: Generation and experience in the co-creation of the smart city are not independent.

8.3 Navigating the Empirical Journey: Unraveling Methodology and Unveiling Findings in Citizen Engagement for Smart Cities

An important factor that shows the level of understanding of the concept of a smart city and the multidimensional relationship between given variables is a survey. A range of data collection and analysis systems were used to gather and interpret the outcomes of the CATI and CAVI surveys. The primary data collection was conducted through a registered data collection agency in Poland. The respondents for the primary data collection were randomly selected based on the Polish CSO database. The data collection was carried out in compliance with European personal data protection laws, particularly the General Data Protection Regulation (GDPR). Safeguarding the privacy and confidentiality of individuals' data is of utmost concern in this study, and it has also taken rigorous measures to ensure that all data collection, storage, and processing procedures align with the principles and requirements outlined in the GDPR.

The primary data consisted of nominal, and ratio scales (see Stevens, 1946). Demographic data, such as age, gender, marital status, and level of education, were collected under the nominal scale (see Table 8.3) as well as citizens' willingness to participate in the co-creation of a smart city and their experiences in the co-creation of a smart city. However, the areas in which citizens could have experienced co-creation and their willingness to co-create were collected under the ratio scale, using a rating scale from 0 to 100, with 0 indicating no previous co-creation experience and no willingness to co-create.

Ratio scale was also used to analyze data on Citizens' perceptional ratings of co-creation experiences and willingness to co-create in areas such as transport, cultural events, green areas, e-office, health, education, environmental protection, local job market, safe city, and the attractiveness of real estate. In addition to the surveys, the Chi-Square test of independence and two-sample Z-tests for population proportion were

Table 8.3 Demographic characteristics

Generation	Level of education	Marital status	Gender
Silent Generation (1928–1945)	Primary	Single	Female
Baby Boomers (1946–1964)	Gymnasium:	Married	Male
Generation X (1965–1980)	High school	Divorced	
Generation Y (1981–1996)	Vocational	In a civil partnership	
Generation Z (1997–2012)	Higher	Widowed	

Source Own research

used. The former was employed to ascertain whether there is a relationship between demographic variables and dependent variables, such as co-creation experience and willingness to co-create, with a significance level of 0.05 (alpha value). The latter was used to compare the co-creation experience and willingness to co-create between female and male citizens.

Data analysis was performed using the Microsoft Excel application package. The summary of the Chi-Square test is presented in Table 8.4. The author conducted the Chi-Square test of independence to examine whether there is a relationship between demographic variables (gender, level of education, marital status, and generation) and dependent variables (willingness to co-create a smart city and experience in co-creating the smart city).

The Chi-square test of independence showed that there is no significant association between gender and willingness to co-create a smart city, χ^2 (1, $N = 427$) = 0.0, $p > 0.05$. Similarly, there is no significant association between the level of education and willingness to co-create a smart city, χ^2 (4, $N = 427$) = 2.60, $p > 0.05$, as well as between marital status and willingness to co-create a smart city, χ^2 (4, $N = 427$) = 3.84, $p > 0.05$. Moreover, no significant association was found between generation and willingness to co-create a smart city, χ^2 (4, $N = 427$) = 2.59, $p > 0.05$. Additionally, there was no significant association between gender and experience in co-creating the smart city, χ^2 (1, $N = 427$) = 0.00, $p > 0.05$, nor between the level of education and experience in co-creating

Table 8.4 Summary of Chi-square test

Hypotheses	Chi-Sq test Statistic	*N*	*df*	α	*p*-value	Observation	Decision
H_{01} H_{a1}	0	427	1	0.05	1	*p*-value > *α*	Fail to reject H_{01}
H_{02} H_{a2}	2.6	427	4	0.05	0.63	*p*-value > *α*	Fail to reject H_{02}
H_{03} H_{a3}	3.48	427	4	0.05	0.48	*p*-value > *α*	Fail to reject H_{03}
H_{04} H_{a4}	2.59	427	4	0.05	0.63	*p*-value > *α*	Fail to reject H_{04}
H_{05} H_{a5}	0	427	1	0.05	1	*p*-value > *α*	Fail to reject H_{05}
H_{06} H_{a6}	7.31	427	4	0.05	0.12	*p*-value > *α*	Fail to reject H_{06}
H_{07} H_{a7}	10.52	427	4	0.05	0.03	*p*-value < *α*	Reject H_{07}
H_{08} H_{a8}	24.23	427	4	0.05	0.00	*p*-value < *α*	Reject H_{08}

Source Own research

the smart city, χ^2 (4, $N = 427$) = 7.31, $p > 0.05$. However, a significant association was observed between marital status and experience in co-creating the smart city, χ^2 (4, $N = 427$) = 10.52, $p > 0.05$, as well as between generation and experience in co-creating the smart city, χ^2 (4, $N = 427$) = 24.23, $p > 0.05$. Table 8.5 presents the results relating to the attitudes of the respondents towards the implementation of the smart city objectives. In the presented research 247 respondents selected the category 'yes' for the question 'Do you want to get involved in the development of your city?'.

Table 8.5 The willingness to co-create the smart city

Categorical variable	Number of respondents	Proportion (Point estimation) (%)	95% confidence interval estimation
Yes	247	58	*0.53 < P < 0.63*
No	180	42	*0.37 < P < 0.47*

Source Own research

Based on the analysis, it was found that fifty-eight percent of the respondents selected 'yes' in response to the question 'Do you want to get involved in the development of your city?' with a ninety-five percent confidence interval of [0.53, 0.63]. Additionally, forty-two percent of the respondents selected 'no' for the same question, with a ninety-five percent confidence interval of [0.37, 0.47]. This indicates that the point estimation for the category 'yes' was fifty-eight percent, and for the category 'no' was forty-two percent. Furthermore, the confidence interval estimation for the categorical variable 'yes' suggests that the population proportion lies between fifty-three percent and sixty-three percent. Similarly, the confidence interval estimation for the categorical variable 'no' indicates a population proportion between thirty-seven percent and forty-seven percent.

Based on Table 8.6, it can be observed that out of 247 female respondents, 137 of them selected the category 'yes' for the question 'Do you want to get involved in the development of your city?' Similarly, out of 180 male respondents, 110 of them selected the same category. The point estimation for the proportion of females who answered 'yes' was fifty-five percent, while for males, it was sixty-one percent. To compare the willingness to co-create between female and male citizens, the author conducted two-sample Z-tests for population proportion.

$$H_0: P_1 - P_2 = 0$$
$$H_a: P_1 - P_2 \neq 0$$

The calculated Z statistic was 0.0483 (with $P_1 = 0.55$, $P_2 = 0.6$, $P = 0.57$, n1 = 247, and n2 = 180). The significance level (alpha) was set at 0.05, and the critical Z-value at the 95% confidence level ($Z_{0.025}$)

Table 8.6 The willingness to co-create the smart city based on the gender group

Gender	Categorical variable = Willingness to Co-create Yes
Female (N = 247)	137
Male (N = 180)	110

Source Own research

was ± 1.95. The obtained *p*-value was 0.480. Since the *p*-value (0.480) is greater than the significance level (0.05), the decision was not to reject the null hypothesis. Therefore, there is enough evidence to suggest that the proportion of females who selected the option 'yes' for the question 'Do you want to get involved in the development of your city?' and the proportion of males who selected the same option for this question are equal. In other words, the population of females and males are equally willing to co-create the smart city.

Based on Table 8.7, the presented data showcases the activities that the analyzed citizens would like to participate in concerning the development of the smart city. It is evident that the highest number of people expressed interest in getting involved in the implementation of actions related to green areas and environmental protection, indicating significant interest in areas concerning sustainable development. This finding highlights the importance of environmental consciousness and the desire for sustainable initiatives among the respondents. Moreover, respondents also provided suggestions for other areas in which they would like to be engaged within the scope of smart city development (see Table 8.7). These individual suggestions could be valuable for identifying new trends emerging among the residents, and emphasize the citizens' strong interest in participating in activities related to green areas and environmental protection. While Table 8.8 presents additional valuable insights gathered from the respondents' suggestions, which can aid in understanding their preferences and aspirations regarding smart city development.

Table 8.9 shows that 154 respondents out of 247 have selected the category 'yes' for the question 'Have you ever been involved in co-creation for the development of a smart city?'.

Based on the analysis, it was found that thirty-six percent of the respondents selected 'yes' in response to the question 'Have you ever been involved in co-creation of the development of a smart city?' with a ninety-five percent confidence interval of [0.32, 0.41]. Similarly, thirty-four percent of the respondents selected 'no' for the same question, with a ninety-five percent confidence interval of [0.59, 0.68]. This indicates that the point estimation for the category 'yes' was thirty-six percent, and for the category 'no' was thirty-four percent.

Table 8.7 The activities in which respondents would like to be involved

Activities	Citizens' total rating percentage (%)
Transport	57.49
Cultural Events	67.10
Green Areas	74.09
E-Office	54.97
Health	66.00
Education	62.70
Environmental Protection	71.61
Local Job Market	60.42
Safe City	69.12
The Attractiveness of Real-Estate	57.41

Source Own research

Table 8.8 Other activities that citizens would like to be involved to co-create a smart city

Other activities	Citizens' total rating percentage (%)
Expand the city limits	0.40
Sports	0.77
I would like to have a greater impact on law enforcement by law enforcement services (Police, Municipal Guard)	0.32
A program for the homeless with a fixed income	0.40
Ecology	0.32
More playgrounds for children	0.36
Islands on Lake Dąbie	0.40
Transport	0.39
Development of motor activity	0.38
Help people with difficulties of various kinds	0.20

Source Own research

Table 8.9 Experience in the co-creation of a smart city

Categorical variable	Number of respondents	Proportion (point estimation) (%)	95% confidence interval estimation
Yes	154	36	$0.32 < P < 0.41$
No	273	34	$0.59 < P < 0.68$

Source Own research

Furthermore, the confidence interval estimation for the categorical variable 'yes' suggests that the population proportion lies between thirty-two percent and forty-one percent. Similarly, the confidence interval estimation for the categorical variable 'no' indicates a population proportion between fifty-nine percent and sixty-eight percent.

According to the research results presented in Table 8.10, out of 247 female respondents, 79 selected the category 'yes' for the question 'Have you ever been involved in co-creation for the development of a smart city?' Likewise, out of 180 male respondents, 75 selected the same category for this question.

The point estimation for the proportion of females who answered 'yes' to the question 'Have you ever been involved in co-creation for the development of a smart city?' was thirty-two percent, while for males, it was forty-two percent.

To compare the experience in co-creation between female and male citizens, the author conducted two-sample Z-tests for population proportion.

H_0: $P_1 - P_2 = 0$
H_a: $P_1 - P_2 \neq 0$

The calculated Z statistic was 0.0470 (with $P_1 = 0.31$, $P_2 = 0.41$, $P = 0.36$, n1 = 247, and n2 = 180). The significance level (alpha) was set at 0.05, and the critical Z-value at the 95% confidence level ($Z_{0.025}$) was ±1.95. The obtained p-value was 0.481.

Since the p-value (0.481) is greater than the significance level (0.05), the decision was not to reject the null hypothesis. Therefore, there is enough evidence to suggest that the proportion of females who selected the option 'yes' for the question of 'Experience in Co-creation' and the

Table 8.10 Citizens' experience in the co-creation of the smart city

Gender	Categorical variable = Experience in co-creation Yes
Female (N = 247)	79
Male (N = 180)	75

Source own research

Table 8.11 Activities that citizens already engaged in to co-create smart city

Activities	Citizen's total rating percentage (%)
Transport	47.68
Cultural Events	61.23
Green Areas	64.65
E-Office	38.34
Health	44.51
Education	56.07
Environmental Protection	60.19
Local Job Market	40.55
Safe City	51.54
The Attractiveness of Real-Estate	37.53
Afforestation (additional answer)	0.64
Purity (additional answer)	0.38

Source Own research

proportion of males who selected the option 'yes' for the question 'Have you ever been involved in co-creation for the development of a smart city?' are equal. In other words, the population of females and males are equally engaged in the co-creation process.

Table 8.11 presents results regarding the participation of analyzed citizens in the process of smart city co-creation. It indicates that residents most frequently co-created actions in the field of culture and green areas. These findings emphasize the importance of these two areas in the co-creation process and highlight the residents' involvement in shaping their smart city.

8.4 From Insights to Impact: An In-Depth Discussion and Conclusions for Smart City Engagement

The main objective of this research was to explore citizens' willingness and engagement in co-creating smart city development and to examine the influence of demographic factors on their participation. The findings have several implications that shed light on the relationship between citizens and smart city initiatives.

Firstly, the study revealed that both female and male populations exhibited equal levels of willingness and engagement to co-create a smart city development. This suggests that gender does not significantly influence citizens' inclination to participate actively in shaping their urban environment.

Secondly, the research findings indicate a significant association between certain independent variables, such as marital status and generation, and the dependent variable of experience in co-creation for smart city development. This implies that individuals from different marital and generational backgrounds may have varying levels of experience in engaging with smart city initiatives.

Interestingly, the results of Chi-square test indicate that generally accepted demographic characteristics do not significantly impact citizens' willingness to co-create smart city development. These findings suggest that willingness to participate is not primarily determined by traditional demographic factors but could be influenced by other factors, such as individual preferences, interests, and perceptions.

With regards to citizens' interests and cooperative activities with the city, the study reveals a similar tendency. It is hypothesized that the designation of the same activities could arise from difficulties in defining potential fields of cooperation. Respondents displayed a willingness to participate in spheres in which they already have experience, which might indicate a preference for familiar areas of involvement. Notably, activities related to e-office, real estate, and the job market sparked the least interest among respondents. These activities are work-related and might not be perceived as directly impacting residents' quality of life. It is essential to raise citizens' awareness and educate them about how their participation in these activities can indeed improve their quality of life.

The involvement of respondents in providing additional input regarding activities they would be keen to participate in as part of smart city co-creation was significant for this study. The listed activities do not constitute separate categories; instead, they represent concrete actions that interest some residents in the analyzed cities.

The research findings not only provide valuable information that can guide decision-making towards sustainable development-oriented initiatives in smart city projects but also offer insights into the relationship between demographic factors and citizen engagement in co-creating smart cities.

The study demonstrates that gender does not influence willingness and engagement in smart city co-creation, while certain demographic factors are associated with the level of experience in participating. This highlights the importance of addressing citizens' interests and raising awareness about their potential impact on various activities to foster meaningful and inclusive smart city co-creation initiatives. By understanding citizens' willingness and engagement levels, city planners and policymakers can adopt a citizen-centric approach in tailoring smart city development strategies. This inclusivity ensures that the initiatives align closely with the preferences and interests of the local community, addressing their real needs and aspirations.

These valuable insights hold significance for city planners and policymakers, providing a foundation for formulating policies that promote active citizen participation and collaboration in smart city projects. Adopting a citizen-centric approach and considering demographic factors can lead to more effective urban initiatives that truly empower residents to shape the future of their urban environment.

In conclusion, this study underscores the importance of city residents as crucial contributors to the innovation chain in ensuring a city's continued development. Citizens possess valuable insights into local issues and demonstrate greater fluency in modern technologies compared to the government (Kresin et al., 2016). While the study explores the association between demographic factors and willingness to co-create a smart city development and co-creation experience using descriptive and non-parametric statistics, further research can enhance the understanding of additional factors not covered in this analysis that may influence these dependent variables.

To comprehensively answer the research question, future studies involving larger study groups should incorporate the Chi-square test for independence and Z-tests for population proportion as a part of quantitative research methods. Additionally, integrating qualitative research can provide deeper insights into citizens' behavior towards willingness to co-create a smart city development and their co-creation experiences. Furthermore, a citizen-centric approach is paramount in creating a smart city 2.0. Cooperation with citizens should commence from the design stage itself, ensuring active inclusion and participation. Emphasizing the role of citizens in the co-creation process fosters greater acceptance and openness to collaborative endeavors, ultimately leading to more effective smart city initiatives.

While this study sheds light on the relationship between demographics and citizen engagement, it is essential to acknowledge its limitations. Future research should strive for a more focused approach and consider a wider range of factors that influence willingness to co-create and co-creation experiences in smart city development. By addressing these limitations and building upon the findings, future research can maximize its impact and offer valuable insights for shaping the future of smart city development effectively.

References

Albino, V., Berardi, U., & Dangelico, R. M. (2015). Smart cities: Definitions, dimensions, performance, and initiatives. *Journal of Urban Technology, 22*(1), 3–21. https://doi.org/10.1080/10630732.2014.942092

Aurigi, A., & Odendaal, N. (2021). From "smart in the box" to "smart in the city": Rethinking the socially sustainable smart city in context. *Journal of Urban Technology, 28*(1–2), 55–70. https://doi.org/10.1080/10630732.2019.1704203

Bakıcı, T., Almirall, E., & Wareham, J. (2013). A smart city initiative: The case of Barcelona. *Journal of the Knowledge Economy, 4*(2), 135–148. https://doi.org/10.1007/s13132-012-0084-9

Caragliu, A., Del Bo, C., & Nijkamp, P. (2011). Smart cities in Europe. *Journal of Urban Technology, 18*(2), 65–82. https://doi.org/10.1080/10630732.2011.601117

Castelnovo, W., Misuraca, G., & Savoldelli, A. (2016). Smart cities governance: The need for a holistic approach to assessing urban participatory policy making. *Social Science Computer Review, 34*(6), 724–739. https://doi.org/10.1177/0894439315611103

Colding, J., & Barthel, S. (2017). An urban ecology critique on the "Smart City" model. *Journal of Cleaner Production, 164*, 95–101. https://doi.org/10.1016/j.jclepro.2017.06.191

Cordella, A., & Paletti, A. (2019). Government as a platform, orchestration, and public value creation: The Italian case. *Government Information Quarterly, 36*(4), 101409. https://doi.org/10.1016/j.giq.2019.101409

Cretu, L.-G. (2012). Smart cities design using event-driven paradigm and semantic web. *Informatica Economica, 16*(4), 57.

El hilali, S., & Azougagh, A. (2021). A netnographic research on citizen's perception of a future smart city. *Cities, 115*, 103233. https://doi.org/10.1016/j.cities.2021.103233

Fernandez-Anez, V., Fernández-Güell, J. M., & Giffinger, R. (2018). Smart city implementation and discourses: An integrated conceptual model. The case of Vienna. *Cities, 78*, 4–16. https://doi.org/10.1016/j.cities.2017.12.004

Freestone, R., & Favaro, P. (2022). The social sustainability of smart cities: A conceptual framework. *City, Culture and Society, 29*, 100460. https://doi.org/10.1016/j.ccs.2022.100460

Giffinger, R., Fertner, C., Kramar, H., & Meijers, E. (2007). City-ranking of European medium-sized cities. *Centre for Regional Science Vienna UT*, *9*(1), 1–12.

Harrison, C., Eckman, B., Hamilton, R., Hartswick, P., Kalagnanam, J., Paraszczak, J., & Williams, P. (2010). Foundations for smarter cities. *IBM Journal of Research and Development, 54*(4), 1–16.

Hollands, R. G. (2015). Critical interventions into the corporate smart city. *Cambridge Journal of Regions, Economy and Society, 8*(1), 61–77. Scopus. https://doi.org/10.1093/cjres/rsu011

Ind, N., & Coates, N. (2013). The meanings of co-creation. *European Business Review, 25*(1), 86–95. https://doi.org/10.1108/09555341311287754

Kitchin, R. (2014). The real-time city? Big data and smart urbanism. *GeoJournal, 79*(1), 1–14.

Kourtit, K., & Nijkamp, P. (2012). Smart cities in the innovation age. *Innovation: The European Journal of Social Science Research, 25*(2), 93–95. https://doi.org/10.1080/13511610.2012.660331

Kresin, F., Mamadouh, V., & van Wageningen, A. (2016). Smart cities value their smart citizens. In G. Marini (Trans.), *Urban Europe: Fifty tales of the city* (pp. 181–186). Amsterdam University Press. https://doi.org/10.1017/9789048535811.022

Kummitha, R. K. R. (2018). Entrepreneurial urbanism and technological panacea: Why smart city planning needs to go beyond corporate visioning?

Technological Forecasting and Social Change, *137*, 330–339. https://doi.org/10.1016/j.techfore.2018.07.010

Lai, C. M. T., & Cole, A. (2022). Measuring progress of smart cities: Indexing the smart city indices. *Urban Governance*. https://doi.org/10.1016/j.ugj.2022.11.004

Lazaroiu, G. C., & Roscia, M. (2012). Definition methodology for the smart cities model. *Energy*, *47*(1), 326–332.

Lombardi, P., Giordano, S., Farouh, H., & Yousef, W. (2012). Modelling the smart city performance. *Innovation: The European Journal of Social Science Research*, *25*(2), 137–149. https://doi.org/10.1080/13511610.2012.660325

Mappiasse, S. (2015). *Looking for social sustainability in a smart city: The case of Makassar city*.

Mark, R., & Anya, G. (2019). Ethics of using smart city AI and Big Data: The case of four large European cities. *The ORBIT Journal*, *2*(2), 1–36. https://doi.org/10.29297/orbit.v2i2.110

Marsal-Llacuna, M.-L. (2016). City indicators on social sustainability as standardization technologies for smarter (Citizen-Centered) governance of cities. *Social Indicators Research*, *128*(3), 1193–1216. Scopus. https://doi.org/10.1007/s11205-015-1075-6

McColl-Kennedy, J. R., Vargo, S. L., Dagger, T. S., Sweeney, J. C., & Kasteren, Y. van. (2012). Health care customer value cocreation practice styles. *Journal of Service Research*, *15*(4), 370–389.

Misiak-Kwit, S. (2020). *Determinants and consequences of entrepreneurship in Poland: Theoretical approach*. Wydawnictwo Naukowe Uniwersytetu Szczecińskiego Szczecin, Poland.

Misiak-Kwit, S., Wiścicka-Fernando, M., & Fernando, K. S. D. (2021). The symbiotic mutualism between co-creation and entrepreneurship. *Sustainability*, *13*(11), Article 11. https://doi.org/10.3390/su13116285

Mohanty, S. P., Choppali, U., & Kougianos, E. (2016). Everything you wanted to know about smart cities: The Internet of things is the backbone. *IEEE Consumer Electronics Magazine*, *5*(3), 60–70.

Monfaredzadeh, T., & Krueger, R. (2015). Investigating social factors of sustainability in a smart city. *Procedia Engineering*, *118*, 1112–1118. https://doi.org/10.1016/j.proeng.2015.08.452

Nam, T., & Pardo, T. A. (2011). Smart city as urban innovation: Focusing on management, policy, and context. *Proceedings of the 5th International Conference on Theory and Practice of Electronic Governance* (pp. 185–194). https://doi.org/10.1145/2072069.2072100

Noga, M. (2015). Smart city. *Polska Energetyka Słoneczna*, *1–4*, 71–76.

Osborne, S. P. (2018). From public service-dominant logic to public service logic: Are public service organizations capable of co-production and value co-creation? *Public Management Review, 20*(2), 225–231. https://doi.org/10.1080/14719037.2017.1350461

Park, S., Lee, S., Park, S., & Park, S. (2019). AI-based physical and virtual platform with 5-layered architecture for sustainable smart energy city development. *Sustainability, 11*(16), 4479.

Paskaleva, K. A. (2011). The smart city: A nexus for open innovation? *Intelligent Buildings International, 3*(3), 153–171. https://doi.org/10.1080/17508975.2011.586672

Prahalad, C. K., & Ramaswamy, V. (2000, January 1). Co-opting customer competence. *Harvard Business Review*. https://hbr.org/2000/01/co-opting-customer-competence

Prahalad, C. K., & Ramaswamy, V. (2004a). Co-creation experiences: The next practice in value creation. *Journal of Interactive Marketing, 18*(3), 5–14. https://doi.org/10.1002/dir.20015

Prahalad, C. K., & Ramaswamy, V. (2004b). *The future of competition: Co-creating unique value with customers*. Harvard Business Press.

Ramaswamy, V. (2011). It's about human experiences… and beyond, to co-creation. *Industrial Marketing Management, 40*(2), 195–196. https://doi.org/10.1016/j.indmarman.2010.06.030

Ramaswamy, V., & Ozcan, K. (2014). *The Co-creation paradigm*. Stanford University Press. http://www.sup.org/books/title/?id=23497

Sager, T. (2011). Neo-liberal urban planning policies: A literature survey 1990–2010. *Progress in Planning, 76*(4), 147–199. https://doi.org/10.1016/j.progress.2011.09.001

Schuch de Azambuja, L. (2021). Drivers and barriers for the development of smart sustainable cities: A systematic literature review. *Proceedings of the 14th International Conference on Theory and Practice of Electronic Governance* (pp. 422–428).

Söderström, O., Paasche, T., & Klauser, F. (2020). Smart cities as corporate storytelling. In *The Routledge companion to smart cities* (pp. 283–300). Routledge.

Stevens, S. S. (1946). On the theory of scales of measurement. *Science, 103*(2684), 677–680. https://doi.org/10.1126/science.103.2684.677

United Nations. (2018). The sustainable development goals report. https://unstats.un.org/sdgs/files/report/2018/thesustainabledevelopmentgoalsreport2018-en.pdf. Retrieved December 12, 2023.

Tochterman, B. (2012). Theorizing neoliberal urban development: A genealogy from Richard Florida to Jane Jacobs. *Radical History Review, 2012*(112), 65–87. https://doi.org/10.1215/01636545-1416169

Townsend, A. M. (2013). *Smart cities: Big data, civic hackers, and the quest for a New Utopia*. W. W. Norton & Company.

Uppström, E., & Lönn, C.-M. (2017). Explaining value co-creation and co-destruction in e-government using boundary object theory. *Government Information Quarterly, 34*(3), 406–420. https://doi.org/10.1016/j.giq.2017.08.001

Wang, K., Zhao, Y., Gangadhari, R. K., & Li, Z. (2021). Analyzing the adoption challenges of the Internet of things (IOT) and artificial intelligence (AI) for smart cities in china. *Sustainability, 13*(19), 10983.

Washburn, D., Sindhu, U., Balaouras, S., Dines, R. A., Hayes, N., & Nelson, L. E. (2009). Helping CIOs understand "smart city" initiatives. *Growth, 17*(2), 1–17.

Yigitcanlar, T. (2015). Smart cities: An effective urban development and management model? *Australian Planner, 52*(1), 27–34. https://doi.org/10.1080/07293682.2015.1019752

Zamponi, M. E., & Barbierato, E. (2022). The dual role of artificial intelligence in developing smart cities. *Smart Cities, 5*(2), 728–755. https://doi.org/10.3390/smartcities5020038

9

Communicated Sustainability Values from Nature-Based Businesses—Different Industries Give Different Perspectives

Anna Sörensson and Maria Bogren

9.1 Introduction

Entrepreneurs within nature-based businesses play an important role in society's sustainable development (Pini, 2005) and this sector is of particular interest for growth and the establishment of new businesses (Bucht, 2017). For nature-based businesses, it is of great importance to develop more sustainable businesses. For a company to be nature-based, its value creation in one way or another must depend on resources from agriculture, forestry, gardening, or other rural environments. Nature-based businesses are important to Sweden's economy, as they employ so many

A. Sörensson (✉)
Mid Sweden University, Östersund, Sweden
e-mail: anna.sorensson@miun.se

Inland Norway University of Applied Science, Rena, Norway

M. Bogren
Nord University, Steinkjer, Norway

© The Author(s), under exclusive license to Springer Nature Switzerland AG 2024
A. Sörensson et al. (eds.), *Creating New Roles for a Sustainable Economy*, Palgrave Studies in Governance, Leadership and Responsibility,
https://doi.org/10.1007/978-3-031-61551-1_9

people: approximately 9% of the workforce in Sweden works in nature-based businesses (Tillväxtverket, 2018). Today, nature-based businesses attract interest from consumers, who are increasingly aware of sustainable issues in relation to businesses (Sörensson and Dalborg, 2017; Sörensson et al., 2018).

Some entrepreneurs in nature-based businesses are currently aware that sustainability might be a value for their business. Sustainable value is today understood as comprising economic, social, and environmental values (Ueda et al., 2009) and value creation is the starting point for companies that want to create value for various stakeholders. The importance of value creation is well-established among researchers (Grönroos, 2011; Grönroos, 2017; Vargo and Lusch, 2008). Value creation is often raised based on different levels such as what value, how value is created as well as value for stakeholders (Freudenreich et al., 2020).

After the Brundtland report (1987) was published, businesses started to supply environmental information and environmental reports as well as including social reports. From the early 2000s, businesses started to introduce sustainability reports that addressed all three sustainability dimensions: economic, social, and environmental. Integrating sustainability reporting is the practice of measuring, disclosing, and being accountable to internal and external stakeholders for organizational performance towards the goal of sustainable development (GRI, 2016). Not all companies supply complete sustainability reports, some just present sustainability information. Regulations concerning sustainability reporting are not clear about what must be included and how reports should be reviewed for instance, whether they should be reviewed, like annual reports.

Previous studies have shown that there might be other values than economic value, such as ecological or social values, that stakeholders look for (Schaltegger et al., 2016). Camilleri (2017) argued that value co-creation creates value not only for businesses themselves, but also for all stakeholders that are willing to participate in co-creation processes. Therefore, value co-creation can contribute to sustainability (Camilleri, 2017). In a study of tourism companies, the result showed that context and prerequisites govern what information they presented for their stakeholders (Bogren and Sörensson, 2021). Moreover, the presented information often was about the social and environmental dimensions in the GRI model.

The aim of this chapter is to explore how nature-based businesses communicate sustainability, regarding economic, social, and environmental sustainability, to their stakeholders.

The following two research questions are discussed:

RQ1: What kind of sustainability value is communicated to the stakeholders of nature-based businesses in Sweden?
RQ2: Is there a difference in what sustainability information nature-based businesses from different categories focus on?

The chapter is structured as follows: Firstly, there is a theoretical review on research about sustainable value for nature-based businesses as well as for its stakeholders. The study method is then described, and subsequently the findings and discussion are presented. Finally, the last section presents conclusions and practical implications.

9.2 Sustainable Value for Stakeholders in Nature-Based Businesses

Research about stakeholders and value creation has often circled around issues such as value creation with and for whom (Freudenreich et al., 2020). Stakeholders include shareholders, banks, investors, customers, employees, the government, and suppliers (Garvare and Johansson, 2010). Firstly, it is often focused on value creation for customers. Customers buy products or services and there should be some value in use for them. The second major stakeholder group is the financial ones (like shareholders or investors). Lately, researchers have focused on other types of stakeholder groups like for instance NGOs as well as other types of values such as for instance sustainable value (Freudenreich et al., 2020). Initially, an understanding of sustainable value focused on economic issues. Today, companies should use value co-creation and integrate social and environmental value for a more holistic understanding of value (Schaltegger et al., 2011). Acs et al. (2013) argued that the creation of social value can be added to economic values and be the driver for social entrepreneurship. A similar perspective views environmental values as combining to create economic values, which is a form of eco-entrepreneurship (Schaltegger and Wagner, 2011). The interests of all stakeholder groups (Evans et al., 2017) are seen as key aspects in the creation of sustainability value. The essential idea of co-creation of value is that companies interact with stakeholders in the creation of value. However, a problem arises when these different values contradict each other.

Evans et al. (2017) argue that economic, social, and environmental aspects are all included, if the stakeholders' needs are in focus. Economic value consists of, for example, profit, business stability, and return on investment (Flammer, 2013). Social value might include development for the community as well as inside an organization, for instance in terms of equality and labour standards. Finally, environmental value might take the form of less pollution and more use of renewable resources. Ara et al. (2020) identified the stakeholders' influence as the dominant factor for SMEs to improve their environmental and social dimensions. Their study showed that stakeholders influence these companies and cause them to change their behaviour. Other studies have shown that SMEs implement sustainability depending on the stakeholders (e.g., the owner's personal interests and motives) and to project a "greener" image towards the stakeholders (Amran et al., 2018; Hasan, 2018; Sharma and Gupta, 2020). The three sustainability dimensions form a combined sustainability value. Sustainability values should take all the stakeholders' views into consideration and not only meet the shareholders' expectations (Stubbs and Cocklin, 2008).

Evans et al. (2017) argue that sustainability value forms in network constellations. Since a company is connected with its suppliers, customers, and society, all these parts form value between them. The process of creating sustainability value must therefore be seen from a system view, wherein all three sub-systems—ecological, social, and economic—must be viable and healthy (Hoffman and Ehrenfeld, 2015). Companies within nature-based business have a number of stakeholders involved in them for different reasons—in some cases, for reasons of sustainability. Stakeholder theory claims that different stakeholders should be presented with different reports about the company, and these reports could, for instance, contain sustainability information (Dienes et al., 2016). Camilleri (2017) argued that stakeholder theory provides opportunities to create business models that meet sustainable environmental needs as well as societal expectations.

Sustainability Reporting in Nature-Based Businesses

In 2017, an EU directive mandated that all companies that fulfil two of the following three criteria must take part in sustainability reporting (GRI, 2016): (1) more than 250 employees, (2) a yearly turnover in excess of 35 million euros and (3) total assets of 17.5 million euros. Until then, sustainability reporting in Sweden had been a voluntary act for privately owned companies. Since it is still voluntary for most companies to present sustainability information, many of them use it more for marketing reasons rather than to supply information.

The reasons behind companies' sustainability reporting varies (Mahoney et al. (2013), and this reporting is often vague. One reason why some do not present sustainability reports might be the lack of a clear framework (Mahoney et al., 2013). Companies also differ in what they include, and "greenwashing"—a practice that involves companies making reports to satisfy the stakeholders rather than to be a more sustainable company—is common. Dumay et al., (2010) argued that companies are reporting more information than in the past, when reports typically only included traditional financial and accounting information (Mahoney et al., 2013). Sweeney and Coughlan (2008) argued that sustainability reporting is done to satisfy stakeholders, present accountability and legitimacy, and also as a way of communicating with the company's stakeholders (Sweeney and Coughlan, 2008).

Companies′ different stakeholders are interested in different economic, social, and environmental issues that determine the success of a company (Buchholz and Rosenthal, 2005; Dilling, 2010; Hahn, and Kühnen, 2013). Often the focus in on annual reports which cover finances and how to maximize revenues (e g economic sustainability). Annual reports are often targeting shareholders, banks, and other credit actors, while sustainability reports are often aimed at customers (e g social and environmental sustainability). Sustainable values may play a key role for all stakeholders (Dumay et al., 2010; Waligo et al., 2013). Sustainability reports can therefore be an active strategic plan for stakeholders to portray a certain image.

With the help of sustainability information, companies can try to meet their stakeholders' demands by presenting information that achieves several aims: increasing transparency; improving brand value, reputation, and legitimacy; motivating employees; and contributing to corporate sustainability (Lozano and Huisingh, 2011). If a business desires to endure, it must be able to create value for itself and its environment (Ramos-González et al., 2017). Sustainability can be much more than a cost, a constraint, or a charitable deed. It should rather be seen as a source of opportunity, innovation, and competitive advantage (Porter and Kramer, 2006). To make the implications of sustainability successful could be affected by the company's size, diversification, research and development, and market conditions (McWilliams and Siegel, 2001). Sustainability information is thus a way for nature-based businesses to communicate their efforts to the stakeholders. There are still few studies that show the importance of sustainable value (Boruchowitch and Fritz, 2022). Research still struggles with the meaning of sustainable value creation and the lack of practical examples.

9.3 Method

The study was conducted with a qualitative and explorative approach. The aim was to explore how nature-based businesses communicate sustainability, regarding economic, social, and environmental sustainability, to their stakeholders. Data were collected from 100 nature-based companies in Sweden, selected from the official homepage of www.allabo lag.se, which is a register of all companies in Sweden. Nature-based businesses were selected from several different categories in order to address the complexity of the industry, which included companies within the agriculture, forestry, hunting, and fishing industries. These companies all had an annual turnover of 1–50 million euros and this is based on

Table 9.1 Selected nature-based companies for the study

Category	$N = 100$
Agriculture	20
Vegetable	20
Egg	10
Fish	10
Forestry	20
Gardening	10
Contract work in forest	10

the categories provided in the Swedish register (Table 9.1). The selected nature-based companies in this study were distributed as follows:

Data were collected from one year using three data sources: annual reports, sustainability reports and websites, and followed certain steps. Firstly, we started by reading each company's annual report to ascertain if any sustainability information was presented there and, if so, what kind of information was included. Annual reports usually focus on economic information, but we focused also on any social and environmental information included. Secondly, we investigated whether the companies provided sustainability reports, and if they did, what kind of information they included. Finally, we examined the companies' websites to see if they provided any sustainability information and, if so, what kind. All data included in the study were secondary data from written documentation provided by the included companies, sourced from annual reports, sustainability reports, and websites.

The data were first divided according to the three data collection sources and then categorized into one of the three areas within sustainability (economic, social, or environmental). The thematic analysis is inspired by Castleberry and Nolen (2018). Firstly, data were grouped into codes that were based on pre-defined codes such as economic, social, or environmental sustainability. Secondly, codes were grouped into themes where data were interpreted, and patterns identified. In the findings, these themes are presented and illustrated with quotes from the webpages. Thirdly and last, conclusions were drawn in relation to the aim and the research questions of the study.

9.4 Findings and Discussion

All the studied nature-based companies must present an annual report with the financial results for the year based on Swedish regulations. One common result is therefore that economic sustainability is not discussed to any great extent. When discussing sustainability, there are other aspects that are addressed concerning economic sustainability, such as market presence and indirect economic impact. These areas are not mentioned in the annual reports, which focuses on the financial results for the year as requested by law.

Another clear result is that many of these companies are family-owned, and many have been in the same family for generations. This leads to a common result that demonstrating economic sustainability to stakeholders is not as important for these nature-based companies since, compared to non-family-owned businesses, they are not as influenced by stakeholders such as stockowners, banks, and investors. Such important stakeholders might request a certain result or quarterly economic reports.

The study found that different types of nature-based businesses focus on different areas of sustainability. When the data were interpreted, the results showed two main groups with similar findings, namely agriculture and food producers (vegetables, eggs, and fish, named group A) and forestry, gardening, and contract work in forests (named group B). The structure of this chapter is therefore based on these two groups.

Group A: Agriculture, Vegetable, Egg and Fish Companies

The study found that companies in group A are particularly focused on environmental sustainability. They are often more detailed about what kind of efforts they make in order to be sustainable. Group A companies, for instance, discuss areas like more sustainable transportation and more ecological types of packaging, the issue of recycling, and the use of compost on farms. Several of the studied companies mentioned the issue of quality; for many of them, quality is equal to environmental sustainability. The issues of quality and quality labeling are important for these companies. Some of the companies are also working on sustainability based on energy consumption and production with the help of renewable energy sources like solar cells and wind turbines. The issue of spraying plants with pesticides and the use of chemicals are addressed. Some of the companies work with carbon dioxide emissions, and the extent to which this issue is debated in the mass media.

"We collect and recycle the eutrophication water to avoid eutrophication in the soil. We also use climate-friendly electricity, produced from renewable raw materials, and the efficiency of transport means that we dare to say that we are a better choice also from an environmental point of view. Other things we do to protect the environment are the use of energy tissue and biological pest control. Every week there are also deliveries of surplus carbon dioxide. Something that would otherwise have gone straight into nature, but which is now used by us" (Case 12).

Social sustainability is mentioned only rarely, especially when compared to environmental sustainability. There are only a few companies that discuss social issues, such as seasonal employment and quality labeling. The issue of gender equality is discussed, since the industry is often portrayed as a male-dominated industry with "men driving the tractors". Another social dimension is that a few companies seem to engage in the local community and make social efforts.

"We support the UN Global Compact's 10 principles on human rights, working conditions, the environment and corruption. We strive for long-term business relationships as a basis for creating customer value, as well as a safe and developing workplace. Our code of conduct describes the requirements and expectations we have in the environments in which we operate, our own actions and conduct, the board, management, and all employees. In the area we have influence, we will strive for our suppliers and other partners to follow the principles in our code of conduct" (Case 56).

Group B: Forestry, Gardening Companies and Contract Work

The companies in this group were among the nature-based businesses that presented the most information to their stakeholders. They are more focused on environmental sustainability and they provided specific sustainability reports annually, in the same way as they provided annual reports. The studied companies often have Program for the Endorsement of Forest Certification (PEFC), which means that the company works towards being a sustainable forestry business. The PEFC is an international, non-profit, non-governmental organization which promotes sustainable forest management through independent third-party certification. It is considered the certification system of choice for small forest owners. The results also show that some companies' vision is to protect animals and nature.

"The quality of work performed is the most important thing for us. The concept of quality means that we are meticulous with details and look after all your wishes. Everyone is different and that's good! Of course, we deliver on time, follow up our results, and give you as a customer a guarantee on the work done. We are your forest's best friend" (Case 90).

The only social sustainability dimension that is mentioned, by a few companies, is the vision to be a great employer. Another conclusion is that the main stakeholder group is not consumers but larger companies that buy the wood or contracting services. These large companies (i.e., stakeholders) are the main target group for sustainability issues for the forestry companies and contracting services companies. The sustainability information seems to be targeted towards the small consumer, who will buy the end products. Since the consumers are more aware of sustainability issues than large businesses of sustainability issues and often choose more sustainable options, it seems important for these nature-based companies to present sustainable information. The sustainability information may lead to more satisfied consumers, thus increasing sales and revenues and improving the nature-based company's economic sustainability.

"We take responsibility! Decent conditions towards our employees and towards you as a customer is a matter of course for us. We care about you and your forest. We care about the world around us and take responsibility for the environment and society. It is natural for us to get involved in various industry forums and industry organizations. If you are looking for a supplier who wants to move forward, has professional pride and is responsible for his actions, you have found the right place. We work to be a good role model for others and to raise the status of the forest industry" (Case 60).

9.5 Conclusions

The aim of this chapter was to explore how nature-based businesses communicate sustainability, regarding economic, social, and environmental sustainability, to their stakeholders. The conclusions that can be drawn from this study are that there seem to be both differences and similarities between the different company categories. Almost none of the included companies showed an interest in social sustainability, with only a few companies mentioning it very briefly. The two main groups that the study has identified showed differences based on the identity of the main stakeholder group (Table 9.2).

This study's first research question concerned what kind of sustainability information nature-based businesses communicate to stakeholders. The conclusion is that they focus mainly on environmental sustainability. The sustainability information provided seems to mainly target the customers as the main stakeholder group. Many nature-based businesses are family owned and are therefore not focused on other stakeholders, such as investors and banks. Environmental aspects are important for many of these businesses, with around 80% of the companies addressing this issue.

The study's second research question was whether there are differences in the kind of sustainability information focused upon by nature-based businesses from different categories. The conclusion is that there are differences but also similarities. One common result is that economic

Table 9.2 Summary for the two groups

Category	Group	Communication to stakeholder
Agriculture Vegetable Egg Fish	Group A	Economic sustainability is a basic prerequisite but is not communicated to stakeholders Social sustainability is not communicated to a great extent, and a major explanation lies in the fact that most companies are family-run Environmental sustainability is the most communicated dimension among the studied companies. The focus is on three sub themes: ecological products, energy, and transport. The key stakeholder group is the customers
Forestry Gardening Contract work in forest	Group B	Economic sustainability is a basic prerequisite but is not communicated to stakeholders Social sustainability is not communicated to a great extent, and the stakeholder group of interest is the employers Environmental sustainability is the most communicated dimension among the studied companies. The focus is on certifications, and this is related to the fact that the key stakeholder group is wood buyers

sustainability value is rarely focused on, and this finding was particularly clear when the nature-based company is family owned. Group A companies are interested in environmental sustainability value but are more eager to present detailed sustainability information. This sustainability information is mainly focused towards food consumers. By contrast, Group B companies have non-consumer-groups, such as wood purchasers, as their main stakeholder group. These companies are focused on environmental sustainability value that interests these stakeholders, such as ecological labels.

The practical implication of these findings is that nature-based businesses could use environmental sustainability as a marketing tool to gain even more customers. Customers today are increasingly aware of and interested in sustainability issues. Making sustainability information available can therefore provide a competitive advantage for nature-based companies.

Future research could study these nature-based companies further through observations and interviews, since the sustainability information that they present may differ from what actually happens in the everyday life of the business. This study has shown the relevance for nature-based businesses of providing different kind of sustainability information to different stakeholders, for example to compare investors or board members view of sustainability information they have as well as wish to receive. Another future study could be to compare nature-based businesses and companies in other industries of similar size.

References

Acs, Z. J., Boardman, M. C., and McNeely, C. L. (2013). The social value of productive entrepreneurship. Small Business Economics, 40(3), 785–796.

Amran, A., Ooi, S. K., Mydin, R. T., and Devi, S. (2018). Use of the web in corporate sustainability disclosure: Malaysian evidence. World Review of Entrepreneurship, Management and Sustainable Development, 14(5), 619–636.

Ara, H., Yeap, J. A. L., and Hassan, S. H. (2020). Does going green really pay off? A sustainability performance view. World Review of Entrepreneurship, Management and Sustainable Development, 16(5), 519–537.

Bogren, M., and Sörensson, A. (2021). Tourism companies' sustainability communication—creating legitimacy and value. Scandinavian Journal of Hospitality and Tourism, 21(5), 475–493.

Boruchowitch, F., and Fritz, M. M. (2022). Who in the firm can create sustainable value and for whom? A single case-study on sustainable procurement and supply chain stakeholders. Journal of Cleaner Production, 363, 132619. https://doi.org/10.1016/j.jclepro.2022.132619

Brundtland Commission. (1987). World commission on environment and development: Our common future. http://www.un-documents.net/wced-ocf.htm.

Buchholz, R. A., and Rosenthal, S. B. (2005). Toward a contemporary conceptual framework for stakeholder theory. Journal of Business Ethics, 58(1), 137–148.

Bucht, S.-E. (2017). Regeringen. http://www.regeringen.se/sveriges-regering/naringsdepartementet/sven-erik-bucht/2017.

Dilling, P. F. (2010). Sustainability reporting in a global context: What are the characteristics of corporations that provide high quality sustainability reports an empirical analysis. International Business and Economics Research Journal (IBER), 9(1).

Camilleri, M. A. (2017). Corporate sustainability and responsibility: Creating value for business, society and the environment. Asian Journal of Sustainability and Social Responsibility, 2(1), 59–74.

Castleberry, A., and Nolen, A. (2018). Thematic analysis of qualitative research data: Is it as easy as it sounds? Currents in pharmacy teaching and learning, 10(6), 807–815.

Dienes, D., Sassen, R., and Fischer, J. (2016). What are the drivers of sustainability reporting? A systematic review. Sustainability Accounting, Management and Policy Journal, 7(2), 154–189.

Dumay, J., Guthrie, J., and Farneti, F. (2010). GRI sustainability reporting guidelines for public and third sector organizations: A critical review. Public Management Review, 12(4), 531–548.

Evans, S., Vladimirova, D., Holgado, M., Van Fossen, K., Yang, M., Silva, E. A., and Barlow, C. Y. (2017). Business model innovation for sustainability: Towards a unified perspective for creation of sustainable business models. Business Strategy and the Environment, 26(5), 597–608.

Flammer, C. (2013). Corporate social responsibility and shareholder reaction: The environmental awareness of investors. Academy of Management Journal, 56(3), 758–781.

Freudenreich, B., Lüdeke-Freund, F., and Schaltegger, S. (2020). A stakeholder theory perspective on business models: Value creation for sustainability. Journal of Business Ethics, 166, 3–18.

Garvare, R., and Johansson, P. (2010). Management for sustainability—A stakeholder theory. Total Quality Management, 21(7), 737–744.

GRI. (2016). GRI. https://www.globalreporting.org/Pages/default.aspx.

Grönroos, C. (2011). Value co-creation in service logic: A critical analysis. Marketing Theory, 11(3), 279–301.

Grönroos, C. (2017). On value and value creation in service: A management perspective. Journal of Creating Value, 3(2), 125–141.https://doi.org/10.1177/2394964317727196

Hahn, R., and Kühnen, M. (2013). Determinants of sustainability reporting: A review of results, trends, theory, and opportunities in an expanding field of research. Journal of cleaner production, 59, 5–21.

Hasan, M. N. (2018). Sustainable and socially responsible business: Doable reality or just a luxury? An exploratory study of the Bangladeshi manufacturing SMEs. World Review of Entrepreneurship, Management and Sustainable Development, 14(4), 473–506.

Hoffman, A. J., and Ehrenfeld, J. R. (2015). The fourth wave: Business management and business education in the age of the Anthropocene. Corporate Stewardship: Organizing for Sustainable Effectiveness (pp. 228–246). Greenleaf Publishing.

Lozano, R., and Huisingh, D. (2011). Inter-linking issues and dimensions in sustainability reporting. Journal of Cleaner Production, 19(2–3), 99–107.

Mahoney, L. S., Thorne, L., Cecil, L., and LaGore, W. (2013). A research note on standalone corporate social responsibility reports: Signaling or greenwashing? Critical Perspectives on Accounting, 24(4–5), 350–359.

McWilliams, A., and Siegel, D. (2001). Profit maximizing corporate social responsibility. Academy of Management Review, 26(4), 504–505.

Pini, B. (2005). Farm women: Driving tractors and negotiating gender. The International Journal of Sociology of Agriculture and Food, 13(1), 1–18.

Porter, M. E., and Kramer, M. R. (2006). The link between competitive advantage and corporate social responsibility. Harvard business review, 84(12), 78–92.

Ramos-González, M., Rubio-Andrés, M., and Sastre-Castillo, M. Á. (2017). Building corporate reputation through sustainable entrepreneurship: The mediating effect of ethical behavior. Sustainability, 9(9), 1663.

Schaltegger, S., Lüdeke-Freund, F., and Hansen, E. G. (2011). Business cases for sustainability and the role of business model innovation: Developing a conceptual framework. Centre for Sustainability Management (CSM), Leuphana Universität Lüneburg.

Schaltegger, S., and Wagner, M. (2011). Sustainable entrepreneurship and sustainability innovation: Categories and interactions. Business strategy and the environment, 20(4), 222–237.

Schaltegger, S., Hansen, E. G., and Lüdeke-Freund, F. (2016). Business models for sustainability: Origins, present research, and future avenues. Organization and Environment, 29(1), 3–10.

Sharma, G., and Gupta, S. (2020). Modelling the impact of corporate sustainability on economic performance with reference to Indian financial industry. World Review of Entrepreneurship, Management and Sustainable Development, 16(3), 317–328.

Stubbs, W., and Cocklin, C. (2008). Conceptualizing a "sustainability business model". Organization and Environment, 21(2), 103–127.

Sweeney, L., and Coughlan, J. (2008). Do different industries report corporate social responsibility differently? An investigation through the lens of stakeholder theory. Journal of Marketing Communications, 14(2), 113–124.
Sörensson, A., and Dalborg, C. (2017). Female entrepreneurs in nature-based businesses: Working conditions, well-being, and everyday life situation. Society, Health and Vulnerability, 8(sup1), 1306905.
Sörensson, A., Dalborg, C., Grande, J., and Carlsson, E. (2018). Entreprenørskap i naturbaserte næringer–faktorer som fremmer og hemmer idéutvikling og sysselsetting. Søkelys på arbeidslivet, 35(03), 186–202.
Tillväxtverket. (2018). Växtkraft för de gröna näringarna. Rapport 0272. https://tillvaxtverket.se/download/18.4b0b6bb11677dcddd156bd3d/1544697114312/0272%20Va%CC%88xtkraft%20fo%CC%88r%20de%20gro%CC%88na%20na%CC%88ringarna2.pdf.
Ueda, K., Takenaka, T., Váncza, J., and Monostori, L. (2009). Value creation and decision-making in sustainable society. CIRP Annals, 58(2), 681–700.
Vargo, S. L., and Lusch, R. F. (2008). Service-dominant logic: Continuing the evolution, Journal of the Academy of Marketing Science, 36(1), 1–10.
Waligo, V. M., Clarke, J., and Hawkins, R. (2013). Implementing sustainable tourism: A multi-stakeholder involvement management framework. Tourism Management, 36, 342–353.

10

Sustainability Developments in Municipalities—What, Why, and How

Anna Sörensson, Anders Lundström, Ida Hallqvist, and Jesper Vestlund

10.1 Introduction

On 25 September 2015, UN member states agreed on new global goals for sustainable development. This came into effect on 1 January 2016 and replaced the previous Millennium Development Goals. These new global goals are called the Sustainable Development Goals (SDGs), and are the part of Agenda 2030 that intends to strive for a more socially, economically, and environmentally sustainable society in all countries of the world. Agenda 2030 is based on the UN's 17 global goals and 169 sub-goals which, based on each country's national conditions and capacity, must be met by the year 2030 (UN, 2015). In Sweden, the

A. Sörensson (✉) · A. Lundström · I. Hallqvist · J. Vestlund
Mid Sweden University, Östersund, Sweden
e-mail: anna.sorensson@miun.se

A. Sörensson
Inland Norway University of Applied Science, Rena, Norway

© The Author(s), under exclusive license to Springer Nature Switzerland AG 2024

A. Sörensson et al. (eds.), *Creating New Roles for a Sustainable Economy*, Palgrave Studies in Governance, Leadership and Responsibility,
https://doi.org/10.1007/978-3-031-61551-1_10

municipalities and regions are responsible for the local implementation of Agenda 2030 and its sub-goals.

Over the past half-century, companies have increasingly worked with social responsibility and sustainable development (Carroll & Shabana, 2010). This work is usually referred to as Corporate Social Responsibility, abbreviated CSR, and can be defined, among other things, as the company's work to contribute to sustainable economic development that works with employees, their families, the local community, and society at large to improve the quality for the inhabitants (Banerjee, 2008). According to Carroll (1991), organizations not only need to work to be on the right side of the law, but also take social, environmental, and ethical responsibility in their strategy implementation and operations in general. Carroll and Shabana (2010) state that companies that want to survive must work actively with actions that create a healthy climate to operate within. Working with CSR is therefore vital for companies, and those who do not prioritize it to a high enough degree risk being left behind and losing their relevance.

There are 290 municipalities in Sweden and the municipalities are responsible for a large part of community services at the local level (SKR, 2022a). In 2021, there were 877,000 employees in the municipalities which is about 17.8 percent of the 4.9 million employed in Sweden. In addition, the number of employees in Sweden's municipalities is increasing, in 2021 the number of employees increased by 1.2 percent (SKR, 2022b). The Swedish municipal organization consists of a political institution in the form of an elected municipal council, and the political work is administered by the municipal board, which consists of politicians. On the other hand, the municipality is managed financially and as an organization to a large extent by public servants, who are not allowed to be politically active. These officials carry out the daily work in the municipalities and their operations. Municipalities in Sweden are not only a political body, but also a public company (Kommunallag, 2017: 725).

Sweden's municipalities have a central role in the implementation of the global goals, as many of the basic tasks that the municipalities stand for are directly linked to the sub-goals in Agenda 2030 (SKR, 2022c). In order to develop the work with Agenda 2030 at the local level, the

Swedish UN Association and SKR started the project "Glokala Sweden" in 2018, which is a communication and education project with the aim of strengthening knowledge and commitment to Agenda 2030 among Sweden's municipalities and regions. This is done by following the work with Agenda 2030 at the national and global level to stimulate and engage the municipalities in their work with sustainable development and Agenda 2030 (Swedish UN Association, u.å.).

Municipalities play a major role in the sustainable development of society. In order for Agenda 2030 to become part of the municipality's strategies, it is required that it become an integrated part of the overall control and management system (SKR, 2022c). According to Dumay et al. (2010), municipalities also have a potential role as guides for sustainable development in society and it is clear that not only private businesses, but also public organizations work with an increasingly widespread and holistic view of responsibility in society. The public sector has become increasingly considerate in relation to environmental issues and the risk posed by environmental problems is now an essential part of the organizational process. Sweden's municipalities have a major impact on the local business climate, and their decisions affect actors operating within the municipality. Since sustainable development has become relevant in both public and private companies, this places particular importance on the municipalities in Sweden implementing sustainable development in its governance in a favorable way for all stakeholders (Alpenberg et al., 2018). According to Slack (2014), it is also important to include stakeholders and have a dialogue with them in the work with sustainable development. In addition to that, there is also an ambivalence in what the sustainability goals really are, who is responsible for them and how they should be implemented (Perry et al., 2021).

Municipalities are tax-financed institutions. This entails a responsibility to have good management of public resources (Kommunallag, 2017: 725). Municipalities thus have a legal duty to take responsibility for the public's tax contribution in the local community, but what has permeated this chapter is that municipalities also have an ethical and moral responsibility towards its stakeholders. Sustainability and sustainable development are taking an ever greater place in society, and with Agenda 2030 the municipalities now have a direct connection to this process. Since municipalities hold a central position as a local social actor, and its impact is so extensive on all stakeholders, it is therefore important to shed light on the municipalities' work in this regard. Furthermore, there is an enormous amount of research that points out that work with sustainability and towards sustainable development is central to all societies creating survival of the planet. It is therefore important to set demands on those who work with sustainable development, and through review and analysis of this also provide an opportunity for improvement.

The purpose is to examine the municipalities' work with Agenda 2030 in their strategic governance, what municipalities are working within sustainable development, why they are working in this particular way, and how they are doing to implement this. The purpose of this is to investigate whether Agenda 2030 has changed the work with sustainable development in municipal operations, whether it is considered sufficient and whether it fulfills the purposes it is intended to do. This study has the intention of contributing to an increased understanding of what drives municipalities in their work with sustainable development and thereby make a contribution to the improvement of future sustainable business development. How do municipalities operationalize and implement Agenda 2030 in the strategic work? Has Agenda 2030 changed the sustainability work in municipalities are two main issues in working with Agenda 2030 and its SDGs. The first part of this paper could therefore be seen as an attempt to connect the different SDGs with the situation in different local communities.

10.2 Sustainable Development

Sustainable development as a concept arose for the first time in the World Charter for Nature (UN, 1982) which the member states of the United Nations (UN) adopted. This report revealed the environmental problems the world was facing at the time, and these problems were addressed by the World Commission on Environment and Development (WCED). In the report our common future (WCED, 1987), informally called the Brundtland Report (Hák et al., 2016). According to Sneddon et al.

(2006), the Brundtland Report was a watershed in the thinking of development, the environment, and governance, as the Brundtland Report called for a recalibration of the activity of economic growth so that it does not endanger the well-being and survival of the planet. The report added a definition of what sustainable development means "Sustainable development is the development that meets the needs of the present without compromising the ability of future generations to meet their needs" (WCED, 1987).

The report shows three different perspectives of sustainable development, which are the social, environmental/ecological, and economic perspectives (WCED, 1987). Lozano (2008) gives examples of what the different perspectives mean in the Brundtland report, where the social aspects can be human rights, corruption, poverty, illiteracy, and child mortality. The environmental/ecological aspect means, for example, not to consume resources beyond their potential for regeneration, and not to generate air pollution beyond nature's capacity to break them down (ibid.). The definition of the economic aspect is influenced by the relationship to which the sustainability model is used as a starting point, where there are mainly two drastically different approaches to sustainable economic growth. The first definition perceives economic sustainability as; economic growth that does not negatively affect environmental/ecological and social sustainability (ibid.). The second definition concerns economic sustainability as economic growth and economic sustainability going hand in hand as long as the amount of capital always increases and suggests that economic growth does not need to take into account the consumption of other assets (such as natural resources and ecosystems) (ibid.). There are additional sustainability perspectives, which can be seen as a middle ground between these two extremes, and where the boundaries between these perspectives are not always explicit (ibid.).

The different sustainability perspectives and how they interact with each other can thus be interpreted differently depending on the viewer's values. One such interpretation is the Triple Bottom Line (TBL) framework first used by Elkington (1998). The framework aims to encourage and provide guidance to organizations to work with the social, environmental/ecological, and economic sustainability perspectives that were presented in the Brundtland Report.

According to Loviscek (2020), TBL is a framework for integrating sustainability goals into corporate strategy. No actor can work towards sustainable development alone, but a favorable and lasting cooperation with several parties is required to succeed (ibid.). The parties must take all three aspects into account in strategic planning, and these aspects must exist together in symbiosis, and not only through the traditional approach of prioritizing financial returns (ibid.). Elkington believes, according to Loviscek (2020), that it is of the outmost importance that organizations generate partnerships that provide aggregated solutions where everyone wins, in order to thus be able to solve the problems that the Brundtland report presents. That it may even be possible to generate solutions that win for everyone is something that goes against the traditional approach that compromises must be made to achieve sustainable development (ibid.).

25 years after the publication of the theory of TBL, Elkington (2018) added a number of reservations about the theory, as companies only report sustainability goals in terms of financial gains and losses without taking human health and the planet's climate into consideration. Furthermore, Elkington (2018) believes that the current paradigm is a failure and that TBL has lost its relevance as the capitalist system does not give enough space to the social and environmental aspects before the economic ones. However, Loviscek (2020) argues that TBL has not lost its relevance in sustainability work, but rather the opposite, as TBL and its calls have reached their zenith in the last five years. The need to work up collaborations, and to generate solutions where all parties win in all aspects of sustainability is something that the literature has recognized as important, despite Elkington's disappointment (ibid.) (Fig. 10.1).

Agenda 2030 works towards a sustainable society where all member countries of the UN strive to achieve 17 global sustainability goals and 169 sub-goals before the end of the year 2030 (Colglazier, 2015). The sustainability goals are related to the pillars of sustainable development and have the intention of realizing the human rights of all people and achieving equality between women and men and that women

Fig. 10.1 Agenda 2030 and its 17 SDGs

should have power over their own bodies (UN, 2015). The basic pillars are the economic, social, and ecological/environmental aspects (Lozano, 2008). The UN's 17 global sustainability goals are of great importance to humanity and the planet. Humans have the right to live in a healthy environment where dignity and equality are a matter of course for everyone. Through sustainable consumption and production, the planet can also be protected from destruction (UN, 2015). Agenda 2030 is an inclusive development agenda that is based on all stakeholders being included in decision-making. The inclusive aspect is important to ensure that the stakeholders will act jointly and uniformly in the commitments of Agenda 2030s goals (Dobrescu, 2017).

Implementation of Agenda 2030

Guarini et al. (2021) developed a five-step model for the implementation of Agenda 2030 at the regional level. The first step of the model is called the political version. For a successful implementation, the political version should either be based on Agenda 2030 or that the strategic management works in symbiosis with the sustainability goals. The second step is to identify which sustainability goals are relevant for the region. Authorities can adapt the sustainability goals and select only relevant goals based on which local issues are pursued and considered important. Guarini et al. (2021) also believe that the strategic management can create a planning structure for how the sustainability goals are to be achieved and develop a plan for how much financial resources should be allocated to achieve each goal. In the third step, management is recommended to carry out a SWOT analysis to identify opportunities for improvement and develop relevant key figures to analyze and compare performance (ibid.). The fourth step is to coordinate the strategies for the sustainability goals with priorities within the region. In this step, the key figures produced in the third step can also be used to assess the implementation of the sustainability goals to be implemented at the regional level. The fifth and final step in the model is to design a control system that will monitor the implementation of the sustainability goals (ibid.).

Municipalities have a central role in Agenda 2030's implementation at the local level (Slack, 2014). In order to work with the sustainability goals, it is beneficial to have a dialogue with citizens and other stakeholders. By having satisfactory sustainability work, it can provide comparative advantages vis-à-vis the outside world. In order for this to be feasible, municipalities must take local conditions into account when implementing Agenda 2030, otherwise there is a risk of an overly demanding and top-down push by the local government towards businesses and citizens, who must also be included for cooperation. Based on these assumptions, Perry et al. (2021) developed value propositions that officials, municipal politicians, and stakeholders in general should take into account when identifying and evaluating the global sustainability goals at the local level. The value propositions that Perry et al. (2021) concluded are:

- Real: Which sustainability goals can be implemented practically?
- Relevant: Which sustainability goals are important locally?
- Relatable: What sustainability goals can the public understand and engage with?
- Relational: What collaborations are necessary?

System-Oriented Theories

According to previous sections, sustainable development in an organizational context should not be worked on completely in isolation, but the organization should take into account the system within which they operate. Organizations already devote a large amount of work to ensure that the interaction with the system in which they operate works satisfactorily. The theories that deal with this phenomenon are called system-oriented theories, of which there are three, the stakeholder theory, the legitimacy theory, and the institutional theory (Unerman & Deegan, 2011). These theories are used in the study to answer why the municipalities do the way they do, and how this affects the exchange of information and cooperation within the society in which they exist.

Stakeholder Theory

The stakeholder theory shows how, with the help of stakeholders, you can create value added for everyone affected by the organization. The theory is based on highlighting and including actors who have an interest in the business, as well as how the actors influence and are influenced by the organization. An organization's stakeholders are actors who have ownership, rights, or interest in the organization, such as customers, employees, suppliers, society, and financiers. The stakeholder model looks different for all organizations depending on who the stakeholders are (Freeman et al., 2010).

According to Unerman and Deegan (2011), there are two different perspectives within the stakeholder model, one normative and one positive. The normative perspective, which is also referred to as the ethical/moral perspective, claims that all stakeholders must be treated fairly and equally by the organization. Unerman and Deegan (2011) believe that how the stakeholders are influenced by the organization, rather than how they influence, should be the most decisive for how the organization acts. Stakeholders have the right to access all information regarding the organization that affects and affects them. The positive perspective is about managers acting in the best interest of the organization. The relationships with the stakeholders are not equal or fair, some stakeholders will be considered more important than others based on what the organization wants to achieve and thus the organization specifically takes into account the interest of those actors (Unerman & Deegan, 2011).

Clarkson (1995) claims that stakeholders can be divided into primary and secondary stakeholders. Primary stakeholders are the actors that the organization cannot survive without, these stakeholders are usually identified as shareholders, investors, employees, customers, and suppliers. If a primary stakeholder withdraws from the organization's operations, it will create consequences for the organization that may be so serious that the entire operation may cease. Secondary stakeholders, on the other hand, are not necessary for the organization's survival, these actors are those who influence or are influenced by the organization but are not involved in the business (Clarkson, 1995).

Legitimacy

Legitimacy theory claims that organizations conduct their activities based on the constantly changing norms and values that exist in the societies in which the organizations are located (O'Donovan, 2002). This is because these organizations constantly strive to conduct a business that is considered legitimate by outside parties (ibid.). According to O'Donovan (2002), legitimacy is something that is treated as a resource within legitimacy theory. The company is also seen to have control over this resource, through manipulation of the corporate strategy. However, the company also has a need for this resource and will seek this resource to the extent of the need that exists within the business (Woodward et al., 1996). The legitimacy theory is also based on the social contract between the organization and other parties in society, which means that in addition to strict financial profits, the organization also has a moral obligation to behave responsibly towards society (O'Donovan, 2002). This is for the reason that if the organization does not conform to the norms and values society expects of them, then they also lose their raison d'être (Deegan, 2002).

Dowling and Pfeffer (1975) define when an organization is perceived as legitimate as: "A corporation is legitimate when it is judged to be 'just and worthy of support'". Suchman (1995) suggests that an organization can maintain its legitimacy through two different types of strategies, which are; predict future changes or protect past performance. Furthermore, Suchman (1995) describes that there are also two approaches to legitimacy in legitimacy theory, the strategic and the institutional approach. The strategic approach describes legitimacy as O'Donovan (2002) does, that it is a resource like any other and that must be managed. The institutional approach instead sees legitimacy not as a conventional resource, but as a set of constitutional and fundamental beliefs (Suchman, 1995).

CSR

Corporate social responsibility (CSR) refers to organizations taking social responsibility, from an economic, legal, ethical, and philanthropic aspect. These four aspects are what form Carroll's CSR pyramid (Carroll, 1991). The financial responsibility is about being cost-effective and offering goods and services to society at a favorable price. It also includes maintaining a strong position among competitors, being consistently profitable, and maintaining high operating efficiency (ibid.). However, organizations cannot only act based on a profit-maximizing purpose, there is also a legal responsibility which means that organizations must follow laws and regulations that have been issued. Organizations have a responsibility towards society to act according to the law. Carroll (1991) emphasizes the importance of organizations being legally compliant, that they fulfill the legal obligations that exist and that goods and services meet the existing legal requirements. The ethical responsibility aims to act according to society's customs and norms beyond the scope of law. Acting in accordance with what is considered moral, as well as with respect for society is an important aspect of ethical responsibility. The last part of Carroll's (1991) CSR pyramid is the philanthropic responsibility which is concerned with social justice and promoting the rights of citizens. Other important parts are harmonizing with society's expectations and being happy to support projects that contribute to a better society (ibid.).

Carroll and Schwartz (2003) believe that the pyramid-shaped model can be perceived as misleading and can be interpreted as a hierarchical order of the four different responsibilities and that the top of the pyramid is the most essential, which is incorrect. Carroll and Schwartz (2003) further claim that financial and legal responsibility are most fundamental, while philanthropic is considered to be less important and that some of them are considered to be an unnecessary category. Carroll also suggests that the philanthropic responsibility may be wrong and has subsequently illustrated a new CSR model called the "three-domain model for CSR" (ibid.). The three-domain model harmonizes with the definition of the responsibilities of the CSR pyramid with the exception that the philanthropic responsibility is not a separate category but is included in the ethical as well as the financial area. The three-domain model is illustrated in a Venn diagram to avoid the areas being perceived as ranked of different importance. The new model's illustration also shows that the responsibilities work in symbiosis, which is a message that the pyramid did not convey.

Grankvist (2012), on the other hand, claims that CSR is fundamentally about economic, environmental, and social responsibility towards society and that these are characterized by an area of ethical responsibility. The financial responsibility is characterized by making as much money as possible from the business that is conducted, which leads to taking responsibility towards the shareholders and securing the company's financial position. Environmental responsibility is largely about ensuring that the business that is carried out should not have a negative impact on the environment. The social includes conducting the business with regard to the health and well-being of stakeholders and society. Grankvist (2012) also believes that these three areas of responsibility must work in symbiosis for the business to achieve long-term sustainability, if any component is excluded an imbalance occurs.

10.3 Methodology

The research strategy underlying this paper is a case study. The study is based on an observation object with the intention of creating an in-depth and detailed understanding of the research area. Based on this intention, a case study was considered best intended because it aims to go in depth and produce detailed information of a specific situation (Bryman & Bell, 2017). By conducting interviews with the subjects of observation, this in-depth understanding that was requested could be achieved. The interview guide that was used was also semi-structured, which left space for the subjects of observation to express their answers freely and also to appropriate their own reasoning and ideas (Merriam, 1994). Bryman and Bell (2017) also believe that understanding increases by conducting semi-structured interviews.

The empirical material has been collected through semi-structured interviews with primary sources via the communication platform Microsoft Teams and by telephone. The interviews take their form based on the interview guide, which in turn is designed based on the theoretical frame of reference. As mentioned in previous sections, semi-structured interviews were considered relevant to the purpose of the study because it gave the subjects of observation space for discussions, to develop reasoning, and to generate new ideas (Merriam, 1994). Before the interviews, an interview guide was created as a starting point, but since the interviews were semi-structured, the order of the questions could be varied if desired. The fact that interviews were chosen as the data collection method can be justified by the desire to create a deeper understanding of the research area. The interviews were transcribed via Microsoft Teams' own tools as well as via Microsoft Word's transcription tool, that both tools were used to ensure that the interviews were indeed transcribed and that the answers given were reported correctly. This was also done to be able to compare the quality of the transcriptions. The interviews were also recorded with the mobile phone as a backup. Afterward, the transcriptions were proofread and compared with the audio files, both those recorded automatically via the transcription tools and from the mobile phone, as an additional element of quality. On the other hand, the interview with Åre municipality was conducted via telephone, we were also connected on Teams at the same time as the interview was conducted and recorded and transcribed the conversation with the respondent via Teams. Bryman and Bell (2017) point out that a more in-depth analysis can be carried out by transcribing the interviews.

The study investigates how municipalities work with Agenda 2030 in the strategic management, a target-driven sample was best suited for the study. Purposive sampling is a form of non-probability sampling and means that the observation objects were strategically selected with the aim of being most relevant to answering the research questions (Bryman & Bell, 2017). By being able to control the selection group, we were able to select the municipalities ourselves. The respondents at the municipalities were chosen based on who had the most knowledge and competence of Agenda 2030, this in order to achieve as relevant and competent answers as possible to the research questions that were asked. The consequences of using a non-probability sample is that the results of this study cannot be generalized to a population (Bryman & Bell, 2017). This study targets municipalities in Jämtland county in central Sweden, the selected municipalities are Berg, Åre, and Östersund.

The Cases

Bergs municipality is geographically located in the southern part of Jämtland county, and has a population of approximately 7150 people, on an area of 5753 km^2. The central town is Svenstavik (Berg municipality, 2022a). The political government since the municipal elections in 2022 consists of the Social Democrats and the Center Party (Berg municipality, 2022b).

Åre municipality is located in western Jämtland County, where 12,206 inhabitants live on an area of 8263 km^2. Järpen is the central town in the municipality (Åre municipality, 2022a). The municipality employed approximople i???n 2019 (Åre municipality, 2019). In connection with the municipal elections in autumn 2022, the Social Democrats, Västjämtlands Väl, and Vänsterpartiet rule (Åre municipality, 2022b).

Östersund municipality is located in the middle of Jämtland county, with a population of 64,566 people on an area of 2517 km2. The municipality also houses the residence city of Östersund, which is also the central location. The municipality's number of employees is approximately 5600 people (Östersund municipality, 2022a). The political government consists of the political parties Social Democrats and the Center Party since the municipal elections in autumn 2022 (Östersund municipality, 2022b).

Municipalities in Sweden and SDGs

In the below table one can see minor differences above all for the span of living concerning the number of years for women and also for men. The differences between gender are 3.7 years for most of the communities. The conclusion will be that there are small differences for this SDG´s making it less interesting to use in the future. The same conclusion can be said for young people below the age of 19 years old in the regions and local communities except for the region of Stockholm. The values for Östersund and Åre are lower. Concerning values for broadband there are high values for the Region of Stockohlm as well as the communities of Östersund and Sundsvall. Low values are for the communities of Berg as well as Åre. Concerning post after school system. We observe very high figures for the Stockholm community as well as the regions of Stockholm and also for Östersund and Sundsvall (Table 10.1).

Secondly, we have been comparing the communities in two regions in Sweden, i.e., the regions of Västernorrland and Jämtland/Härjedalen. In these two regions there are in total 15 local communities of different sizes and levels of the SDGn used in this report. See Table 10.2. In this table we have used a ranking procedure. The first eight communities belonging to the region of Jämtland/Härjedalen and the remaining 7 communities representing the region of Västernorrland.

Note that in the table above we use five different SDGn. Furthermore, the different SDG values are not independent of each other. If we however compare the total ranking values with the ranking values for the number of citizens we can see that the communities of Åre, Berg, Härjedalen, and Krokom have better total rankings than expected while Kramfors, Sollefteå, Timrå, and Sundsvall have lower total ranking

Table 10.1 SDGs—values for some regions and local communities

	Poverty (%)	Span of living women	Span of living men	Education (%)	Born out (%)	Broadband (%)
Region Stockholm	12.6	85.2	81.5	54.9	27.1	96.0
Region Jämtland/ Berg	6. 4	84.1	80.6	40. 6	10. 5	82.8
Region Väster- norrland	7.3	83.6	80.0	39.0	11.5	84.2
Stockholm	6.3	85.2	81.3	62.2	Na	99.3
Östersund	5.6	84.4	80.7	47.2	Na	94.4
Berg	7.8	83.9	80.1	29.9	Na	74.9
Åre	5.1	86.0	82.3	44.7	Na	79.5
Sundsvall	6.5	83.9	80.5	43.5	Na	90.6
Timrå	6.4	82.7	78.9	32.5	Na	86.6

Table 10.2 Different rankings for different SDGs in the regions of Västernorrland and Jämtland/Härjedalen

Community	Poverty ranking	Expectancy women ranking	Expectancy men ranking	Post secondary educa- tion ranking	Gainfully employed ranking	Ranking sum
Berg	4	10	11	6	2	33
Bräcke	12	10	11	7	12	52
Härjedalen	1	2	6	7	4	20
Krokom	2	7	2	10	1	22
Ragunda	6	4	13	15	8	46
Strömsund	14	13	10	13	10	60
Åre	2	1	1	3	3	10
Östersund	7	2	3	1	5	18
Härnösand	5	8	9	5	14	41
Kramfors	15	15	14	9	15	68
Sollefteå	8	13	15	2	13	51
Timrå	9	12	13	14	7	55
Sundsvall	13	4	6	4	8	35
Ånge	5	9	14	11	11	50
Örnsköldsvik	9	4	8	12	6	39
Interval						

than expected. How the municipalities implement Agenda 2030 in the strategic management is different. Berg municipality has an unstructured process that takes place in consultation with stakeholders. Åre municipality used backcasting before, but currently the strategy is somewhat unclear and Östersund municipality works from a horizontal perspective. The conclusion is that each municipality must work with sustainable development and Agenda 2030 based on their respective conditions. The network Glokala Sverige has a significant role for the municipalities, and the municipalities' cooperation partners are an important part of the sustainability work. Agenda 2030 seems to have changed the work with sustainability in municipalities fundamentally. According to Parris and Kates (2003), the interpretation of the concept of sustainable development is broad and unspecific, as many advocates of the concept have different emphases on what should be sustainable. Furthermore, sustainability and sustainable development are used interchangeably, as sustainability is sometimes used as a synonym for sustainable development (Meadowcroft, 2022). Despite the ambiguity of sustainable development, a large amount of research has been done concerning the concept due to its relevance (Parris & Kates, 2003).

The Three Municipalities

Brundtland's definition (WCED, 1987) of sustainable development has shaped how all three municipalities choose to define sustainable development. On the other hand, the relationship to the definition varies strongly from municipality to municipality. In the municipality of Berg, they choose to use Brundtland's definition as the basis for their own definition but have then chosen to add a quality of life aspect, as it is important to them. Åre municipality also stated that Brundtland's definition of sustainable development is in good agreement with how they view sustainable development. Although Östersund municipality also considers that Brundtland's definition is dominant in their organizations, it can be perceived as having a slightly looser connection to it based on the respondents' answers, as they also choose to define it loosely depending on which geographic, demographic, and economic challenges you face, and that based on these challenges you yourself can decide how you choose to define sustainable development.

All municipalities are working on some form of sustainability projects. The two relatively smaller municipalities have relatively small projects which are also newly started or which have not even been started yet, while the relatively larger Östersund municipality has a variety of projects, which have also been ongoing for two decades. Berg municipality has projects that focus on local development in the municipality's towns, they run a biogas company and also a recycling project. Åre municipality is waiting for their application to run a project on urban development to be approved. The municipality of Östersund runs a project in electric aviation and autonomous aircraft, a project that deals with energy consulting for business and the region, and more.

When it comes to the municipalities' partners, it is clear that none of the surveyed municipalities work alone and in isolation with their sustainability work, and there does not seem to be any clear difference between the municipalities. All municipalities are members of the Glokala Sweden network, which offers training and advice in the field of sustainable development. The municipality of Berg also works a lot together with the region and the county board on sustainability issues, and also has a company together with the municipality of Härjedalen. Östersund municipality also works a lot with the region and the municipality. On the other hand, Åre did not mention any specific cooperation partners apart from Glokala Sweden. That these municipalities value collaboration in their sustainability work is clearly visible. Even though the municipalities work differently with sustainability right now and are in different phases in the implementation of sustainability in their strategies, they undeniably see the importance of generating solutions together with other parties. This is something that Elkington (1998) considered important in sustainability work.

The municipality of Berg and Östersund works overall with all 17 sustainability goals, while the municipality of Åre could not say concretely which goals they are working on because the work is relatively new for the municipality. However, it is possible to see tendencies towards prioritizing certain sub-goals over others, as all municipalities point out that some of the sub-goals are part of the municipality's basic mission to fulfill, for example Goal 4: Good education and Goal 6: Clean water. The difference between the municipalities here, however, is that Åre municipality did not have a clear answer to this, as the municipality is at an early stage in the implementation of the milestones in their sustainability work. This is in contrast to the municipality of Berg and Östersund, which could explicitly admit that all sub-goals affected their strategy implementation to some extent, but that certain sustainability goals are self-evident to work with as a municipality.

The municipalities' opinion on the adequacy of Agenda 2030 is, on the whole, very consistent, even if there are minor differences of opinion between the respondents, on the other hand, Östersund municipality did not have a really developed answer to this. Berg municipality believes that there is a lack of trust in the sustainability goals, as metrics and indicators are not sufficient when it comes to how people feel, and their experience of being involved. Berg municipality also thinks that Agenda 2030 is too international and that many of the sustainability goals are already self-evident in Sweden. But on the whole, they think Agenda 2030 is a good and holistic framework for sustainability work. The municipality of Östersund believes that Agenda 2030 is comprehensive and indivisible as a construction. Åre municipality thinks Agenda 2030 is a brilliant idea as a model and construction, as it has succeeded in concentrating the three dimensions of sustainability in 17 different areas.

Stakeholders, Legitimacy, and CSR

Based on the respondents' answers to which stakeholders are relevant to the municipality, there was a clear and consistent pattern that there were four main stakeholders that they could identify. Citizens, however, seem to be the main stakeholder according to the respondents, even though all municipalities have expressed the central role of the other three stakeholders in the municipality's operations. It can be interpreted that all stakeholders can be classified as primary stakeholders based on the respondents' answers. The citizens bring tax funds that the municipality cannot survive without. Business adds workplaces, tax funds, and business opportunities via public procurement. The authorities provide project funds and development support. State and region provide advice and capital. Together with this, it can also be interpreted as the respondents looking at the stakeholders from a mainly normative perspective, as all municipalities work with citizen and business dialogue for transparency and participation. The municipalities also work actively to promote society in the first place and not the organization alone, which also indicates a normative perspective (Unerman & Deegan, 2011).

The respondents demonstrated consensus on which stakeholders are affected by the municipality's sustainability work. The municipalities also unanimously considered that all stakeholders are affected. The municipality of Berg is concerned that it could potentially interfere with the municipality's business life if the sustainability work is too strict and the requirements too harsh. However, they still see the need to be able to make demands on companies through sustainability requirements in public procurement. Åre municipality has already dealt with this problem when developers in the municipality have shown their dissatisfaction because the municipality's sustainability work has worked against them and caused financial strain. Östersund municipality finds it difficult to answer how the stakeholders are affected and whether it is positive or negative as it depends on the perspective from which you look at it.

Legitimacy

None of the municipalities consider that their work with Agenda 2030 and sustainable development is sufficient and they think that more resources must be put into the work. It is important to know how additional resources can be used. The municipality of Berg believes that due to a reduction in residents in the municipality, and not a sufficiently high focus on environmental sustainability, there is still a lack of sustainable work that can be perceived as sufficient by the public. They need to work more on expanding agriculture and housing with the county board's consent, as well as having the public's consent to major changes. Åre Municipality believes that the whole country is backing down in relation to important issues within sustainability issues. The municipality of Östersund believes that they are doing enough in relation to the resources they have, even though there is potential for improvement, as a constant development of the work is required in order not to take revenge on other municipalities. It is possible to interpret the municipalities' stance on whether their sustainability work is sufficient or not by looking at the discussion climate that exists today. It would most likely be unwise to claim that the ongoing sustainability work is sufficient at some point, as there is ever-increasing pressure on institutions and companies to broaden their sustainability work. Going against public norms and values would, according to Deegan (2002), destroy the legitimacy of the municipality, which in turn would put the survival of both the ruling political mandate and its officials in question.

Berg's municipality can be perceived as working with sustainability in the institutional approach to maintaining the organization's legitimacy, as they work a lot to take society's various conditions and citizens' opinions into account in their sustainability work. The same can be said about Åre municipality's sustainability work, as their sustainability work has been influenced by citizen proposals, as well as citizen dialogues that have put pressure on the municipality to work more explicitly with sustainability issues, and come up with new solutions. On the other hand, the municipality of Östersund can instead be perceived as working with sustainability as a resource to create competitive advantages, as they mention that Agenda 2030 is a bit like brand building for them. This is in line with the strategic approach to maintaining the organization's legitimacy according to Suchman (1995).

CSR

The CSR pyramid that Carroll (1991) created was intended to make organizations and companies understand that there is a social responsibility that should be taken into account. When the question of social responsibility was raised during the interviews, all respondents answered that social responsibility is part of the municipalities' basic mission. Bergs municipality believes that as a municipality you must work in a sustainable way that lasts over time and that social responsibility is always taken into account in the work that the municipality does. Grankvist (2012) and Carroll and Schwartz (2003) highlight that the three areas of responsibility within social responsibility must work together for the business to achieve long-term sustainability. One of the respondent points out that in the municipality's work with growth programs, economic, social, and environmental social responsibility has been an important part of the development. Furthermore, the municipality of Berg believes that in order to achieve a sustainable society, the actors in the municipality must also take their social responsibility. The municipality of Åre and Östersund believes that it is difficult to apply the CSR model to municipal operations because the municipalities' work is based on social responsibility and promoting a better society for everyone. Åre municipality believes that the sustainability work has taken over the work with social responsibility, but that social responsibility is still an important part of the municipality's sustainability work. Respondent 2 from Östersund municipality believes that Agenda 2030 and social responsibility fulfill the same function.

Implementation of Agenda 2030

According to Guarini et al. (2021) five-step model, municipalities should work circularly with the implementation of Agenda 2030 and its sustainability goals. The political vision should go hand in hand with the sustainability work, alternatively the strategic management should work in symbiosis with the sustainability goals. Then the sustainability goals that are relevant should be identified. After that, they should conduct a SWOT analysis, then coordinate the strategies for the sustainability goals with priorities within the region. Finally, they should design a control system that will monitor the implementation of the sustainability goals. Based on the respondents' answers, the real process does not seem to be structured, and the different cases also seem to work somewhat differently with the implementation and operationalization of Agenda 2030. The municipality of Berg believes that their strategic implementation is an unstructured process that takes place in consultation with the stakeholders, and the respondents believe that it is what works best for the municipality based on the conditions. Åre municipality has previously used backcasting to work with sustainability. This is something the municipality has not continued with, however, due to staff shortages. The municipality of Östersund is very hesitant to create an implementation model based on Agenda 2030, instead they have a horizontal perspective based on Agenda 2030 that permeates all work within the municipality. The municipality of Östersund also thought that one should not work on rigidly structured models of sustainability work, as it must constantly change in step with varying conditions.

According to Perry et al. (2021), municipalities should locate the sustainability goals that they should work on by starting from four different value propositions in the municipality. These are: Which sustainability goals can be implemented practically? Which sustainability goals are important locally? What sustainability goals can the public understand and engage with? Which collaborations are necessary? It can be interpreted that the municipality of Bergs and Östersund seems to have taken these value propositions into account in decisions about the relevance of the sustainability goals for their operations. On the other hand, it cannot be seen that it has opted out of certain sustainability goals over others, and that there has been some kind of exclusion process, as both two of these municipalities have chosen to work with all 17 sustainability goals in some form. Instead, it is rather possible to see a tendency towards a prioritization and ranking of all sustainability goals in these two municipalities. Åre municipality currently has no implemented process for working with the sustainability goals, and thus does not seem to have made an assessment of them that the respondent could comment on.

Agenda 2030 seems to have had a big impact on the relatively smaller municipalities of Berg and Åre, but not as big an impact on a relatively larger municipality like Östersund. The municipality of Bergs and Åre points out that their work with sustainability and sustainable development has been non-existent to minimal before Agenda 2030 was presented, and only then has their work taken off in earnest. In Östersund, there was existing work with sustainability and sustainable development already before 2015, and its impact does not seem to have been as great as in Bergs and Åre municipalities.

10.4 Conclusions

The purpose of this study has been to investigate what, why, and how municipalities work with sustainable development and Agenda 2030. We also wanted to investigate whether Agenda 2030 has changed sustainability work in municipalities, and whether the global sustainability goals are considered sufficient for the purpose they are intended to fulfill, according to those who actually work on this. With this, we wanted to contribute to an increased understanding of what drives municipalities in their work with sustainable development and make a contribution to improve sustainable development as a business process.

At the outset, we would like to point out that Gro Harlem Brundtland's definition of sustainable development seems to have remained relevant after more than a quarter of a century since its inception, as it is the backbone of the sustainability work of all the municipalities examined. All municipalities carry out some form of work with sustainability, but with varying breadth and number depending on population size. Berg, on the other hand, stands out in this aspect, as their sustainability work seems to have progressed much further than in Åre, even though they are of comparable size. What this is due to is not fully clarified, and may well be worth further research, however, the respondent in Åre mentioned that their environmental strategist had to leave his post a few years ago, and after this their work with sustainable development has slowed down in speed. This should reasonably have an explanation for why Åre has fallen behind in its sustainability work compared to the other research objects, as it is a relatively small municipality, with limited resources, and where expertise may not always be readily available. The Glokala Sweden network seems to have played a significant role in the sustainability work of the surveyed municipalities, as they were mentioned by all respondents when asked who their collaboration partners are when it comes to their sustainability work. There is also evidence that Åre seems to be behind in the implementation of sustainable development, as the municipality of Berg and Östersund had many examples of cooperation partners, but also when it comes to which sustainability goals the municipalities are working with. All respondents seem to agree that Agenda 2030 is broadly sufficient, even if there are things that could have been better or added. This should be seen as a success for the UN, as its sustainability goals are seen in such an exemplary way by its implementers.

All municipalities seem to work with mainly four stakeholders, all of whom seem to have a huge impact on municipal operations and their sustainability work. This should reasonably be able to explain why the municipalities carry out such close-knit sustainability work with all stakeholders, and that the stakeholders' opinions are taken into account with great consideration. The municipalities' sustainability work should reasonably have a legitimacy-creating purpose, as the conversational climate that exists in today's society means that its absence from one's municipality's operations would put the political mandate in question. This should be an explanation for why none of the surveyed municipalities lacks sustainability work. On the other hand, judging from the results, it differs in how Berg and Åre municipality works to achieve legitimacy from how Östersund municipality works in our opinion, as Berg and Åre municipality works with wanting to contribute social benefit to achieve legitimacy, while Östersund municipality seems to want to build a brand to achieve legitimacy. The municipalities seem to take their social responsibility for granted, as their basic mission requires them to work with it. Therefore, we can think that it is difficult to apply CSR to municipalities, even if the aspect of social responsibility is central to them in the sustainability work.

None of the municipalities use any specific model when implementing Agenda 2030 in the municipality's operations. There is a lack of evidence in the results to draw a conclusion about any kind of structured model that was used in the sustainability work in the investigated municipalities. Rather, they seem to work in a more open and circular process, rather than in a linear and punctual approach. Therefore, we believe that Guarini et al. (2021) five-step model is not used in practice by the investigated research objects. In contrast, they seem to have worked on identifying and locating the global sustainability goals similar to Perry et al. (2021) value propositions, but we believe that they rather use these value propositions to rank and prioritize the sustainability goals, rather than strictly exclude them.

Finally, we would like to state that the sustainability work in the surveyed municipalities seems to have completely changed in connection with Agenda 2030's adoption by the UN member states. Although fixed size seems to have played a role in its importance, all the municipalities examined have felt compelled to relate to it in their work with sustainability. We believe that it gave the investigated municipalities an incentive to work on the most important issue of our time, and that those who had no direct connection and relation to sustainable development actually took hold of it.

Since the work on Agenda 2030 is only halfway through its intended lifespan, and that it is still a relatively unexplored area, we have a number of interesting suggestions for continued research:

- A qualitative study on the work with Agenda 2030's evolution during its lifetime after the year 2030.
- A quantitative study on key figures in the Kolada database, and its impact on the municipalities' work with Agenda 2030.
- A qualitative study on the business community's relationship to the municipalities' work with Agenda 2030.
- A qualitative follow-up study on how the municipalities finally managed to implement the sustainability goals in Agenda 2030, and whether it produced the desired

A ranking study of the results of different SDGs and e.g., relationships with the total number of inhabitants in the community. In this study we can observe SDGs dependency as well as no such relationships. Such relationships could be tested for the investment in broadbands or the number of educated inhabitants.

A study of the level of entrepreneurship in a community related to different SDGs as well as the awareness in the business sector of the different SDGs.

References

Alpenberg, J., Wnuk-Pel, T., & Henebäck, A. (2018). Environmental orientation in Swedish local governments. *Sustainability, 10*(2), 459.

Banerjee, S. B. (2008). Corporate social responsibility: The good, the bad and the ugly. *Critical Sociology, 34*(1), 51–79.

Bryman, A., & Bell, E. (2017). *Företagsekonomiska forskningsmetoder* (Uppl. 3). Stockholm: Liber.

Carroll, A. B. (1991). The pyramid of corporate social responsibility: Toward the moral management of organizational stakeholders. *Business Horizons, 34*(4), 39–48.

Carroll, A. B., & Shabana, K. M. (2010). The business case for corporate social responsibility: A review of concepts, research and practice. *International Journal of Management Reviews, 12*(1), 85–105.

Carroll, A. B., & Schwartz, M. S. (2003). Corporate social responsibility: A three-domain approach. In *Business Ethics and Strategy* (pp. 55–82). Routledge.

Clarkson, M. E. (1995). A stakeholder framework for analyzing and evaluating corporate social performance. *Academy of Management Review, 20*(1), 92–117.

Colglazier, W. (2015). Sustainable development agenda: 2030. *Science, 349*(6252), 1048–1050.

Deegan, C. (2002). Introduction: The legitimising effect of social and environmental disclosures—A theoretical foundation. *Accounting, Auditing & Accountability Journal*.

Dobrescu, E. M. (2017). Agenda 2030. New perspectives. *Journal of Defense Resources Management* (JoDRM), *8*(1), 165–180.

Dowling, J., & Pfeffer, J. (1975). Organizational legitimacy: Social values and organizational behavior. *Pacific Sociological Review, 18*(1), 122–136.

Dumay, J., Guthrie, J., & Farneti, F. (2010). GRI sustainability reporting guidelines for public and third sector organizations: A critical review. *Public Management Review, 12*(4), 531–548.

Elkington, J. (2018). 25 years ago I coined the phrase "triple bottom line." Here's why it's time to rethink it. *Harvard Business Review, 25*, 2–5.

Freeman, R. E., Harrison, J. S., Wicks, A. C., Parmar, B. L., & De Colle, S. (2010). *Stakeholder theory: The state of the art* (pp. 9, 24–25). Cambridge: University Press.

Grankvist, P. (2012). *CSR i praktiken: Hur företaget kan jobba med hållbarhet för att tjäna pengar* (Uppl. 2:1). Malmö: Liber.

Guarini, E., Mori, E., & Zuffada, E. (2021). New development: Embedding the SDGs in city strategic planning and management. *Public Money & Management, 41*(6), 494–497.

Hák, T., Janoušková, S., & Moldan, B. (2016). Sustainable development goals: A need for relevant indicators. *Ecological Indicators, 60*, 565–573.

Kommunallag. (2017). Sveriges riksdag. https://www.riksdagen.se.

Loviscek, V. (2020). Triple bottom line toward a holistic framework for sustainability: A systematic review. *Revista de Administração Contemporânea*, 25.

Lozano, R. (2008). Envisioning sustainability three-dimensionally. *Journal of Cleaner Production, 16*(17), 1838–1846.

Merriam, B. S. (1994). *Fallstudien som forskningsmetod*. Lund: Studentlitteratur.

O'Donovan, G. (2002). Environmental disclosures in the annual report: Extending the applicability and predictive power of legitimacy theory. *Accounting, Auditing & Accountability Journal, 15*(3), 344–371.

Parris, T. M., & Kates, R. W. (2003). Characterizing and measuring sustainable development. *Annual Review of Environment and Resources, 28*(1), 559–586.

Perry, B., Diprose, K., Taylor Buck, N., & Simon, D. (2021). Localizing the SDGs in England: Challenges and value propositions for local government. *Frontiers in Sustainable Cities*, 3.

Slack, L. (2014). The post-2015 global agenda-a role for local government. *Commonwealth Journal of Local Governance, 15*, 173–177.

Sneddon, C., Howarth, R. B., & Norgaard, R. B. (2006). Sustainable development in a post-Brundtland world. *Ecological Economics, 57*(2), 253–268.

Suchman, M. C. (1995). Managing legitimacy: Strategic and institutional approaches. *Academy of Management Review, 20*(3), 571–610.

Unerman, J., & Deegan, C. (2011). *Financial accounting theory*. Maidenhead: McGraw-Hill.

Woodward, D. G., Edwards, P., & Birkin, F. (1996). Organizational legitimacy and stakeholder information provision 1. *British Journal of Management, 7*(4), 329–347.

Övriga dokument

Elkington, J. (1998). Accounting for the triple bottom line. *Measuring Business Excellence.*

Förenta nationerna (FN). (1982). *World charter for nature.* A/RES/37/7 28:e oktober 1982. New York: United Nations.
Förenta nationerna (FN). (2015). *Resolution adopted by the General Assembly on 11 September 2015.* A/RES/70/1 25:e september 2015. New York: United Nations.
The World Commission on Environment and Development (WCED). (1987). *Our common future.* Oxford: Oxford University Press.

Elektroniska källor

Meadowcroft, J. (2022–09–07). *Sustainability. Encyclopedia Britannica.* https://www.britannica.com/science/sustainability Hämtad 2022–11–24.
Bergs kommun. (2022–09–30a). *Kommunfakta.* https://www.berg.se/48/kommun-och-politik/verksamhet-och-organisation/kommunfakta. Hämtad 2022–12–13.
Bergs kommun. (2022–11–18b). *Politisk organisation, möten och protokoll.* https://www.berg.se/48/kommun-och-politik/politisk-organisation-moten-och-protokoll. Hämtad 2022–12–15.
Bergs kommun. (2022–12–01c). *Utvecklingsarbete.* https://www.berg.se/48/kommun-och-politik/verksamhet-och-organisation/utvecklingsarbete. Hämtad 2022–12–15.
Regeringen. (2015–12–01). *Sveriges arbete med Agenda 2030.* https://www.regeringen.se/regeringens-politik/globala-malen-och-agenda-2030/globala-mal-for-hallbar-utveckling/. Hämtad 2022–11–25.
Sveriges kommuner och regioner (SKR). (2022–10–27a). *Fakta om kommuner och regioner.* https://skr.se/skr/tjanster/kommunerochregioner/faktakommunerochregioner.1022.html. Hämtad 2022–11–28.
Sveriges kommuner och regioner (SKR). (2022–04–07b). *Personalen i välfärden 2021.* https://skr.se/skr/tjanster/rapporterochskrifter/publikationer/personalenivalfarden2021.65353.html. Hämtad 2022–12–05.
Sveriges kommuner och regioner (SKR). (2022–10–31c). *Agenda 2030—för hållbar utveckling.* https://skr.se/skr/omskr/agenda2030.19225.html. Hämtad 2022–12–05.
Svenska FN-förbundet. (u.å.). *DET HÄR ÄR GLOKALA SVERIGE.* https://fn.se/glokalasverige/om-glokala-sverige/. Hämtad 2022–12–05.
UN. (2023). https://www.un.org/development/desa/dspd/wp-content/uploads/sites/22/2018/08/E_2018_SDG_Poster_with_UN_emblem.png. Accessed 2023–05–28.

Åre kommun. (2019–08–13). *Din kommun*. https://are.se/kommunpolitik/din kommun. Hämtad 2022–12–15.
Åre kommun. (2020–09–07a). *Hållbar utveckling*. https://are.se/miljotrafik/hal lbar-utveckling. Hämtad 2022–12–15.
Åre kommun. (2020–12–07b). *Folkhälsa*. https://are.se/miljotrafik/hallbar-utv eckling/folkhaelsa. Hämtad 2022–12–15.
Åre kommun. (2022–10–14a). *Befolkningsstatistik*. https://are.se/kommunpol itik/dinkommun/befolkningsstatistik. Hämtad 2022–12–15.
Åre kommun. (2022–11–16b). *Kommun och politik*. https://are.se/kommunpol itik. Hämtad 2022–12–15.
Östersunds kommun. (2022–11–14a). *Kommunfakta*. https://www.ostersund. se/kommun-och-politik/kommunfakta.html. Hämtad 2022–12–13.
Östersunds kommun. (2022–12–09b). *Valresultat och mandatfördelning*. https://www.ostersund.se/kommun-och-politik/kommunfakta/valresultat-och-mandatfordelning.html. Hämtad 2022–12–15.
Östersunds kommun. (2022–08–08c). *Kommunens mål och budget*. https:// www.ostersund.se/kommun-och-politik/kommunens-mal-och-budget.html. Hämtad 2022–12–15.

Muntliga källor

Respondent 1. Utvecklingsstrateg. Bergs kommun. Microsoft Teams. Intervju 28 november 2022.
Respondent 2. Miljöstrateg. Östersunds kommun. Microsoft Teams. Intervju 30 november 2022.
Respondent 3. Verksamhetscontroller. Östersunds kommun. Microsoft Teams. Intervju 30 november 2022.
Respondent 4. Kommundirektör. Bergs kommun. Microsoft Teams. Intervju 30 november 2022.
Respondent 5. Hållbarhetsstrategi. Åre kommun. Telefonsamtal. Intervju 14 december 2022.

Index

A

Agenda 2030 6, 219–222, 224–226, 232, 235, 237–244

B

bibliometric analysis 4, 37, 39, 42, 61

C

Citizens' engagement 6
coffee 4, 5, 71–77, 79–96
convenience 4, 71, 77, 78, 81, 82, 84–86, 88–92, 95, 96
CSR 2, 4, 5, 37–40, 43, 49, 59–62, 84, 121–129, 131–136, 220, 229, 230, 237, 239, 243

D

digitalization 3, 4

E

e-commerce 4, 36–40, 43, 45, 46, 48–51, 53, 54, 56, 57, 59–62
entrepreneur 102, 104, 105

G

green businesses 3, 4

M

municipality 6, 101, 103, 108, 220, 221, 231, 232, 235–243

© The Editor(s) (if applicable) and The Author(s), under exclusive license to Springer Nature Switzerland AG 2024
A. Sörensson et al. (eds.), *Creating New Roles for a Sustainable Economy*, Palgrave Studies in Governance, Leadership and Responsibility,
https://doi.org/10.1007/978-3-031-61551-1

N
nature-based businesses 6, 203–205, 208, 210, 212–215

Q
Quadruple Helix 5, 105, 107, 111, 113–115

R
regional development 5, 102, 103, 105–111, 114, 116

S
SDGs 6, 101, 219, 222, 225, 233, 234, 244
smart city 6, 177–197
SMEs 3, 4, 20, 122–129, 133–136, 206
social entrepreneur 105
social entrepreneurship 3, 4, 103–105, 108–111, 114–116, 206
sustainability 2–5, 11–13, 15, 17, 19, 21, 24, 27, 37, 38, 48–51, 56, 57, 59, 72, 73, 77, 78, 80, 83–91, 95, 96, 101, 105, 143, 144, 146–148, 157, 159, 161, 165, 166, 168–172, 179, 181, 182, 204–214, 221–224, 226, 230, 235–244
systematic sustainable business model 5

SPRINGER NATURE

GPSR Compliance

The European Union's (EU) General Product Safety Regulation (GPSR) is a set of rules that requires consumer products to be safe and our obligations to ensure this.

If you have any concerns about our products, you can contact us on ProductSafety@springernature.com

In case Publisher is established outside the EU, the EU authorized representative is:

Springer Nature Customer Service Center GmbH
Europaplatz 3
69115 Heidelberg, Germany

The manufacturer's authorised representative in the EU is Springer Nature Customer Service Centre GmbH, Europaplatz 3, 69115 Heidelberg, Germany. If you have any concerns regarding our products, please contact ProductSafety@springernature.com

Printed and bound by CPI Group (UK) Ltd, Croydon, CR0 4YY
28/09/2026
02224083-0004